Rewarding people

People's behaviour can be rewarding to others through what they say or do: it may be no more than an appreciative smile, a sympathetic touch or a word of praise, but the impact can be highly significant. *Rewarding People* is an in-depth exploration of these social rewards and their relevance to the practice of those in the inter-personal professions.

While much of its content is relevant to everyday life, the essential focus of the book is on the ways in which an understanding of the working of social rewards can benefit such groups as teachers, doctors, social workers, counsellors, nurses and managers in their interactions with their patients, clients and pupils.

In exploring the nature and distribution of social rewards, the authors introduce the concept of interpersonal skill, and discuss a range of theoretical perspectives to account for the consequences of responding positively to others. The effects of social rewards in promoting interpersonal attraction, establishing and regulating relationships, and the ethical issues involved in conferring power and facilitating influence are also discussed.

With its discussion of theory and research linked to explicit practical applica-tions, *Rewarding People* will be of interest to advanced level students in the area of communication skills and psychology, as well as those professionals for whom interpersonal relations are central to their working lives.

David Dickson and **Christine Saunders** work in the Department of Communica-tion, and **Maurice Stringer** works in the Department of Psychology, at the University of Ulster.

International Series on Communication Skills

Edited by Owen Hargie
Head of the Department of Communication
University of Ulster

Already published

The Practice of Questioning
J.T. Dillon

Assertive Behavior: Theory, Research, and Training
Richard F. Rakos

Professional Interviewing
Rob Millar, Valerie Crute and Owen Hargie

Rewarding people

The skill of responding positively

David Dickson,
Christine Saunders
and Maurice Stringer

London and New York

First published in 1993
by Routledge
11 New Fetter Lane, London EC4P 4EE

Simultaneously published in the USA and Canada
by Routledge
29 West 35th Street, New York, NY 10001

Typeset in Times New Roman by Michael Mepham, Frome, Somerset
Printed and bound in Great Britain by
Mackays of Chatham PLC, Chatham, Kent

British Library Cataloguing in Publication Data
A catalogue record for this book is available from the British Library.

Library of Congress Cataloging in Publication Data
Dickson, David.
　Rewarding people : the skill of responding positively / David Dickson,
　Christine Saunders, and Maurice Stringer.
　　p.　cm. — (International series on communication skills)
　Includes bibliographical references and index.
　1. Reward (Psychology) 2. Interpersonal communication.
　3. Reinforcement (Psychology) I. Saunders, Christine. II. Stringer,
　Maurice. III. Title. IV. Series.
　BF505.R48D53　1993
　153.6—dc20
　　　　　　　　　　　　　　　　　　　　　　　　　　　92-27563
　　　　　　　　　　　　　　　　　　　　　　　　　　　CIP

ISBN 0–415–04094–9
　　　0–415–04095–7 (pbk)

This book is dedicated to our families

Contents

Figures and tables

Editorial introduction

INTERNATIONAL SERIES ON COMMUNICATION SKILLS

In recent years increasing attention has been devoted to the analysis of social interaction in terms of the communicative competence of the participants. In particular, the conceptualisation of interpersonal communication as skilled performance has resulted in a veritable flood of empirical, scientific and descriptive publications regarding the nature of interpersonal skills. However, these publications have been disseminated over a wide spectrum of discipline areas including psychology, communication, sociology, education, business, and counselling. As a result, there is a clear need for a new series of books designed specifically to draw together this material, from disparate sources, into a meaningful evaluation and analysis of a range of identified communication skill areas.

Each book in this series contains a blend of theory, research and practice pertaining to a particular area of communication. However, the emphasis throughout the series is upon the practical application of communication skills to social interaction *per se*. The books are written by authors of international repute, chosen for their knowledge of, and publications in, the specific topic under consideration. As such, this series will make a significant contribution to the rapidly expanding field of interpersonal communication.

The books in the series therefore represent a major addition to the literature, and will be of interest to students and researchers in communication, psychology and other disciplines. They will also prove valuable to the vast range of people in the 'interpersonal professions' (doctors, nurses, therapists, etc.) whose day-to-day work so depends upon effective communication.

Taken as a whole, this series represents an encyclopaedia of information regarding our current knowledge of communication skills. It is certainly the most comprehensive attempt to date to chart the existing state of this field of study. As such it is both a privilege and a pleasure to have been involved in the conception and execution of this series.

REWARDING PEOPLE: THE SKILL OF RESPONDING POSITIVELY

It is very likely the case that no other concept has provoked so much debate or generated as much research within the field of psychology as that of reinforcement. The exact nature, functions and outcomes of different types and patterns of reinforcement have been the subject of academic study since the early part of this century. A voluminous number of papers, articles, book chapters and books have been devoted to this topic. However, while the potency of reinforcers as techniques for influencing behaviour has long been recognised, the conceptualisation of reinforcement as a form of social skill, involving verbal and nonverbal behaviour, is a relatively recent phenomenon. The publication of this text is therefore timely in that it draws together for the first time the many and sometimes diverse strands associated with this area.

The coverage of the topic of rewardingness in this text is exhaustive. This concept is traced back to the early work in the field of reinforcement and the reader is taken on a lucid voyage of discovery through Thorndike's law of effect, Skinner's operant conditioning and Bandura's social learning theory and on to the more recent humanistic approaches of theorists such as Rogers. Throughout these accounts, topical issues of concern are raised. For example, in relation to the behaviourist approach to reward, issues of mentalism and the role of cognition are explored, as is the heavy reliance on animal studies and their uncritical extrapolation to humans. In this way, the core importance of both intra- and inter-personal domains is recognised.

Thereafter, the book embraces a wide sweep of issues within the psychology of communication, all of which pertain directly to rewardingness. This includes an examination of approaches such as transactional analysis, person-centred therapy and cognitive psychology. It also incorporates a comprehensive analysis of the influence of a wide panoply of other central variables, including the self and self-concept, locus of control, self-monitoring, attribution theory, learned helplessness, power, attractiveness and social influence. At the same time, the influence of impinging variables such as gender, age, class, socioeconomic background and personality upon rewardingness is explored.

The authors of this text have a breadth and depth of knowledge of research, theory and practice in the area of interpersonal communication. Dr David Dickson is Head of the Social Skills Centre and Christine Saunders is Senior Lecturer, within the Department of Communication, and Dr Maurice Stringer is Lecturer in the Department of Psychology, all at the University of Ulster. They are highly respected academics who have published widely in the field of the psychology of communication. They also have considerable experience as trainers in the design, operation and evaluation of communication skills training programmes, particularly for professional groups. This has undoubtedly been a positive force within the present text, where theory and research are consistently and directly linked to explicit practical applications. This is exemplified by the final chapter in which a cogent summative analysis is provided of research findings pertaining to rewardingness. These findings are reviewed in relation to four main variables: aspects concerning the nature of the rewards *per se*; factors relating to the person delivering the reward and to the person receiving it; and related circumstantial factors. This section is a most valuable *aide-mémoire* for the reader. The ethical responsibilities of those possessing such knowledge about rewarding powers are also recognised in this chapter.

Overall, the content of this book provides the most detailed, informed and informative account to date of research, theory and practice in the field of reward-ingness. As the authors point out and demonstrate, the contents of the book are directly relevant to professionals in many settings. However, since this is an area of study which is of widespread and more general interest, the information presented will be of relevance, and benefit, to academics in many contexts. Furthermore, the theoretical and research material covered results in a fine balance of academic and applied perspectives on the study of reinforcement and reward-ingness. In this way the book is, in every sense, comprehensive.

It should be noted that where either the masculine or feminine gender is referred to throughout this text this should be taken as encompassing both genders as appropriate.

Owen Hargie
Professor and Head of the Department of Communication
University of Ulster

Chapter 1

Introduction

In the play *Huis Clos*, Jean-Paul Sartre is responsible for the well-known statement that 'Hell is other people'. The three characters, Garcin and the two females Estelle and Inès, find themselves in hell, death having brought an end to different life projects. For Garcin, being regarded as a man of bravery and honour had been important, yet, in a moment of crisis which required acting on a matter of principle, he had turned coward and fled. Having died before he could redeem himself, his abiding concern is that he will be forever regarded by those who knew him as a coward and there is nothing that can now be done about it. There is one glimmer of hope though, offered by Estelle. She might be influenced to look upon Garcin as a hero if, in turn, he redefined the circumstances of her murdering her two children in such a way as to absolve her of all blame. Unfortunately the success of this complicity in mutual bad faith is compromised by Inès, a lesbian. She died as a result of a suicide pact with her girl friend having previously been the cause of the death of her friend's husband at his own hand. Were it not for Garcin, Inès could engineer an affair with Estelle. Were it not for Estelle the intense rivalry between Garcin and Inès would subside. They are trapped in an enduring internecine web of destructive interrelationships wherein each acts as the torturer of the other two – hell is indeed other people!

The play may strike a chord in many to the extent that we can reflect upon personal liaisons which, while less dramatically extreme than that sketched by Sartre, have been irredeemably frustrating and limiting experiences. Through our associations with those with whom we establish bonds, we can be exposed to a great deal of pain, anger, disappointment and anguish. But by the same token, the most precious moments of sublime joy and fulfilment also frequently stem from the social nature of our existence. We all readily recognise the benefits which are derivable. Freedman (1978) discovered that people, when asked what makes them most happy, offers most satisfaction and provides most meaning to their lives, placed close relationships ahead of other areas of importance such as work, leisure, money or even health. This book resonates with these sentiments, drawing upon possibilities for beneficial and constructive mutual influence residing in interpersonal contact. As such, and without wishing to address the deeper existentialist assumptions upon which that play is founded, it is premised upon a view of human relations which is diametrically opposed to the starkly gloomy and depressing depiction in *Huis Clos*.

This book accentuates the positivity of social fellowship in the mutuality of rewards through which that fellowship is perpetuated and which, in turn, it facilitates. The central objective, however ambitiously conceived, is to increase the reader's appreciation of the significance of social rewards in dealing with others, to heighten his or her self-awareness as a rewarding agent and to draw more extensively on that potential, utilising it with greater efficiency in interpersonal transactions. While essentially we have in mind interactions between professionals and those for whom a service is provided, much of what is said is directly relevant to everyday relationships.

In this introductory chapter, we will reflect more fully upon the importance of social rewards in directing our relationships with others, influencing our attitudes and feelings towards them and shaping our behaviour. Since the book is fundamentally about interaction in professional settings, some initial thought is devoted to the interpersonal dimension of much of professional practice and the role of rewarding transactions in a range of professional contexts including education, social work, speech therapy, counselling, management, coaching and health care. Some of the different personal and social outcomes associated with the exchange of rewards are outlined before turning to look more closely at the process of interpersonal communication *per se* and the concept of communication skill. To this end a model of interpersonal transaction as skilled enterprise is elaborated which has important implications for the business of rewarding. For the moment, however, let's give some thought to elaborating this idea of rewards which we make available and, in turn, receive from others with whom we engage.

WHAT IS SOCIAL REWARDINGNESS?

We can think of people being rewarding in various ways. In the complexly differentiated social and occupational worlds in which we live, many of the material things for which we strive are not directly accessible to us. In the main they are obtainable only through the intervention of another party. More money, represented by increases in pay, comes courtesy of employers who usually have to be prevailed upon to recognise employees' contributions in some such tangible manner. Additional or alternative recompenses and incentives at the disposal of management have been alluded to by Komaki (1982), and include promotion, job assignments, and training opportunities as well as a variety of 'perks' such as a company car, more time off, insurance schemes, etc. Apart from the world of work, we may have our meals made for us, our pain relieved for us, and if we are lucky our clothes, jewellery, cars, etc. bought for us. In so doing, employers, spouses, doctors, parents, etc. may come to be positively valued (although hopefully not only for those reasons) through being instrumental in providing things or making possible events which we seek. Being able to occasion such desired states of affairs can also confer upon them a certain power over us. (See Chapter Eight.)

But the rewards that people bestow can be of a completely different nature. No doubt we can all think of individuals whose company we seek out, not because it is necessarily of any material benefit, but rather that it is enjoyable, stimulating, even enriching. What is important is the way in which they relate to us, their enlivening conversation and amusing anecdotes, the fact that they are ready to appreciate us and what we try to do, perhaps because they seem to recognise and engage with some facet of self that others have failed to identify or have even denied. Thus, as described by Argyle (1983, p. 65), 'A person can be rewarding in a large variety of ways – by being warm and friendly, taking an interest in the other, admiring him, being submissive, showing sexual approval, helping with his problems, or by being interesting and cheerful.'

Moreover, it isn't only what is said that matters. Rewards are revealed more broadly in the different forms which communication can take. They could be conveyed in a genuinely appreciative tone of voice, a caring touch, fascinated look, or delighted smile, depending on the context of the interchange. In addressing the topics of rewards and rewarding in this book, we will be concerned not so much with the effects of material incentives like money, but rather with what people say and how they behave to each other.

IMPORTANCE OF REWARDS IN SOCIAL LIVES

Social rewards are of the utmost importance in interpersonal transactions and their effects wide-ranging. They can help shape the friendships that we foster, the attitudes we form, the degree of liking felt towards others and indeed how we come to view and accept ourselves, our abilities and attributes. Moreover the things that we do, habits adopted, and activities pursued, are partly determined by the rewards and reinforcers that are brought about courtesy of others, when we behave in those ways. We are much more likely to do things that elicit positive outcomes from those who matter to us. These actions are reinforced in consequence while others that clearly displease or lead to some other negatively valued rebuke will probably be avoided in future.

Sensitivity to the reactions of others and the ability to regulate our behaviour in this manner so as to make it more likely that we are reacted to positively rather than negatively by those whom we encounter is considered to be fundamental to successful social life. This is reflected in the definitional basis which some have advocated for the concept of social skill. Libet and Lewinsohn (1973, p. 304) for instance, in one of the earliest attempts, defined social skill as, 'the complex ability both to emit behaviours which are positively or negatively reinforced and not to emit behaviours that are punished or extinguished by others'. In other words, and while these terms will be explained fully in the next chapter, social skill hinges on being able to equip oneself so as to influence others to do things that we value positively or to stop doing things that we value negatively, and also to refrain from alternative actions that bring about either negative outcomes or no worthwhile outcomes at all. Michelson et al. (1983) also refer to the maximisation of social reinforcement from others in evaluating the key features of social skill, while Phillips (1985, p. 3) reflecting upon this line of thought, concluded that, 'Social competence or skill pivots on positively reinforced exchanges with others and few or no punished or ignored exchanges'.

The notion of interpersonal skill will be returned to shortly and considered in greater depth. Its inclusion at this juncture, and the point to bear in mind, is the centrality of rewards to competent social functioning.

So far most of the talk has centred on how *we* go about extracting rewards from *others* with whom we have dealings. Given that the focus of the book is primarily upon professional interaction, it might be more appropriate to turn this thinking around lest we lose sight of the fact that, as professionals, we are also those 'others' with whom someone else (patient, client, pupil, etc.) interacts. We are the source of significant consequences for them. Depending upon how we react, decisions will be reached by them about the extent of further contact (assuming that there is freedom of choice), feelings and attitudes towards us formed, types of future conduct possibly shaped, and perhaps new insights into aspects of their own make-up gleaned. Being skilled with people, we believe, requires not only the wherewithal to extract social rewards in the course of transactions but to provide them as well. This latter proposition is fundamental to the underlying rationale for the book. When Faraone and Hurtig (1985) examined what those regarded as highly socially skilled actually did, compared with their low social skill counterparts, when they conversed with a stranger of the opposite sex, they found, among other things, that the highly skilled were more rewarding in the way in which they reduced uncertainty, and therefore possible unease in the situation, and in reacting positively to the other through what was said and topics introduced.

INTERACTION IN PROFESSIONAL CONTEXTS

The past decade has witnessed a burgeoning awareness of the indispensability of effective levels of interpersonal communication to acceptable standards of practice in many professional circles. Ellis and Whittington (1981) coined the term 'the Interpersonal Professions' to identify those occupations where the major proportion of the professional's day is spent in face-to-face interaction with others and where the fundamental objectives of the service offered are achieved essentially by this means. Without making any attempt at a comprehensive listing, examples include managers, teachers, counsellors, lawyers, and doctors together with a whole range of other health workers and carers. Social work has a special significance in this respect according to Dickson and Mullan (1990). Likewise, Baldock and Prior (1981) stress that 'doing' social work is inextricably bound up with talking. It is not only that social workers arguably spent more of their time with clients engaged in this activity but that interacting in the context of the client interview is 'the basic resource for social work practice' (p. 20). Similar views are espoused by Davies (1985) in describing interpersonal communication as the basic tool at the disposal of the social worker.

The import of the interpersonal dimension in other sectors of professional practice has been readily acknowledged. Those who have attempted, in reflecting upon its nature, to analyse how skilled practitioners characteristically relate, frequently identify responding positively to those with whom they engage so as to reward and reinforce appropriately. Following earlier work by the likes of Flanders and Simon (1969), Turney *et al.* (1983) included reinforcement in their anthology of basic teaching skills. They describe how teachers can increase pupils' attention and motivation, improve classroom behaviour and promote achievement by various verbal and nonverbal means including praise and encouragement, touch, gestures, adjusting physical proximity, and making available the opportunity to take part in other activities such as playing class games with peers.

Shifting the focus from teaching to interviewing and counselling, Ivey and Authier (1978), in their quest to develop a taxonomy of microskills embodied in these activities, specified attending and listening as being of fundamental importance: 'The most basic unit of microcounselling is attending behaviour, the careful listening to the client. The beginning counsellor who is able to attend to and hear the client is equipped to start counselling sessions. Without the ability to attend, the helping interview – regardless of theoretical orientation – becomes an empty sham' (p. 64). Based on the premise that people will only talk about what others are prepared to listen to, they outline how clients can be encouraged to disclose issues of concern through the use of attending behaviour and the reinforcing effects in this endeavour of selective listening on the part of the counsellor.

In operational terms, attending relies upon acceptable patterns of eye contact, a relaxed yet involved posture, and the maintenance of the thematic coherence of the conversation by refraining from introducing intrusive changes in topic. The use of minimal encourages to talk including expressions like 'I See', 'Right', 'OK', and vocalisations such as 'mm-hmm', along with consonant nonverbal indices (e.g. head-nods, congruent facial expressions, gestures, etc.) are also implicated. At more advanced levels, selective attention to factual or affective areas for exploration, for instance, can be effected through the use of listening skills. Listed among these are reflection of feeling which involves isolating the core affective message being communicated by the client and mirroring it back in the form of a statement; paraphrasing which is similar in many ways but taps the cognitive domain of discourse; and summarisation which 'involves attending to the client, accurately sensing the feelings and content being expressed, and meaningfully integrating the various responses to the client' (Ivey and Authier, 1978, p. 87).

Reinforcement has also been identified as playing a prominent role in the practice of Speech Therapy. In a significant piece of research, Saunders and Caves (1986) undertook to unearth the key communication skills utilised by members of this profession in conducting therapy with both child and adult clients. Therapists were videotaped during consultations and this material was then subjected to peer analysis. From isolated positive and negative instances, the object was to reach consensus on a set of behavioural categories of effective practice. 'Using positive reinforcement' was one of the categories to so emerge from interactions with children as well as adults. Verbal and nonverbal sub-types were specified.

Social rewards including praise make a potentially beneficial contribution to other and diverse areas of professional activity such as management and coaching. In the former setting there is some evidence that when properly programmed, improvements in absenteeism, motivation, job satisfaction and productivity can result (Davey, 1981; Rapp *et al.*, 1983). Sports coaches who employ these techniques have been found to be popular, especially with younger competitors; to enhance levels of skill; and to improve results among those with whom they work (Martin and Hrycaiko, 1983; Smith and Smoll, 1990).

Finally, in the field of health care, recognition has been made by DiMatteo and DiNicola (1982) and Raven (1988), among others, of health-worker social rewards in the form of attention, praise, approval, compliments, etc. as one (but only one) approach to increasing, for example, patient satisfaction and tackling the abiding problem of improving compliance with prescribed drug regimens or recommended courses of action. The scale of this problem was illustrated by Ley (1988). Having collated a broad spectrum of the research findings he concluded that on average between 40 per cent and 50 per cent of patients would appear to be non-compliant, representing an estimated drain on health expenditure, in US figures, of a staggering 400 million to 800 million dollars! By taking steps to monitor patient behaviour and reinforce compliance when it does take place, health workers can go some way to rectifying this situation. This may be particularly impactful in cases of adherence to difficult or stressful courses of action when, 'the here-and-now reward value of maintaining contact with a respected helper can tip the balance in favour of good intentions when the client is tempted to avoid the here-and-now costs and suffering' (Janis, 1983, p. 148). Both Janis (1983) and Raven (1988) emphasise that influencing change along these lines presupposes the prior establishment of a relationship of trust, acceptance and respect. It is only in this context that praise and approval are likely to be valued.

There is accumulating research evidence to support these propositions. Having reviewed over forty independent studies into practitioner behaviour in medical consultations and its effects, Hall *et al.* (1988) reached the conclusion that reacting positively towards patients through both verbal and nonverbal behaviour led to important outcomes. Positive talk, defined as showing approval, agreeing, offering support, giving reassurance, attending, encouraging, facilitating, empathising, and so on, was associated not only with compliance but also with the recall and understanding of information given and, very significantly, with patient satisfaction over how they had been treated. The expression of greater intimacy and attention as revealed nonverbally in more eye contact, touch, forward leaning posture, closer interpersonal distance and direct orientation was also linked to this latter variable. Likewise, what Buller and Buller (1987) refer to as an affirmative style on the part of the physician was found to be predictive of the degree of satisfaction which patients expressed with the service received.

EFFECTS OF SOCIAL REWARDS

It may be worthwhile at this juncture to bring into sharper focus the sorts of outcomes that tend to be associated with social rewards and reinforcers. As listed by Hargie *et al.* (1987), these include:

1 Promoting interaction and maintaining relationships;
2 Increasing the involvement of the interactive partner;
3 Influencing the contribution of the partner to the interaction;
4 Demonstrating a genuine interest in the ideas, thoughts and feelings of the other;
5 Making interaction interesting and enjoyable;
6 Creating an impression of warmth and understanding;
7 Increasing the social attractiveness of the source of rewards;
8 Improving the confidence and self-esteem of the recipient;
9 Exercising power.

During social encounters we not only welcome but demand a certain basic level of reward. If it is not forthcoming we may treat this as sufficient grounds for abandoning the relationship in favour of more attractive alternatives. In a study undertaken by Jones *et al.* (1982), college students who were lonely, in comparison to their more gregarious peers, were found to be strikingly less attentive to conversational partners. Trower *et al.* (1978) have noted the marked lack of reinforcement which characterises the conversations of certain groups of mental patient. It is suggested that their condition may be exacerbated by a lack of social rewards leading to reduced contact with others as relationships begin to crumble. The increased social isolation which results leads to a further deterioration in their mental state with fewer opportunities for interpersonal involvement, thus creating a debilitating downward spiral. The role of rewards in the formation, maintenance and termination of relationships will be addressed in Chapter Nine.

For professionals and paraprofessionals who work mainly with other people, simply maintaining the interactive episode, while necessary, is not sufficient. It is important that the recipient of the service be encouraged to be fully involved in what takes place if the goals of the encounter are to be actualised. Promoting active participation in the classroom is a good example. Costs incurred by pupils, in the form of energy expended, lack of opportunity to devote time to competing activities, fear of getting it wrong, etc., must be offset by the availability of rewards. In some learning situations e.g. acquiring a novel skill, intrinsic rewards from efficient task performance may be initially limited. Teacher reinforcement is therefore one method of increasing pupil commitment to what is taking place.

Apart from extending the general level of participation, rewards can be administered in a planned and systematic fashion to selectively reinforce and shape contributions along particular lines. When interviewing, the interviewee can be influenced in this way to continue with the detailed exploration of certain topics or issues to the exclusion of others regarded as being of lesser relevance or even counterproductive. In a medical setting, for instance, White and Sanders (1986) demonstrated how patients suffering from chronic pain conversationally focused more on their pain when the interviewer responded with attention and praise. Selectively reinforcing 'well talk', on the other hand, had the opposite effect. Using the same principles, teachers can increase the incidence of appropriate pupil behaviour in class (Wheldall and Glynn, 1989). Further research in this tradition is reviewed in Chapters Three and Four.

Before progressing, it should be acknowledged that, when worded in this way, there is little which is either original or profound in the proposition that people are inclined to do things that lead to positive outcomes and avoid other courses of action that produce unwanted consequences. This much is widely known. Indeed the statement may seem so obvious as to be trivial. But Lieberman (1990) makes the more interesting observation that, despite this general awareness, individuals are often remarkably unsuccessful in bringing about behavioural change both in themselves and in other people. The conclusion drawn is that, 'Clearly the principle of reward cannot be quite as simple as it sounds' (p. 157). As we shall see in subsequent chapters, when it comes to interactions by professionals, many simply do not make particularly effective use of this aspect of communication.

In addition to influencing what interactors say or do, providing rewards also conveys information about the source. Providers of substantial amounts of social reinforcement are usually perceived to be keenly interested in those with whom they interact and what they have to say. They also typically create an impression of being warm, accepting and understanding. (See Chapter Five for more information.) By contrast those who, for the most part, dispense few social rewards are often regarded as cold, aloof, depressed, bored or even boring.

Extending this thinking, some investigators, including Lott and Lott (1968) and Clore and Byrne (1974), have made use of the concept of reinforcement in attempting to account for interpersonal attraction. Responses and pleasurable feelings which stem from receiving rewards become associated, it is proposed, with the provider, or even with a third party who happens to be consistently present when they are dispensed. Indeed a number of studies have determined, perhaps predictably, that people like to receive praise, compliments and other similar positive evaluations and tend to like those who give them (Aronson, 1984). The circumstances surrounding interpersonal attraction will be explored in Chapter Six.

Positive reactions may not only produce more favourable impressions towards those who offer them (under certain conditions), but may also result in heightened feelings of self-esteem in the recipient. Self-esteem refers to the sense of personal worth that an individual entertains ranging from love and acceptance to hate and rejection. It can, in part, be based upon the persistent evaluations of significant others as will be examined in more depth in the following chapter. Impressions about self as well as the other can therefore be formed from rewards received or denied.

Finally the possibility of the distribution of rewards as an exercise in power and authority should not be overlooked. Raven and Rubin (1983) mention this as one of six recognisably different forms of social power. Being in a position to determine whether or not another receives something valued confers on that individual the ability to exert influence and determine what the other does. When the giving of rewards is interpreted as an attempt at control, however, with the putative recipient valuing autonomy more highly than what is on offer, resistance to such manipulation may be provoked. These issues will be returned to in Chapter Eight.

INTERPERSONAL COMMUNICATION AND SKILL

Much of what has already been said has been about communication. Indeed it would be difficult to imagine any informed comment on topics such as social interaction and relationship work which ignored this concept. But what, in fact, is communication? How does it operate? What does it mean to describe communication as being skilled? These are some of the questions to be taken up in this sub-section.

Picking up on the first question, maybe the most immediately striking feature of communication is its ubiquity – it appears to be everywhere and ever present. This has led Ellis and Beattie (1986) to describe it as a 'fuzzy' concept with boundaries that are blurred and uncertain. In the interests of simplicity and mindful of the criterion of relevancy, we can largely ignore representational media (e.g. reports, books, files, etc.) and mechanical/electronic media (e.g. TV, telex, electronic mail, etc.) to concentrate primarily on communication which is face-to-face. What we are left with has been defined by Brooks and Heath (1985, p. 8) as, 'the process by which information, meanings and feelings are shared by persons through the exchange of verbal and nonverbal messages'.

Several aspects are worth further mention. Wiemann and Giles (1988) highlight the fact that communication is a process. It requires that at least two contribute to the ongoing and dynamic sequence of events in which each affects, and is affected by, the other in a system of reciprocal determination. As we shall see shortly, each at the same time makes perceptions of the other in context, makes some sort of sense of what is happening, comes to a decision as to how to react, and responds accordingly.

Another commonly cited characteristic of communication is its purposefulness. Those who take part do so with some end in mind (Berger, 1989). Broadly speaking, these goals may be instrumental or consummatory (Ruffner and Burgoon, 1981). The former is carried out in order to achieve some further outcome, e.g. a supervisor may reward effort to increase productivity. Consummatory communication, on the other hand, satisfies the communicator without the *active* intervention of another, e.g. the supervisor may reward because it makes him feel good to distribute largesse. In reviewing some of the determinants of the deployment of rewards with subordinates, Podsakoff (1982) draws attention to the meeting of supervisors' personal needs.

The purposeful nature of professional communication can also be considered in terms of the six categories of intervention identified by Heron (1990) as:

1 prescriptive: seeking to direct and ordain behaviour of the client, usually behaviour occurring outside the relationship with the professional;
2 informative: providing information and promoting understanding of facts or concerns of which the client was previously ignorant;
3 confronting: heightening awareness of personal beliefs, attitudes and behaviour;
4 cathartic: enabling the expression and discharge of strong emotions like anger, grief and fear;
5 catalytic: encouraging the quest for self-reflection, self-discovery and self-direction;
6 supportive: affirming the worth and value of clients, their attitudes, values and actions.

Heron specifies praise as an instance of the latter type of intervention. Moreover, this category would appear to enjoy a uniquely prominent position in relation to the rest. Based upon work requiring nurses to rate their level of interpersonal skill according to each of these six modes of relating to patients, Morrison et al. (1991) exposed a pattern of interrelationships in which supportive involvement underpinned all the others. Rewarding, as we have construed it, can be additionally implicated in at least the prescriptive and catalytic categories.

To what extent does communication presuppose intention and conscious involvement? One school of thought stresses that some level of intentional coding of symbols and conscious action is a necessary condition for communication to take place. In fact the act of communicating has been distinguished from the mere manifestation of expressive behaviour on these grounds (Wiener et al., 1972; Wiemann and Giles, 1988). Other theorists, including Watzlawick et al. (1967), take a much more inclusive view of communication as occurring when people are simply aware of the presence of others and are influenced in what they do as a consequence.

Borden (1972) furthermore argues that purposive behaviour implies consciousness. Likewise Klinger et al. (1981) believe that convictions of the existence of unconscious goals do not match the evidence, concluding that 'life would be far more chaotic than it is if substantial portions of people's goal strivings were for goals about which the striver was unconscious' (p. 171). Emmons (1989) has summarised the current thinking by suggesting that it is commonly accepted that people have considerable access to their goals and can readily report them but are less aware of the underlying motivational basis upon which they are founded. This does not imply, however, that for individuals acting to attain fixed ends, the entirety of the communicative act must have prominence in the ongoing stream of consciousness. While intention, control and awareness are central to general conceptualisations of communication as skilled activity, it seems that many well-rehearsed sequences can be run off with only limited attention (Berscheid, 1983). When skills are well-honed, they can often be executed on the 'back burner' of conscious thought.

Another significant feature of communication is its multidimensionality –

messages exchanged are seldom unitary or discrete. Watzlawick *et al.* (1967) drew attention to the fact that the process takes place at two separate, but interrelated, levels. One has to do with substantive matters, the other with relational concerns and helps determine how participants define their association *vis-à-vis*, for instance, degree of affiliation, status relationship, and the balance of power. This has important ramifications for the exchange of rewards. While it is perfectly acceptable for the teacher to praise a junior pupil for a commendable effort in class, were the pupil to address the teacher in like manner it would be seen as presumptuous or even discourteous. Before moving on, it should also be appreciated, as previously intimated, that personal identities are projected through styles of relating to others. Being recognised as the provider of valued commodities, whether material or social, constitutes evidence upon which the reputation of being a generous person can be constructed.

The idea of interpersonal skill has already been encountered as involving the acquisition of rewards from the social milieu. The possibility of the conferment of rewards being similarly skilled was also posited. Here this line of thought will be extended by elaborating some additional features of communication as a skilled undertaking. These centre around four core themes, which are:

1 Utility. The goal-directed nature of communication has been stressed. Communication which, other things being equal, succeeds in effectively and efficiently accomplishing a certain preordained goal is held to be more highly skilled than that which fails (Argyle, 1983).
2 Behavioural facility. The label 'skill' carries with it connotations of behavioural facility. It is not enough that things are accomplished, they have to be accomplished in a particular fashion. Some of the performative characteristics of interpersonal skill have been outlined by Hargie *et al.* (1987), and include behavioural organisation, synchrony and control.
3 Contextual propriety. Although facility is a necessary behavioural condition, it is not sufficient. Going back to the example of the junior pupil praising the teacher, it may have been effected with considerable aplomb, but this alone does not make it a significant piece of skilled interaction. What is said and done must be in accordance with expectations of appropriate conduct given the situation, participants and the nature of their relationship, together with the conventions which apply.
4 Normativity. This consideration extends the previous one. It has to do not only with acceptability of conduct but also with the warrantability of goals as legitimate projections worthy of pursuit. Interactors are cast as morally accountable agents. Ethical issues surrounding rewarding as skilled activity in professional settings will be returned to in the final chapter.

In sum, and as proposed by Dickson (1988), skilled communication relies upon the use of contextually appropriate and behaviourally facilitative means of relating effectively and efficiently to others so as to accomplish warrantable outcomes.

We will continue by taking a closer look at some of the components processes of skilled communication sketched by Hargie and Marshall (1986) and Dickson *et al.* (1989) in a conceptual model based upon earlier theorising by Argyle (1983).

A SKILL MODEL OF INTERPERSONAL COMMUNICATION

By way of an overview, the model presented in Figure 1.1 depicts dyadic interaction within a person–situation framework. What takes place is partly a feature of the particular participants and the personal 'baggage' that they bring to the encounter; their knowledge, values, emotions, attitudes, expectations and dispositions. The way in which they have come to regard themselves (their self-concept) and the beliefs that they have formed about their abilities to succeed in various types of enterprise (their feelings of self-efficacy) will also determine the sorts of encounters contemplated, how they are conducted and rewards derivable from them.

Interaction is also co-determined by parameters of the situation within which individuals find themselves, including role demands and the rules which pertain. Hargie and Marshall (1986) also discuss the potential effects which physical constraints of the environment, such as organisation of space and how it is adorned, can exert upon the communicative process. Furthermore these sources of influence are bidirectional. It is not only the case that personal characteristics and situational factors have a bearing on behaviour. What transpires during social contact can also effect changes in interactors. As we will see in the following chapter, the manner in which the individual is typically reacted to by others, the interpersonal rewards that are enjoyed or punishments endured, can serve to mould how that person comes to regard him/herself. Thus involvement with others can lead to modifications in individual knowledge, beliefs, attitudes, etc. (indeed the success of educational and counselling endeavours typically depends on it), and can also, within limits, serve to redefine the social situation.

Within this person–situation framework, three basic claims are made about interpersonal behaviour and its organisation. The first, as already specified, is that people act purposefully. Secondly, that they are sensitive to the effects of what they do. And thirdly, that they take steps to modify subsequent behaviour in the light of this information. Thus one of the features of social activity is that it is goal-driven. It is entered into in order to achieve some end-state even if this amounts to little more than the pleasure to be had from conversing. Accordingly, strategies projected to accomplish these outcomes are formulated and, through operationalisation, lead to the production of corresponding messages expressed in commensurate action (Argyle, 1983). The interactive nature of the procedure is such that each interactor, in reacting to the other, provides information of relevance to arriving at decisions on goal attainment. Additional to this mediated facility, each has a direct channel of feedback on performance enabling monitoring of self to take place.

While feedback makes information available, it can only be acted upon if it is actually received by the recipient. *Person perception* is central to skilful interaction yet its intrinsically selective and inferential nature results, in many cases, in

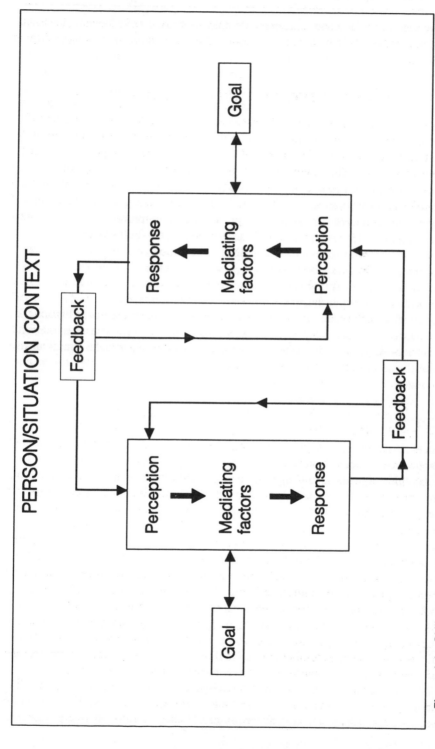

Figure 1.1 Skill model of interpersonal communication

perceptual inaccuracy and miscommunication (Forgas, 1985). Notwithstanding, information stemming from perceptions of self, the situation, and the other inter-actor, is considered in accordance with a complex of mediating processes, the outcome of which is a plan to govern action. As already mentioned, this plan of action, deemed to maximise opportunities for goal attainment under the prevailing circumstances, is represented in strategies to be behaviourally implemented in action thereby determining individual responses.

It should be realised that, firstly, due to the dynamic and changing character of communication, both participants are, at one and the same time, senders and receivers of information. Each is, even when silent, acting and reacting to the other. Secondly, and as recognised by Trower *et al.* (1978), potential barriers to successful communication exist at each of the different stages outlined. This may be particu-larly pronounced when translated into a professional environment where, as noted by Barnlund (1976) with reference to health care, the complexities of problems faced together with assessment, diagnosis and subsequent treatment, militate against the successful sharing of messages, without ambiguity or information loss. Practitioners and patients typically differ in the language, concepts, and knowledge base with which they respectively make sense of these matters.

A detailed and systematic unpacking of the entire model presented in Figure 1.1 lies beyond the scope of this book. Those who are interested are advised to consult the referenced sources. Nevertheless several elements have particular significance to the theme of social rewards and rewarding and will therefore be selectively elaborated.

Goals

A useful starting point is with the notion of goal which is taken to contribute direction and impetus to the interactive process. Following Dillard (1990, p. 70), we can think of goals quite simply as ' desired future states which an individual is committed to achieving or maintaining'. This basic proposition is embellished somewhat by Pervin (1989), in the suggestion that representations of end states have both cognitive and affective features. The former articulate and specify the nature of that anticipated future state while the latter address the extent and vigour of movement towards it. Persistence to achievement is an important characteristic of goal-directed behaviour and this motivational effect is perhaps the one that has received most attention from researchers. Once commitment to reach an outcome has been given, the normal development is for a course of action, designed to bring about that object or state of affairs, to be set in place and perpetuated, with continued checking to enable degree of success to be decided upon (Deci and Porac, 1978). This does not mean, however, that all goal aspirations are necessarily translated into action. Whether or not they are is dependent upon an appreciation of a variety of external and internal factors and these figure strongly in the deliberations of Bandura (1986), for instance, on the topic. They include assessments of how conducive environmental circumstances are at that time to goal achievement together with judgements of *self-efficacy* which determine the extent to which individuals concerned believe that they have the abilities and resources at hand to succeed. Furthermore, Bandura stresses the motivational impetus derivable from perceived progress either towards or away from projected goals. Perceptions of succeeding implicate personal standards and lead to positive self-evaluations; it is these which count. Information from others which indicates that a course of action is effective may presumably carry rewarding connotations in these terms.

One of the assumptions underlying any goals-based account of human endeavour is, in the view of Dillard (1990), that individuals are typically striving to actualise a multiplicity of outcomes in their dealings with their material and interpersonal environs. These end states can be organised according to at least three dimensions. Firstly, they can be hierarchically structured. This possibility is a common theme in the literature although some authors have formulated more complex arrangements than others. Dillard believes that a three-level structure is adequate with broad motives leading to goals which, in turn, govern subgoals. But what are these underlying needs that impel us to establish goals in directing our activities with others? Again different classificatory systems exist. Emmons (1989), nevertheless, believes that in essence these can be rendered down to three basic concerns: the need to feel in control and to be able to predict events of which one is part; the need for a sense of belonging to, and intimate involvement with, others making possible approval from them; and the need to exercise mastery and display competence in one's strivings thereby experiencing a sense of self-worth. Eventualities which satisfy these needs are another basis upon which rewardingness can be construed. These ideas as to why rewards have the impact that they do will be taken up and pursued in the following chapter.

A second dimension along which goals can be placed is that of importance. Quite simply, certain goals will be attached more weight than others and it will be these which exercise most impact upon action at any particular juncture. The processes involved in goal selection have been discussed by Deci and Porac (1978). Decisions reached depend very much on the psychological value attached to the accomplishment of that outcome together with estimates of the likelihood of various anticipated courses of action being successful in this respect, possible costs which may ensue, and so on. The value or valence of an outcome, Deci and Porac believe, is a feature of the satisfaction of particular motives. Atkinson and Raynor (1974) hold that these may reflect largely internal needs such as feelings of mastery and competence, while Vroom (1964) has stressed alternatives which are more externally oriented. The fact that people can be rewarding due to their instrumentality in the acquisition of other positively valued but tangible products such as money, promotion, etc. has already been mentioned. No doubt there is some form of ongoing assessment and reprioritising as certain outcomes are achieved, other projects possibly abandoned, and as circumstances alter. (The topics of *Expectancy-value* theories of Motivation, *Reinforcement value* and *Intrinsic motivation* will be returned to in the next chapter.)

Returning to the deliberations of Dillard, he mentions a third, temporal dimension. This, together with hierarchical orderings, is in keeping with the views of Hargie and Marshall (1986) when they talk about long-term and short-term goals. The example they give is of a personnel officer interviewing a job applicant. The principal goal directing this activity is, of course, to reach a proper decision as to the suitability of the interviewee. An appropriate short-term goal might be to establish rapport and put the candidate at ease. Actions are generally under the immediate control of goals at this level although long-term goals must not be lost sight of (Von Cranach *et al.*, 1982).

Depending on the time-frame, a long-term aim may be worked towards over a series of encounters. To continue with our selection example, if the job is sufficiently high-powered, the process of picking the right person may not be completed in a single interview. So far we have tended to assume that the goal must be reached within some interactive episode. This may not happen. It may be that the ultimate outcome of professional involvement is actualised by the client outwith direct interpersonal contact with the professional in question. While the coach's intensive work with the athlete may have been geared to winning a gold medal or breaking a record, these are things that the athlete must ultimately accomplish on the track, alone.

In discussing the nature of goals, Schlenker and Weigold (1989) make the further point that they may be quite precise and clearly specified or rather vague and indeterminate. Thus a junior nurse may have as a goal to be more assertive in transactions with other staff or to politely but firmly refuse to swap shifts with Doreen the next time she asks! In the context of the identification of objectives for educational or therapeutic interventions, one of the commonly accepted recommendations is that they be precisely articulated in assessable terms (Kanfer and Goldstein, 1986).

We have paid scant regard to the fact that, as suggested in the model in Figure 1.1, both parties involved in an interaction are likely to be acting in pursuit of goals. How these different goals relate has obvious and extremely important implications for the encounter and what transpires during it. Wilensky (1983) proposed that they may be either:

(a) competitive, in which case they will be negatively related in that the goals of one interactor can only be satisfied at the expense of those of the other; or
(b) concordant, where the relationship is positive and the achievement of one person's goal will facilitate the others.

An important part of the initial contact with clients in different professional settings is the business of locating, clarifying and establishing the suitability and compatibility of expectations (Saunders, 1986). Dinkmeyer (1971) called the creation of this framework of common purpose 'goal alignment', and without it little of benefit can be contemplated. In many instances, this agreement is formalised in the business of contracting (Lang and van der Molen, 1990). This has also significant ramifications for rewarding. When both parties are pursuing a joint goal, the rewards provided by each as feedback on goal attainment during the course of interaction derive from the same source and are offered in pursuit of a joint cause. When goals are discordant it is possible for individuals to provide rewards with ulterior motives in mind. The intention may be to deceive the other into acting in ways that are in the best interests of the rewarder rather than 'the rewarded'. The ethical issues here are quite conspicuous.

Mediating processes

These mediate between the goal which is being pursued, perceptions of information contributed through feedback, and the responses which are made in consequence. As we have seen, they play a part in the formulation of goals, influence the way in which people and events are perceived, and reflect the capacity of the individual to assimilate, deal with and respond to the circumstances of social encounters. Some of the intrapersonal components of interpersonal interaction operating at this stage are discussed by Kreps (1988) in terms of the organisation, processing and evaluation of information, the formulation or reassessment of alternative ways of reacting, decision-making and the selection of action strategies. One important criterion in deciding the most appropriate course of action to embark upon is based on expectations and anticipated consequences of so doing for attaining the set goal. Strategies will be selected which are thought likely to be rewarded in this manner while others will be dropped or held in abeyance. One of the foremost theoretical accounts of how rewards operate to influence what people do makes use of this concept of incentive value.

The complexities involved at this stage are still the subject of much speculation. In any case we can be sure that they are grossly under-represented in this brief overview. Knowledge structures and metacognitions are held to play a part by Hewes and Planalp (1987). As far as the latter are concerned, in order to interact successfully we must be able to form cognitive representations of others' cognitions. We must be able to think about and form an opinion on how they think and how they go about making sense of the world which they experience. The way in which messages are encoded by skilled communicators will reflect judgements along these lines. While all of this depends on an ability to retain and successfully retrieve information, the role of memory as a mediating process will not be gone into here. It is explored by, for example, Hargie and Marshall (1986). In broader terms, the ability to recollect a history of rewards, made available by various activities within past and enduring social liaisons, is obviously of fundamental importance in accounting for current interpersonal conduct, and will be returned to in Chapter Nine.

Responses

Plans and strategies are implemented at this stage. A common categorisation of social action, and one which has already been referred to, is that which distinguishes between the verbal and the nonverbal. While closely connected, verbal communication has to do with the purely linguistic message, with the actual words used. Nonverbal behaviour encompasses a whole range of body movements and facial expressions, together with vocal aspects of speech. This facet may be worth elaborating. Laver and Hutcheson (1972) differentiate between vocal and non-vocal, and verbal and nonverbal communication. Vocal refers to language and accompanying vocalisations. Verbal communication, on the other hand, is taken to mean, as we have seen, only the actual words and language used. The nonverbal category, therefore, subsumes nonvocal behaviour in the form of what is sometimes called body language, i.e. gestures, posture, facial expressions, etc., together with vocal communication such as moans and sighs along with intonation features which are not verbal in the sense defined above.

Chapters Three and Four will be devoted to outlining a variety of classes of social reward in the form of verbal and nonverbal behaviour respectively.

Feedback

Feedback is a fundamental feature of communication and without it prospects of skilled engagement are denied. Having acted, individuals rely on knowledge of their performance together with outcomes that may have accrued in order to reach decisions as to what to do next and alter subsequent responses accordingly. In the model presented in Figure 1.1, two sources of feedback are depicted. The more direct channel acknowledges that we have access, through proprioceptive and kinaesthetic means as well as visually (to a certain extent) and aurally (albeit with distortion), to what we say and do when communicating with others. Perhaps of greater interest is the thesis that, as interaction takes place, each member, as well as pursuing personal goals for the exchange, is at the same time, in what they say and do, providing the other with information which can act as feedback relevant to that other's goal quests. Perhaps Haslett and Ogilvie (1988, p. 385) express it more succinctly and elegantly when they define feedback, in the interpersonal setting, as, 'the response listeners give to others about their behaviour.... Feedback from others enables us to understand how our behaviour affects them, and allows us to modify our behaviour to achieve our desired goals.' Gudykunst (1991) asserts furthermore that convergence towards mutual understanding and shared meaning is proportional to the degree to which feedback is put to effective use. Limited provision and/or reception increase(s) the chances of divergence and misunderstanding. Corresponding to the different aspects of responding, feedback can be provided verbally or nonverbally, the latter in nonvocal and vocal forms. Although both are typically implicated, nonverbal modes may be particularly salient when it comes to affective or evaluative matters, while cognitive or substantive feedback relies more heavily upon the verbal (Zajonc, 1980).

Fitts and Posner (1973) identify three possible methods by means of which feedback can operate to influence further behaviour. It may, firstly, contribute *knowledge* about the results of performance; secondly, it can generate *motivation* to persist with a course of action; and thirdly, it may provide *reinforcement*, thereby strengthening the behaviour that led to it and increasing the chances that the individual will behave in a like manner in the future. Let's take the example of a teacher who praises a pupil for the successful completion of some task, say getting all her spellings correct. Those who conceptualise feedback in terms of giving information would hold that the beneficial effects of such praise are due to the fact that it confirms for the pupil that those particular ways of spelling the set words were indeed the correct ones and that the task has been successfully accomplished. Someone taking a motivational stance would interpret what happened differently. In this case subsequent improvements in performance are seen as a result of pupils having increased interest in, and enthusiasm for, tasks that they are doing, and being more committed to invest greater effort and to make a better job of them when there is an anticipation that they will lead to a recognised and accepted positive outcome. Finally, feedback can be looked on as a means of reinforcement, acting to increase the frequency of the behaviour that brought it about. There are differing views on just how this is accomplished. A more radical interpretation proposes that rein- forcement may function in a largely automatic, reflexive manner in accordance with operant conditioning principles (Skinner, 1953). Cairns (1986) has argued that the feedback concept in most theories of communication can be cast in this latter way, although there are many who would disagree with this assertion. (A strictly Skinnerian interpretation of reinforcement would also draw a distinction between performance feedback and operant conditioning (Skinner, 1974). These theoretical issues will be returned to in Chapter Two.)

While it is relatively easy to distinguish conceptually between these three modes of operation, the practical problems of doing so in any specific instance will be recognised. The feedback given to the pupil perhaps informed, motivated and reinforced at one and the same time. This possibility is readily accepted by Salmoni *et al.* (1984), in their discussion of the elusive functional mechanism of feedback, when they conclude with the suggestion that, 'It acts in many ways simultaneously' (p. 382).

How do social rewards fit into this picture? As a form of feedback they may well inform, motivate and reinforce to varying degrees and on different occasions. However, while feedback can be positive or negative, rewards have a typically affirmative connotation. Moreover, it could also be argued that, perhaps in a situation where goals are shared, the actions and reactions of each as both work successfully towards an agreed end will be mutually rewarding. Nevertheless, rewards are more often and obviously thought of not merely as routine reactions in the pursuit of goals, but as reactions that specify the behaviour of the other and in some way pass comment on it. This is most evident in acts of praising, approving, complimenting, etc. to be examined in Chapter Three. Rewards are therefore a special sub-type of feedback that can possibly serve to inform as to goal accom- plishment, motivate continued effort, or even reinforce specific patterns of performance, as the case may be.

Perception

Not all information potentially available via feedback is perceived; not all information perceived is perceived accurately. But it is only through the perceptual apparatus that information about the internal and external environment, including other people, can be taken into account and acted upon through making judgements and decisions in relation to the goals being sought. Person perception is one of the most significant yet complex challenges we face as social animals. Forgas (1985, p. 21) reminds us that, 'it is the first crucial stage in any interaction between people. We must first perceive and interpret other people before we can meaningfully relate to them.'

There are a number of related processes that we need to take into account when reflecting upon perception and the part that it plays in social interaction, generally, and the exchange of rewards in particular. One of these concerns the business of *attribution*, whereby we locate the reasons for and causes of behaviour – our own and that of others. Jones (1990) proposes that perceiving people is inextricably bound up with attaching meaning to them and what they do. Judgments have to be reached about what makes them act in the ways witnessed. Perhaps the two most fundamental alternatives are between identifying the cause as residing in the individual (i.e. he did it because he is that type of person) or in the situation and circumstances in which he found himself (i.e. he did it because he had no choice) (Heider, 1958). The resolution of this dilemma has tremendously pertinent consequences for rewarding and the interpretation of rewards. Whether or not we regard an action as praiseworthy will depend on the personal and situational factors that are adjudged to have brought it about. To what extent was it due to luck, effort or ability? Was the actor a free agent? Would most others have acted in a similar manner if faced with that set of circumstances? Again when in receipt of rewards it makes sense to establish the intentions underlying such largesse. Is it a genuine and spontaneous expression of appreciation and admiration? Is it a statement of solidarity or an attempt to guide and support? Or is it something altogether more sinister; a bid to control or manipulate? Answers to such questions will obviously offer different translations of the rewarding process and dictate contrasting courses of action in response. These are some of the considerations which will be focused upon in Chapter Seven.

How people are perceived is also a feature of the expectations that are entertained of them. We often see in others what we expect to find there. Jones (1990) points out that expectations can be category-based when we have little personal detail to go on. Prior knowledge of a name may surface ethnic or religious presumptions. An address which locates the individual in a certain part of town may do likewise. Familiarity leads to these giving way to target-based alternatives when our expectations stem from all that we have come to know of that individual.

It has also been proposed that what we believe others to be like or what we think they will do is mediated by *implicit personality theories* that we come to hold (Bruner and Taguiri, 1954). This refers to the grouping of traits and characteristics into internally consistent complexes. It could be that ambitious people are believed to be able, scheming, devious, ruthless and not to be trusted. With this view of how people operate, being rewarded by someone looked upon as ambitious will mean something quite different than would be the case were that person labelled in some other way.

In addition to perceptions of others, skilled interpersonal behaviour also requires accurate perceptions of self and of how one is being perceived or *metaperception*. As already mentioned, beliefs in one's abilities and dispositions will have a bearing on projects embarked upon and reactions to feedback received. The importance of self-efficacy in social transactions has been highlighted by Bandura (1986). In a more general sense, people differ in their beliefs that they are the instigators of the rewards that come their way, rather than putting these windfalls simply down to chance. *Locus of control*, as it is called, is a further consideration in the operation of rewards (Rotter, 1966), which will also be explored in Chapter Seven.

Being mindful of the public image portrayed must not be overlooked. Snyder (1987) uses the term *self-monitoring* to refer to the observation, regulation and control of identity projected in public. While some endeavour to create and maintain an impression in keeping with the situation and to earn approbation, others seem less preoccupied by these concerns. Again there are clear implications here for the utility of social rewards.

CONCLUSION

It has become increasingly recognised over recent years that interpersonal communicative competence is an integral part of effective practice in many professional circles including education, management, counselling and health care, to name but a few. Furthermore, the extent to which practitioners are capable of acting as skilled rewarding agents has been identified as making a fundamental contribution to the overall quality of service proffered. Patient and client effects can range from, at the macro level, the shaping of personal and social being, to the micro-level modification of subtle elements of verbal and nonverbal behaviour during encounters. Such rewards can influence not only what people do, but also what they learn, the decisions that they take, their feelings and attitudes towards themselves and others – in short, and depending upon duration of exposure, the sorts of people they become. It is, therefore, all the more surprising that many practitioners seem to make particularly poor use of social rewards in their professional, perhaps even personal lives.

Effective rewarding can be cast as an instance of skilled communication. Some of the key criteria of communication as a skilful undertaking include utility, behavioural facility, contextual propriety, and normativity. In the model of skilled interaction depicted, the centrality of the concept of goal and goal-directed action is accordingly highlighted. The roles of additional components including mediating processes, responses, feedback, and perceptual factors, together with person–situation contextual variables, are also sketched.

Chapter 2

Contrasting theoretical perspectives on interpersonal rewards and rewarding

INTRODUCTION

In the model of interpersonal interaction sketched in the last chapter, we have already encountered a conceptual framework within which the utilisation of social rewards and the process of responding positively to bring about a desired outcome can be interpreted. It is the intention here to extend that thinking by exploring further the psychological background to the notion of social rewards. A range of contrasting theoretical perspectives and paradigms will be considered to further illuminate our understanding of the nature of the phenomenon and its operation in interpersonal contexts pertinent to professional enterprise. The impact of this aspect of communication as it affects the recipient will be considered within the loose categories of firstly, learning and behaviour; secondly, social performance; and thirdly, personality and self-concept. While the first is principally dealt with from a behaviourist point of view, the second that of social learning theory, and the third a combination of psychological humanism and cognitivism, it should, nevertheless, be recognised from the outset that these category boundaries are quite permeable to paradigmatic influence.

EFFECTS OF REWARDS ON LEARNING AND BEHAVIOUR

There can be little doubt that those psychologists down the years interested in the processes involved in creating learning and bringing about behavioural change have made an invaluable contribution to the systematic, empirical investigation and theoretical analysis of the positive consequences of action. The import of the early work of Edward Thorndike in laying the foundations of this rich tradition of scientific inquiry, is frequently acknowledged (Kimble and Schlesinger, 1985).

Thorndike and the Law of Effect

Thorndike's original interest was in exploring the parameters of animal intelligence. At that time, in the late 1890s, a view was held that animals negotiate their environment in an essentially similar way to humans. Thorndike remained unconvinced and determined to subject this anthropomorphic theorising to a more rigorous scrutiny. A programme of experimentation was embarked upon (Thorndike, 1898), the results of which pointed to the role of external rewards rather than internal thought processes in the way in which animals go about solving problems.

A typical experiment presented the experimental subject, frequently a cat, with the task of obtaining a tasty morsel of food, perhaps a portion of fish, while restrained in a piece of apparatus called a puzzle-box. A puzzle-box is, to all intents and purposes, a cage with a door which is the only means of exit. This door can be opened with a simple latch mechanism located inside the box. A hungry cat was placed in the apparatus within sight and smell, but out of reach of the food. In order to obtain the much-prized reward, it was therefore necessary to learn to unlatch the door.

Initial attempts to obtain the food were characterised by much pawing between the bars of the apparatus and equally ill-fated scratching, biting, meowing, etc. However eventually, and often, it seemed, almost by accident, the latch would be tripped, the cat released and the food rapidly consumed. Over the course of a number of trials, the time taken to open the door and receive the reward gradually declined as many of the initial faltering attempts to escape were abandoned. Were the animal operating on the basis of some profound insight into the nature of its predicament and the solution to it, one would have expected a more hasty exit on the second attempt! Rather Thorndike explained these observations in terms of the progressive strengthening of an association between the response that led to the reward and stimuli provided by the box in the presence of which the successful response was made. By contrast potential connections with alternative but unsuccessful responses were not sustained. A more general statement of this line of thought is enshrined in *The Law of Effect* (Thorndike, 1911), which asserts that those behaviours closely followed by rewarding consequences (believed by Thorndike to produce satisfying or pleasurable states of affairs for the recipient) become 'stamped-in' or strengthened and are therefore more likely to recur in the future under similar circumstances.

By this stage the reader might begin to question the relevance of animal intelligence and cats in puzzle boxes to the exploration of rewards as a social phenomenon. It should be appreciated that, for Thorndike as an avowed Darwinian, all learning regardless of the species in question adheres to the same fundamental principles. While human behaviour, together with the types of events that can have a rewarding influence on it, may be much more sophisticated than that found in the animal kingdom, the same basic processes are at work. This supposition will be returned to shortly.

What of the current status of the Law of Effect? Few contemporary theorists would now accord with it, in the way that it was originally envisaged, as an acceptable statement of the essential nature of the learning process. Notwithstanding, Thorndike made a significant contribution to work in this area, the legacy of which is still current within the behaviourist tradition of psychological enquiry (Leahey, 1987).

The Behaviourist tradition

Various shades of Behaviourism presently existing make a brief, definitive statement of underlying philosophy difficult. Since the values and assumptions which
underpin it contrast quite sharply with alternative paradigms to be confronted later
in the chapter, an attempt is worth the effort.

According to Day (1980), modern behaviourism has at its core four indispensable tenets. The first is a commitment to behaviour as an intrinsically worthy
domain of scientific study. The second is a refutation of mentalism. In attempting
to account for what people do, one should look not to inner thoughts, intentions
and feelings, but to the objective world of physical reality. It is perhaps with this
belief that behaviourism is most closely associated and around which much
controversy has centred. Thirdly, behaviourists eschew notions of free will as a
satisfactory means of explaining people's actions. Again this stance has attracted
vigorous criticism. Finally, there is an adherence to biological evolutionism. As
with Thorndike, an inter-species continuity is countenanced making possible, as
has been mentioned, the identification of general principles governing learning that
hold not only between different types of animal, but furthermore between the
animal kingdom and man. Contemporary learning theorists, however, are less
committed to the search for broad laws concentrating instead on researching limited
aspects of learned behaviour (Mowrer and Klein, 1989).

One of the central figures in psychology this century was B.F. Skinner, an
uncompromising behaviourist. Like Thorndike, he believed that the consequences
of instrumental behaviour (behaviour which is instrumental in bringing about
certain states of affairs) have a profound significance when it comes to explaining
and predicting what people do. He is perhaps best remembered for his early work
with mainly pigeons. By making pellets of food available on condition that the bird
displayed a particular response, e.g. pecking a button, he showed that predictable
patterns of behaviour could be set in place. While disagreeing with Thorndike's
account of how this happens, he concurred that positive outcomes increase the
likelihood of those actions being repeated under comparable conditions. Skinner
(1938), however, preferred the more technical term *reinforcement* to that of reward
in referring to this process due to its greater semantic precision and lack of
mentalistic trappings. The application of reinforcement procedures in this way is
also called *operant* or *instrumental conditioning*.

Behaviour and its consequences

We have already seen that, according to the Behaviourist ethos, an understanding
of people's actions can be gleaned from a consideration of happenings in their
surroundings to which they have been exposed. (The causal influence of biological
factors are also recognised.) For any particular piece of behaviour, we can think,
firstly, of environmental stimuli which precede or accompany it and, secondly, of
others which take place afterwards. Take the classroom example of a teacher asking

the class a question to which a child raises its hand. As far as the child's act is concerned, the most conspicuous antecedent stimulus is obviously the posed question. The pupil's response also takes place within the context of a plethora of stimuli which constitute the classroom environment. Other stimuli follow on from it and are made available as a consequence of the behaviour having been performed, e.g. the teacher may react enthusiastically, the child may be offered the opportunity to display its knowledge by answering, etc. The role of antecedent stimuli will be returned to, but for the moment those events which are the products of performance will be further considered.

In broadest terms the relationship between a response and its consequences may be such that that type of response is subsequently either, (i) increased in frequency; (ii) decreased in frequency; or, (iii) left largely unaffected. As to the first of these eventualities, reinforcement, as has been mentioned, is the process taking place. Reinforcers serve to make preceding actions more likely to recur. Reinforcement, however, can take a positive or a negative form, as will be explained shortly. *Punishment* has the effect of suppressing behaviour thus making it less likely that those acts leading to it will be repeated. Indeed, it too can operate in either a positive or a negative way, the former through the administration of a noxious stimulus contingent upon the appearance of the targeted behaviour, the latter by withdrawing some benefit which, had the individual not acted in that way, would continue to have been enjoyed.

Attempts at control and influence through punishment are common in everyday interaction and may be subtly exercised. They can involve sarcasm, ridicule, derision, reprimands and threat, to specify but a few. However, since these practices are the antitheses of rewarding, coupled with the fact that unsanctioned negative behaviour can often be regarded as stemming from a lack of social skill (Spence, 1982), we shall leave the topic of punishment.

When actions previously reinforced cease, for whatever reason, to produce customarily positively valued outcomes, the likely long-term effect will also be a reduction in those activities. This occurs through the phenomenon of *extinction*. Thus while there are important differences between punishment and extinction, both serve to reduce the rate of a response (Hulse *et al.*, 1980).

Finally, given that behaviour can have several predictable outcomes, it may be that some are of little importance one way or another to the person concerned and therefore of no functional significance.

Positive reinforcement

It was mentioned earlier that reinforcement can be engineered through positive or negative means. When behaving in a particular way leads to the introduction of some event that would not have occurred otherwise, any increase in this type of behaviour as a result is due to positive reinforcement. Thus both Thorndike's cat and the pupil in the earlier example had their respective responses positively reinforced by, on the one hand, food and, on the other, teacher acknowledgement, etc. Rewarding is most commonly associated with this kind of relationship whereby an action leads to the introduction of a positively valued outcome that was not available heretofore. Moreover Kimble (1961) called this procedure reward training. Since it will feature largely in the remainder of this part of the chapter, little more need be said about it at this point.

Negative reinforcement

Here an act is associated with the avoidance, termination or reduction of an aversive stimulus which would have either occurred or continued at some existing level had the response not taken place. Negative reinforcement and punishment must not be confused despite the fact that the terms are sometimes treated interchangeably in the literature (Green, 1977). Although both involve aversive states, in the case of punishment this state is made contingent on the occurrence of the behaviour under focus and has the effect of making that behaviour *less* likely to recur. With negative reinforcement, behaviour resulting in the noxious stimulus being reduced, eliminated or avoided will be *more* probable. The effects of people earning rewards of this negative kind for doing certain tasks have been well researched and documented but mostly as part of organised programmes of intervention in such institutional settings as mental hospitals, prisons, and special schools. Allen and Stokes (1987) introduced this approach to manage the disruptive and uncooperative behaviour of children receiving restorative dental treatment. In this case children were asked to be 'Big Helpers' by lying still and being quiet. This led to the temporary suspension of treatment. Gradually children had to be 'Big Helpers' for longer periods of time in order to have treatment stopped. Not only were children markedly more compliant by the last visit but, from readings of heart rate and blood pressure, were also significantly less stressed by the experience.

But opportunities, in day-to-day interactions, for controlling social behaviour through negative reinforcement can also be found. Bringing to an end as quickly as possible an interchange with someone found unpleasant, uninteresting, or just difficult to relate to, could presumably be accounted for in this way (Cipani, 1990). Some evidence for this interpretation emerged from a laboratory-based experiment undertaken by Cramer *et al.* (1989), in which it was discovered that female subjects preferred males who espoused less traditional male values and attitudes. Within the experimental procedure, characteristics of females' switching as they changed from listening over an intercom to a 'macho' male, to listening to one who adhered less rigidly to the traditional male stereotype, was consistent with what would be expected if the former experience was aversive, making the negative reinforcement of switching behaviour possible. A similar explanation for the phenomenon of speaking in reply, especially in conversations where one's opinion has been challenged by the other party, has been put forward by Weiss *et al.* (1971) and Lombardo *et al.* (1973). Again, disagreement with one's point-of-view can be aversive; having the chance to subsequently defend it can bring relief and therefore make responding more likely.

Conversational 'repair' is a further feature of talk (McLaughlin, 1984). Apologies and disclaimers, as examples, are brought into play when participants unwittingly break a conversational or societal rule thereby running the risk of losing face. Approaching this interpersonal activity from a behavioural perspective, Baldwin and Baldwin (1981) see negative reinforcement at work. Thus breaking the rule may cause embarrassment or discomfort which is assuaged by an apology or disclaimer, thereby making it likely that these forms of repairs will be relied upon in similar situations in future.

For negative reinforcement to work, there must be an existing state of unease or discomfort which can be reduced or eliminated through some action. What happens in situations where nothing that individuals do seems to bring relief, where the aversive stimuli to which they are subjected seem to be beyond their powers to control? According to Seligman (1975), when what we do appears to persistently bear no relationship to outcome, making it impossible to control unpleasant experiences to which we are subjected, *learned helplessness* often results. People become passive, apathetic and simply give up trying. Furthermore, and particularly when the cause is attributed to personal inability, this helplessness can generalise to other situations (Mikulineer, 1986), and give rise to stress (Glass and Singer, 1972) and depression (Seligman, 1975).

Categories of positive reinforcer

The vast range of things that we do as we go about our workaday lives gives rise to a multiplicity of differing outcomes, both physical and social. Many of these exert a controlling influence through the operation of positive reinforcement. Is it possible to begin to impose order on these innumerable instances of specific reinforcing event by classifying them according to some pertinent criterion? Among psychologists who respond affirmatively to this question, Sherman (1990) suggests that at least five categories can be identified.

Primary reinforcers

These can be thought of as stimuli, the positive value and reinforcing potential of which do not rely upon a process of prior learning. Ones that spring most readily to mind include food, drink, sex, etc. These are things that we depend on for survival due to our biological make-up. Despite their fundamental indispensability, the limitations of these as a direct means of influencing the complexities of interpersonal behaviour in modern society will be quickly appreciated. Here the rewards tend to be less basic.

Conditioned reinforcers

This grouping, which is also labelled secondary reinforcers, is in sharp contrast to the previous. It includes events that have no intrinsic worth but whose power to control behaviour is ultimately derived from an earlier association with primary reinforcers. Contrasting theoretical accounts of just how this happens are offered by Fantino (1977). Tokens, stickers, vouchers, stamps, badges, stars, etc. have been incorporated into organised programmes called *token economies* where they are earned for engaging in certain tasks and subsequently exchanged for something of greater appeal. (For reviews see Ayllon and Azrin, 1968; McLaughlin and Williams, 1988; and Kazdin, 1988.)

Under certain circumstances, an originally neutral stimulus can become associated with a plurality of primary reinforcers. Money, to cite one example, can be used to obtain food, drink, heat, sex, etc. Skinner (1953) gave the name *generalised reinforcers* to refer to this special class.

Social reinforcers

Social behaviour, by definition, presupposes the involvement of other people. In the main, the types of reward that govern and shape it are also contributed by those with whom we mix and intermingle. These rewards, Buss (1983) suggests, can be thought of as either process or content. The former are an inherent part of interpersonal contact and include, in order of increasing potency, the mere presence of others, attention from them, and their conversational responsivity. An interesting observation is that too much or too little of these activities can be aversive; it is only at a notional intermediate level that they become reinforcing. This view is echoed by Epling and Pierce (1988), who comment that the attention given by a teacher to a pupil in the same environment may well change from being reinforcing to punishing as a function of the increase or decrease in frequency of delivery.

What takes place within interaction has also rewarding ramifications. Here Buss pays particular heed to the acts of showing deference, praising, extending sympathy, and expressing affection. Unlike their process equivalents, these are thought to operate along unipolar dimensions, and additionally presuppose a certain type of interpersonal relationship to be relevant and effective. We seldom praise or show affection to complete strangers, for instance. As well as process and content rewards, individuals can find, variously reinforcing, opportunities to compare themselves to others, compete, dominate or self-disclose, and may seek out situations and occasions to indulge themselves accordingly.

Skinner (1974) and Bandura (1986), among others, speak of individuals being moulded as social beings through the influence of the social milieu of which they are a part. As we have seen, the subtleties of the process make use of the judicious distribution, by significant members, of attention, interest, approval, affection, and so on. It is these sorts of activities that lie at the heart of positive responding conceived of as an interpersonal skill. Through them one person can determine what another does without constant recourse to physical intervention. Furthermore, since many of the projects with which we concern ourselves are long-term, a great deal of initial effort may be expended with few tangible results to show in return.

Here Bandura (1986) stresses the role of support from others in sustaining goal-directed performance.

According to Skinner positive social reactions can be used to shape interpersonal behaviour because they serve as generalised reinforcers. Of 'approval' he wrote, 'A common generalised reinforcer is approval.... It may be little more than a nod of the head or a smile on the part of someone who characteristically supplies a variety of reinforcers. Sometimes... it has a verbal form "Right! or Good!"' (Skinner, 1957, p. 53). Similarly, 'The attention of people is reinforcing because it is a necessary condition for other reinforcements from them. In general, only those who are attending to us reinforce our behaviour' (Skinner, 1953, p. 78).

For Lieberman (1990), among others, these aspects of social performance, in that they can be thought of at all as reinforcers in the Skinnerian sense, embrace both learned and unlearned dimensions. To be more specific, the suggestion is that some of the nonverbal features such as smiles and hugs may not depend upon prior experience to be positively valued.

Sensory reinforcers

One need only think of the attractions of, for example, listening to beautiful music, looking at a striking painting, attending the theatre, or watching an exciting rugby match, together with the effort and expense that devotees will often sustain to do so, to appreciate that certain quantities and qualities of sensory stimulation can be rewarding.

This fact was exploited by Mizes (1985) in treating an adolescent girl who was hospitalised following complaints of chronic lower-back pain. The extent of this pain was such that she was virtually bed-ridden. Tests and examinations having failed to locate any physical cause, the case was treated as a conversion disorder which was being inadvertently held in place through operant conditioning. When opportunities to watch TV, have access to the telephone, and receive parental visits were made conditional upon demonstrably increased mobility, symptoms gradually subsided.

Buss (1983) seems to claim that those kinds of social reward which he categorised as process, including the presence of others, attention from them, and their degree of responsivity, are found attractive because of their stimulation value. As such they would appear to be a special case of sensory reinforcer.

Activity reinforcers

According to David Premack, activities rather than things are reinforcing. It is eating, drinking, etc., that is of significance rather than food or drink, as such. Stated formally, the *Premack Principle*, as it is commonly known, proposes that activities of low probability can be increased in likelihood if activities of high probability are made contingent upon them (Premack, 1965).

Activity reinforcement can be a powerful means of organising work routines and maximising commitment in a diversity of professional settings including management, industry and education. Pupils may prefer practical classes to more didactic instruction but given the freedom to choose they would probably fill their time in some other way. This likelihood was put to good use by Hutchins *et al.* (1989), to improve low achieving secondary pupils' punctuality and readiness to begin lessons on time. The agreement was that if the entire class was present and prepared to begin work within one minute of the bell to signal the beginning of the period, the last four minutes would be set aside for members to do whatever they pleased. The effect of this group contingent free-time procedure was an average five-fold improvement in good time-keeping. Pupils also reacted favourably to it and teachers reported that more academic work got completed as a result.

The potential for these principles to enhance managerial effectiveness and raise output has been recognised by Komaki (1982). She suggested that time off work which would become available upon completion of certain targets could be an appealing activity reinforcer. The reinforcing implications of personnel training as part of organisations' human resource development systems have also been identified (Nordhaug, 1989). Productivity can also be improved, as demonstrated by Gupton and LeBow (1971), through an internal rearrangement of the various types of task that workers carry out. In this case the workers were part-time telephone sales personnel in industry who sold both new and renewal service contracts. On average the success rate for attempts at renewals was more than twice that for new sales, so sales personnel tended to devote most of their energies to the former. As far as the firm was concerned this resulted in a general failure to attract new customers. By imposing the Premack Principle, five new calls were required before the representatives had an opportunity to make attempts at renewal sales. This contingency resulted in a substantial increase not only in the number of new contracts sold but renewals as well.

It shouldn't be assumed, however, that only certain activities can reinforce. Premack stressed that any behaviour can increase the likelihood of any other provided that the former tends to occur more frequently and, in order to perform it, the latter has to be carried out. Instrumental and reinforcing actions are not intrinsically different: reinforcement is relative rather than absolute. These ideas have been further developed, particularly in the study of animals, by including concepts from economics to account for how behavioural resources are regulated to maximise outcome (Allison, 1989).

Frequency of reinforcement

As we go about our daily lives the things that we do don't invariably produce the rewards that we seek. Putting considerable effort into a successful project at work may sometimes lead to special recognition from the manager, raising your hand in class may sometimes attract the teacher's attention, investing in the stock market may sometimes produce profits, telephoning a customer may sometimes win a sale, listening single-mindedly to an anxious patient's symptoms may sometimes encourage a disclosure of the real concern – but often it does not! In the early stages of coming to appreciate the advantages of these ways of doing things, frequent failure can severely jeopardise the acquisition process. Once established, however, they can be kept in place even if desired outcomes are only occasionally achieved.

The effects of *intermittent reinforcement* were first noted and systematically investigated in the laboratory by Skinner during his work with pigeons. Much concerted research subsequently identified consistently distinct patterns of responding associated with different *schedules of reinforcement* (Ferster and Skinner, 1957). A schedule in this sense can be thought of as a stipulation of the circumstances under which a reward will be made available following an appropriate response.

Ratio schedules

Here the availability of reinforcement is dependent on the number of responses that are made. The specified behaviour has to be repeated a predetermined number of times before a reward becomes available. This may be arranged on a *fixed* basis whereby say every tenth response is consistently rewarded or be made *variable* so that *on average* every tenth response brings success. Piecework can be thought of as an example of the former. Factory workers may be paid a certain amount for every twenty screws inserted, hems stitched, or tins packed. Gambling is often held to be maintained through the influence of variable ratio systems. Put to more productive ends, Wallin and Johnson (1976) reported how absenteeism was radically reduced resulting in a savings to the firm of over three thousand dollars in less than a year, when staff were given the chance to enter a monthly lottery if they had a perfect attendance record for that period. The winner received the recognition of management and workers through public acknowledgement of their achievement and was given a small monetary prize.

Ratio schedules, particularly of the variable type, produce extremely high performance output. When rewards are distributed in a fixed fashion, rates of responding tend to be less consistent, with characteristic dips in performance immediately after each reinforcement is delivered (Ferster and Skinner, 1957).

Interval schedules

We can no doubt think of instances where the positive outcomes we seek are only available at particular times. The number of responses *per se* is not the determining feature but rather *when* they occur. *Fixed-interval schedules* reinforce the next response after a designated period of time has elapsed, while with *variable-interval schedules* that time period is averaged making the delivery of the reinforcer less predictable.

Interval schedules are generally less effective than ratio alternatives in motivating high levels of performance and encouraging persistence in the face of failure, but are usually much more successful in these respects than continuous reinforcement. This finding is reflected in recommendations to practitioners. Thus Brophy (1981) advised teachers to use praise sparingly thereby maximising its reinforcing capabilities. (This advice would seem to be at odds, however, with that derivable from Buss's conceptualisation of praise as an instance of the class of content social rewards!)

Before leaving the topic, a cautionary note should be sounded. Much of the work which has given rise to the recognition of these four distinct patterns of responding characterising the schedules mentioned has emerged from controlled, laboratory-based animal experimentation. Just how widely these schedules generalise to account for what people do is subject to current debate. There is evidence that people are, perhaps surprisingly, less sensitive than animals to schedule differences and, when exposed to fixed-interval arrangements, often respond at either consistently high or low levels. Lowe (1979) suggested that these differences largely reflect the way in which the relationship between response and reward is interpreted by the individual together with subsequent self-instructions as to how to approach the task.

Accounting for choice

Contemplating behavioural options brings us inexorably to the possibility of choice. Since this notion carries heavy mentalistic connotations it poses particular problems for behaviourists. One attempt to get around this difficulty, while retaining a belief in the causal potency of the environment in accounting for what people finally end up doing, focuses on the relative richness of different but concurrent sources and types of reward often delivered according to contrasting schedules. In situations of this sort, studies (mostly with animals in two-choice arrangements) have led to the formulation of the 'Matching Law' equating response and reinforcement variability. Simply stated, it predicts that response rate for a particular behaviour will be directly proportional to the rate of reinforcement accruing (Herrnstein, 1970).

One interesting application of the Matching Law in a group discussion context was completed by Conger and Killeen (1974). Subjects ostensibly took part, with three other members, in a discussion on student attitudes towards drugs. In fact the other members were 'plants', one of whom had the task of keeping the conversation going while the other two rewarded the subject's contributions by means of contingent approval. While both were approving in accordance with variable-interval schedules, one schedule dispensed more than twice the amount of rewards compared to the other. Members took turns at being more or less rewarding to eliminate the contaminating influence of any individual idiosyncrasies. An analysis of the extent of subjects' responding to these two was discovered to match the proportion of rewards received. The member who was more approving of subjects' opinions, as determined by the richer schedule, tended to be engaged correspondingly more frequently by them. The authors nevertheless question the degree to which these findings are replicable in naturally occurring groups. However, Martens *et al.* (1990) reported that the Matching Law which acknowledged teacher's reinforcement through contingent attention of both on-task and off-task pupil behaviour was a better predictor of appropriate classroom participation than an analysis restricted to the rewarding of positive behaviour alone. A review of several further applications of Matching principles in natural settings is offered by McDowell (1988).

Magnitude of reinforcement

Do large rewards have a greater impact on behaviour than smaller ones? Attempts to answer this question are mainly derived from animal experimentation where significant inconsistencies in findings have emerged (Bonem and Crossman, 1988). It seems that, in the main, sheer extent of reward is not the crucial factor. A relativistic approach is required embracing the relationships between present amount and both past experiences of that reinforcer (Flaherty, 1982), and the totality of concurrent reinforcement also available (Martens *et al.*, 1990). The relationship between the amount of reward received and that felt to be warranted also seems to be important (Lawler, 1983). In an organisational setting, workers expressed less satisfaction with inequitable arrangements including those which furnished them with *higher* rewards than they thought was appropriate. In any case, Lieberman (1990) suggests that magnitude of reward makes a greater difference to performance because of motivational rather than learning effects.

With social reinforcers ideas of absolute amount are fraught with even greater problems. There is some research evidence to testify that the reinforcing potential of conversationalists depends on the timing of their verbal and nonverbal contributions and where they place them in the ongoing interaction, rather than on how much they offer *per se* (Schroeder and Rakos, 1983). The situational context within which it occurs also imposes meaning on social behaviour to determine its reinforcing potential. As pointed out by Epling and Pierce (1988), teacher attention may be a highly desirable reward for a child in the classroom but may be shunned by that same child in the playground.

Stimulus control

It will be recalled from earlier in the chapter that behaviour can be set in a context of, on the one hand, preceding and accompanying stimuli, and, on the other, consequent events. We have also acknowledged that a particular response sometimes produces a rewarding consequence but at other times fails to. When a certain action only succeeds in eliciting reinforcement in the presence of particular accompanying stimuli, then that piece of behaviour is said to be under *stimulus control* (Domjan and Burkhard, 1986) and those stimuli have become *discriminative stimuli* in respect of it. They signal the availability of a reinforcer for behaving in that way.

Many examples of stimulus control spring to mind. Fisher and Groce (1990) describe the doctor–patient consultation as a typically one-sided affair in which, 'Physicians solicit technical information from patients who provide the information requested, responding in a relatively passive fashion' (p. 226). Here the doctor is the one who asks the questions and introduces topics for discussion; blatant attempts by patients to negotiate their own agendas meet with little success. In this setting, doctor questions perhaps serve as discriminative stimuli indicating to patients when their contributions will be welcomed and when not! The perspicacious employee who learns to read the subtle cues that suggest the likelihood of his manager being receptive to new ideas, and accordingly picks his opportunity to propose some innovation, is also being influenced by stimulus control.

Shaping

Reinforcement operates by increasing the future probability of an action that it is made contingent upon. Any possible effect, therefore, presupposes the performance of that piece of behaviour. If the action is never performed it obviously can't be reinforced. But in some cases one might wait a long time for certain behaviours to appear spontaneously. *Shaping* permits nascent attempts at the end performance to be rewarded. By systematically demanding higher standards for rewards to be granted, performances can be shaped to attain acceptable levels of excellence. The acquisition of most everyday skills like swimming, driving a car, writing a letter, and so on involve an element of shaping (Schwartz, 1989). While early behaviourists believed that behaviour was almost infinitely malleable in this way, such optimism has been replaced by a more realistic assessment of the limits of shaping and conditioning (Breland and Breland, 1961).

How does reinforcement work?

It is widely accepted that reinforcement modifies the future probability of the behaviour that led to it as we have seen. There is much less agreement, however, about just how this is brought about. Miller (1963) reviewed nine contrasting theoretical attempts to explain the mechanisms which are at the basis of the phenomenon. Some of these have since fallen from favour while other contenders have emerged to take their place. Furthermore, recent theorists have also shown a greater willingness to contemplate the possibility that the reinforcing outcomes of instrumental conditioning, under contrasting circumstances, may reflect different underlying processes (Davey, 1988). There may be no one correct answer to the question of how reinforcement has its effect. A more fulsome exploration of these matters together with an overview of extant theories and models is well beyond the scope of this chapter. Nevertheless several issues around which current debate still centres will be briefly mentioned.

Automatic effect

Some theorists, including Thorndike and Skinner, held that reinforcement functions largely automatically to bring about behavioural change. Two important implications stem from this view, each of which will be considered. The first is that the individual's awareness of what is taking place is not a prerequisite of reinforcement. The second concerns the nature of the relationship between the targeted response and the reinforcing event.

Awareness

Does there have to be a conscious awareness of the relationship between what one does and the rewarding outcome which results for reinforcement to function? For Thorndike the answer to this question was an emphatic 'No'. In keeping with the Law of Effect, satisfying or pleasurable consequences acted in an entirely automatic, unconscious way to 'stamp in' connections between representations of situational stimuli and responses.

Neither was conscious deliberation a necessary prerequisite for operant conditioning to be manifested, as far as Skinner was concerned. This belief was held just as steadfastly in reference to people as to animals. The results of a series of verbal operant conditioning experiments offered some (although not necessarily the strongest) support for this stance. One such was conducted by Greenspoon (1955), who found that the number of plural nouns given by subjects, during interactions with an experimenter, could be systematically increased by making the experimenter utterance 'mm-hmm' contingent upon this class of verbalisation. When asked afterwards, subjects seemed to have had little knowledge of the response/reinforcer connection to which they had been subjected.

Others have criticised many of these experiments on methodological grounds, arguing that the procedures adopted to determine awareness on the part of subjects were inadequate (DeNike and Spielberger, 1963). When a more incisive approach is taken to assess this variable, the case in favour of automaticity of reinforcement is less impressive (Dulany, 1968; Brewer, 1974). According to Dulany (1968), conditioning results can be better explained in terms of subjects trying to figure out the connection between what they do and the outcomes they experience in a sort of puzzle-solving exercise. Engineering further consequences then becomes a volitional activity.

While conclusive proof is lacking to resolve this difference in position, the present consensus of opinion appears to be that, as far as social performance is concerned, probably little instrumental conditioning takes place without at least some minimal level of conscious involvement (Bower and Hilgard, 1981).

Relationship between response and reinforcer

The issue at stake here is whether reinforcement depends on the behaviour in question bringing about a positive outcome (contingency) or simply being followed by one (contiguity). We can think of many natural effects of actions that only take place some time afterwards. The successful salesperson has to wait until the end of the month to collect a bonus for surpassing set targets. On the other hand it sometimes happens that sought-after states of affairs arrive entirely fortuitously but directly following the completion of some irrelevant task. Once the rain-dance has ended it begins to rain!

A belief in contiguity as a necessary and sufficient condition for reinforcement to take place is commonly associated with its unconscious operation. Skinner (1977, p. 4), for instance, wrote that, 'Coincidence is the heart of operant conditioning. A response is strengthened by certain kinds of consequences, but not necessarily because they are actually produced by it.' Superstition is explicable in this way. No doubt there are instances when we are seduced by the immediacy of events that occur into believing that we have bought them about by our own efforts. Indeed, people seem generally to differ in their predisposition to regard themselves as being in control of things that happen to them. (See discussion of Locus of Control in Chapter Seven.) It is also commonly recommended that rewards be administered directly after the desired response, particularly where delay might lead to a disassociation between the two (O'Leary and O'Leary, 1977). Nevertheless, not only people but also animals appear to be, for the most part, quite adept at identifying causal connections between what they do and environmental circumstances. If it were not so, if we were at the mercy of the myriad of events that happen to co-occur with what we do, our behaviour would be bizarre and our lives chaotic. While acknowledging exceptions, the effects of reinforcement seem to rely more upon a contingent than a mere contiguous association between behaviour and reward (Schwartz, 1989; Maier, 1989).

It can be concluded, therefore, that, in the main, rewards work best when the individuals involved are aware of a causal relationship between what they have done, or are doing, and the outcomes that are sought. In the main, according to such as Bandura (1977), those outcomes operate to motivate and inform, rather than to strengthen behaviour in an automatic and mechanistic fashion.

Motivation

Motivation as a factor in interpersonally skilled performance has already been considered in the last chapter. We will return to the topic and further consider its contribution to our understanding of the nature of reinforcement. The histories of the study of reinforcement and motivation are closely interwoven. Prominent among the earlier theorists who came to place great importance on the contribution of deprivation to the mechanisms of reinforcement was Clark Hull. Accordingly, deprivation was envisaged causing an imbalance in the organism's underlying physiological state. Since an innate predilection exists to maintain internal systems in homeostasis, a *drive* to reverse the effects of insufficiency is created. The end result is to motivate the organism through energising behavioural resources to do whatever is necessary to restore an internal harmony. Whatever succeeds becomes a reinforcer by dint of its drive-reducing properties (Hull, 1943).

How far does this take us in understanding notions of reward in social interaction? An attempt was made by Miller and Dollard (1941) to develop many of Hull's ideas and apply them more fully to the human condition. Following Hull, they equated reinforcement with a drive-reducing capacity. In addition to *primary drives* such as hunger, thirst, sex, pain, etc., a category of *secondary drive*, including, for example, fear and anger as well as sociability, need for approval, and the need for a sense of personal competence, was postulated. These motives are learned through association with the satisfaction of primary drives and are ultimately derivable from them. Indeed, Miller (1951) came to believe that any stimulus, internal or external, if intense enough, could constitute a drive and impel action.

Accordingly, attention has rewarding properties because it can reduce the learned drive for recognition from others. In situations where such recognition has been consistently connected with an aversive experience, a quite different drive will emerge and attention cease to reinforce. Indeed it might even become a source of punishment under these circumstances (Sajwaj and Dillon, 1977).

This notion of learned or secondary drives has been invoked by different authors in explaining varied aspects of interpersonal interaction which are regarded as stemming from social reinforcement. The reinforcing effects of speaking in reply when one's views are challenged, which were researched by such as Weiss *et al.* (1971) and Lombardo *et al.* (1973), and were referred to earlier, were thought to be possibly due to an effectance drive. One is thereby motivated to be consistent and correct in one's beliefs and dealings with the environment. Steigleder *et al.* (1980) also claimed that competing with others has drive-like qualities such that bringing competition to an end produces negative reinforcing consequences. Further work in this tradition is outlined by Gergen (1969), who mentions that if need for recognition, approval, etc., really are drives similar in nature to the need for food, water, and so on, and if social reinforcers including attention and praise operate by bringing about reductions in these states, then they should be subject to the same parameters among which are satiation and deprivation. In other words, being deprived of attention should heighten its reinforcing impact; too much should have the opposite effect. Despite evidence that this might be so in some cases (Gergen, 1969; Cook, 1985), many would rebutt this general stance. Rotter (1982), for instance, is adamant that, 'Drive reduction as an alternative view of reinforcement ceases to be useful in the study of complex social behaviour' (p. 9).

The concept of drive has largely fallen into disrepute as a useful intervening variable in the understanding of how animals learn and why they behave in the ways that they do (Bolles, 1975). In the study of personality and interpersonal relations, however, the role of the related ideas of social needs and motives is very much to the fore, as mentioned in the previous chapter. There is no assumption though that they operate in accordance with a Hullian conceptualisation of drive reduction (Buck, 1988). Neither is it the case that the motivational basis of rewards must ultimately rest on their capacity to reduce drive states in the way that this theorist suggested.

The common counter to drive-based theories of motivation focuses on the inducement of an *incentive*. Kelly (1955) characterised these approaches as the stick and the carrot; the former emphasising the goad of enduring, unpleasant states, the latter the pull of attractive possibilities. What we do, claimed Logan (1971), is determined not so much by the push of internal drives as the pull of anticipated and positively valued incentives. Social rewards are also believed to influence how people act interpersonally on the basis of their incentive value (Bandura, 1977). Individuals behave in decided ways, adopt particular practices, and engage with certain others due to an anticipation of attention, interest, approval, affection, or other favoured outcomes from them in consequence.

Notice how far this incentive view of rewards takes us from the idea of reinforcers acting in an automatic and mechanical manner to strengthen preceding behaviour. Here, by experiencing event y having done x, individuals come to anticipate that in the future doing x will make y available. Continuing to do x in consequence is, therefore, a result of such expectations and predictions. These cognitive processes mediate between features of the environment and the individual's behaviour, and play an indispensable part in determining courses of action taken. More will be said about them in both this chapter and the chapters to follow.

Before leaving this discussion of the motivational bases of reinforcement, it will be recalled from Chapter One that the concept of goal has implications for energising the agent (Pervin, 1989). Bandura (1989) differentiates between the motivating effects of external incentives representing the projected attainment of tangible outcomes, including the approval of others, etc., and those of a self-generated nature stemming from anticipations of positive self-evaluation arising from the application of internal standards to successful goal-directed performance. In so far as the reactions of others furnish feedback of relevance to such judgements, they are likely to be welcomed. It is not only the attainment of the goal which is rewarding, evidence of progress towards it will be positively valued in these terms.

Information

Rewards can serve to heighten motivation either through reducing drive levels or, as is now more commonly accepted, by providing incentives for designated courses of action. But reinforcers, particularly secondary reinforcers, also carry information about impending events. In the words of Estes (1971), 'for the adult learner, rewards and punishments serve to an important extent as carriers of information quite independently of any effect they may have as satisfiers or arousers of drives or motives' (p. 19). Could it be that their major influence on behaviour is due to this fact?

Conditioning studies with people are often arranged so that response-contingent points are allocated which can then be exchanged for back-up reinforcers like food or money. The material value of these is usually quite small. Wearden (1988), for example, draws attention to the fact that, in some instances, subjects have worked diligently on variable schedules for, in real terms, as little as five pence an hour! When food is the reward, it is often left unconsumed, indeed sometimes discarded without being tasted, and yet at the same time subjects continue to earn more. These findings are difficult to reconcile in motivational terms if money or food is thought of as the key inducement. A more plausible explanation offered by Wearden (1988) portrays the conditioning procedure as a problem-solving exercise, in the eyes of the subjects. Points received for an appropriate move are prized, not hedonistically through association with money or food, but on account of the information they contribute to finding a solution to the 'puzzle'.

Thought of in this light, social rewards such as praise take on a different complexion. By praising pupils' responses, teachers make them aware of the acceptability of the goals towards which they strive, together with feedback on their efforts in respect of attaining them. We can speculate that, in situations where neither might be immediately evident, this knowledge will be particularly valuable.

The basis of a model of reinforcement working in this way has been sketched by Schwartz (1989). This author makes the point, however, that positive feedback often signals that one should move on to the next stage of a sequence of activities that will be concluded when the goal is reached, rather than repeating the same response as a traditional interpretation of reinforcement would suggest. Glaser (1971) proposes, however, that what is being modified when this happens are perhaps strategies that inform behaviour rather than the specific responses themselves.

An important distinction is drawn by Deci and Porac (1978), with reference to the informational nature of rewards. On the one hand, they can enable conclusions to be drawn about the level of efficacy with which a course of action is being prosecuted. The more frequently individuals are praised for doing a task well, let's say, the greater their feelings of self-competence and self-confidence, and the more likely their persistence with this type of endeavour. Alternatively, rewards can connote attempts to control and influence, in which case those in receipt may come to regard what they do as entirely due to this external inducement and be less inclined to continue with the activity. O'Donnell et al. (1983) found that those subjects who reported an awareness of the experimental contingency in a verbal conditioning procedure, but did not display the expected increase in the reinforced response, tended to regard the experiment as an attempt at social influence. This may be a manifestation of what Brehm and Brehm (1981) called *reactance* which is an attempt to reassert personal freedom perceived to be compromised. The way in which information carried by rewards is interpreted seems, therefore, to be a crucially important intervening factor in determining their probable effects.

Summing up this section, it would appear that while rewards may operate in an automatic, mechanistic fashion to modify behaviour unbeknown to the person concerned, this is atypical. For the most part, in everyday and professional life, rewards serve to influence through acting as incentives to pursue one action path rather than another, together with furnishing information on the utility and acceptability of behaviour in pursuit of goals. These ideas will be further developed as the chapter unfolds.

Rewards, reinforcement and intrinsic motivation

Most would readily agree that we are influenced by rewards, no matter how this happens, to continue with those activities that elicit them. But is this invariably the case? Some would claim not. A widely reported finding is that when rewards that are not part of the intrinsic nature of a task are given for what is inherently motivating and would have been done in any case, people may be subsequently *less*, rather than *more* likely to take part in those activities for their own sake. One instance of this phenomenon, reported by Upton (1973), involved giving a ten dollar inducement to donors for offering blood. It was discovered, perhaps rather surprisingly, that initially highly committed volunteers were less likely to come forward when paid. Lepper and Greene (1978) explain this finding in terms of an external reward bringing about a decline in the degree of intrinsic motivation that was once held for the task. It would seem, however, that this is less likely to occur when the extrinsic incentive is social rather than material. Furthermore, there is evidence that verbal rewards may even promote intrinsic interest when they are perceived as sincere, relevant to the targeted activity and specifying its approval (Kruglanski, 1978; Sakurai, 1990). Why are some tasks intrinsically motivating? Deci and Ryan (1980) believe that it has to do with opportunities provided for manifesting competence and self-determination. In an earlier and highly influential publication, White (1959) also posited an in-built need to deal effectively with the environment thereby exercising personal competence. It will be recalled from Chapter One, of course, that this is one of the fundamental needs identified by Emmons (1989) as leading to the establishment of interpersonal goals.

The implications of this research on the influence of external incentives on intrinsically motivating tasks are two-fold. Firstly, at the practical level, it opens the possibility of behaviour leading to rewards being less likely to be repeated in the future. Secondly, this has important conceptual ramifications for the nature of the relationship between rewards and reinforcement. If rewards are thought of in essentially objective terms as the mere giving of money, etc., and reinforcers are defined along strictly behavioural lines as stimuli that increase the probability of preceding behaviour, we arrive at a situation where rewards do not necessarily reinforce (Dickinson, 1989).

In the following section, and in subsequent chapters, we will consider how the expectations and meanings attributed to rewarding episodes have a bearing upon how individuals react to them, and the extent to which they are found attractive and consequently sought out. There can be no guarantee of a one-to-one correspondence between the value bestowed upon a reward by the giver, or indeed a third party, and that of the person at the receiving end (Mischel, 1990).

EFFECTS OF REWARDS ON SOCIAL PERFORMANCE

Some of our speculations on how rewards as reinforcers might operate to produce learning and modify behaviour rest somewhat uncomfortably with the fundamental behaviouristic assumptions, such as an avowed antimentalism, which were sketched at the beginning of the last section and broadly characterised much of the content of it. For many theorists, the view emerging from this behaviourist tradition of how people as social entities are formed, shaped and controlled is profoundly lacking in a number of respects. These are summarised by Phares (1984). Firstly, it denies a role to the rich cognitive panoply which pervades so much of human functioning as it mediates responses to that which is confronted. Rewards which are encountered are not responded to in a typically inflexible, robotic manner. Rather they are interpreted, assessed and reacted to in an essentially considered style. This was borne out in an experiment conducted by Kaufman *et al.* (1966), in which the patterns of responding to emerge were more in keeping with subjects' beliefs about reinforcing consequences rather than the actual schedules of reinforcement which pertained.

Secondly, the derivation of broad principles of learning from mainly laboratory-based experiments with animals has been a cause for concern in some quarters (Wearden, 1988). A very small proportion of basic research has in fact featured people. Rather the tendency has been to assume direct applicability to the human condition and proceed accordingly (Lowe, 1979).

Thirdly, and associated with the previous point, Phares (1984) acknowledges a further weakness in a relative neglect of the inescapable social domain of the majority of human conduct. Most of the rewards that matter are given by us to others with whom we come in contact, not gleaned by them from apersonal surroundings.

Finally, a strictly behaviouristic model characterises a passive exposure to the world, as our behaviour is moulded to meet the demands which are imposed. But the fact that individuals are influenced by their surroundings is only part of the picture; they also make changes and can choose where to locate. This is particularly the case in the interpersonal context. At the micro level of face-to-face interaction, 'Person A responds to the stimulus properties of Person B, but Person B in turn is responsive to the behaviour of Person A, which he has in part determined' (Wachtel, 1973, p. 330). People are active agents in the business of seeking out rewards and making them happen. This can extend to the implementation of self-presentation strategies such as ingratiation.

Disquiet surrounding these sorts of issues has spurred modifications and extensions of basic behaviouristic conceptualisations of, among other matters, the role and operation of rewards in behavioural acquisition and regulation, leading to what has come to be referred to as *Social Learning Theory* or, recently, *Social Cognitive Theory* (Bandura, 1986). Although the roots of this movement can be traced back to the psychology of the turn of the century and beyond (Woodward, 1982), it is with the work of three contemporary theorists that it is commonly associated. They are Albert Bandura (Bandura, 1977), Julian Rotter (Rotter, 1982), and Walter Mischel (Mischel, 1973), each of whom has developed a unique, yet broadly consistent and complementary theory subsumable under this general rubric. No attempt will be made to sketch the extent of their individual contributions. Instead several of the ideas which recast views of social reward and which have come to typify this genre will be briefly presented.

Observation learning

Much of what we know and do, as social animals, is due to observational learning rather than directly experiencing the consequences of action. It is accomplished by watching what others do, noting what happens to them because of it, evaluating whether one could act similarly, and deciding if it is worth the effort. The efficacy of learning by this means has been extensively researched across a broad swath of social behaviour (Bandura, 1986). Nor does the model have to be in the physical presence of the observer for this to take place. Mediated models presented via videotape, audiotape, or the written medium can be highly influential (Dickson *et al.*, 1989).

How does observation learning come about? Bandura (1977) stipulated that four related sub-processes were involved, namely, attention, retention, motor reproduction, and, finally, motivation.

Attention

A necessary prerequisite for behaviour to be acquired in this way is that the model be attended to. Unless the observer can orient to, perceive and successfully discriminate the relevant features of the model's performance from the frequent confusion of competing and distracting stimuli also present, the overall imitative process will suffer.

Retention

While attention to pertinent cues is necessary for successful imitation, it is not sufficient. Information so gained must be remembered long enough, in the absence of the source, to be acted upon. Bandura (1977) asserts that what persists, once the model is no longer present or acting, are internal symbolic representations of the observed external stimuli. These can be either imaginal or verbal in form. As far as the former mode of encoding is concerned, we create mental images of the event which provide long-lasting and easily retrievable sources of knowledge. The verbal representational system plays a more important role in most learning by this method. By creating and logging away a sort of 'internal description' of what took place, vast amounts of detail can be quickly learned and retrieved after lengthy periods of time.

Rehearsal operations also aid retention. This can be done either overtly, when the observer actually performs the modelled response pattern, or covertly. In the latter case the performance is merely gone through in the 'mind's eye'. Both have been found to be useful.

Motor reproduction processes

Here symbolic representations of the witnessed performance are translated into corresponding behaviour.

Motivation

By now it may be wondered where the role of rewards fits into this picture of social learning. A fundamental differentiation made by Bandura (1977) is that between, on the one hand, the acquisition of knowledge and, on the other, its implementation in performance. The mere fact that there is an understanding of how to behave in a particular way does not entail that a decision will be taken to do so. Only those actions that are expected to produce positive outcomes, based either on observations or past experiences, are likely to be carried out. It is in this anticipatory respect that rewards proffered create sufficient incentives for people to determine whether it is worthwhile to make use of their know-how.

Does this mean that the prospects of being rewarded are irrelevant as far as the actual *learning* component is concerned? No, not quite. While directly rewarding consequences are not essential in order for knowledge of how to act in particular situations to be picked up, they facilitate this process in several respects. The anticipation of what is happening leading to desirable outcomes will, at the attention stage, enhance the importance of this event relative to co-existing alternatives, increase the likelihood that it will be contemplated, and direct concerted attention to the crucial cues of the modelled display by assisting in their discrimination. This is especially so in the case of events that are not particularly striking in and of themselves and would, therefore, be unlikely to have much impact on this account (Bandura, 1986). Interestingly, some presentations, such as television, are so intrinsically rewarding that even children can be held enthralled for long periods. No doubt this lies behind the concern felt by many over children's exposure to scenes of explicit sex or violence.

The prospect of rewards also has a bearing on the retention stage. Although it may mean that the individual applies himself more diligently to the accurate symbolic encoding of what is attended to, perhaps the greatest effect of such incentives is on the amount of rehearsal undertaken and consequently the extent to which acquisitions are strengthened and stabilised. Following on from that, it is unlikely that at the motor reproduction stage considerable effort will be invested in transforming internal representations into a veridical construction of what was witnessed, bearing in mind that this may demand ongoing attempts and refinements, unless it is thought to make available opportunities that would otherwise be denied. In this indirect way, rewards can therefore facilitate social performance based upon the observation of others.

Finally, lest it be thought that observational learning only operates in behavioural terms, it should be recognised that one of the most important methods by which the rules and conventions that pertain in different social situations are realised and adopted is through observing how others equip themselves and how they are received as a result.

Bandura (1986) also maintains that much of what people do is in this way self-regulated. As we have already seen, interventions and the effects that accrue are monitored with comparisons made between what has been accomplished and internalised standards so that subsequent activity can be modified accordingly. These standards of conduct are partly laid down by copying those manifested by salient others but also, especially although not exclusively in the formative years, through the rewards and punishments bestowed by such people in reacting to us. Under circumstances where a paucity of affirmative responses results in the adoption of extremely rigorous standards of self-evaluation, making self-defined success infrequent and unlikely, feelings of depression and worthlessness can develop. The effects of the evaluative reactions of others on self-concept will be taken up in the next section.

Vicarious rewards

So far we have discussed the direct impact of positive outcome on the acquisition and regulation of the behaviour that brought it about. But the influence of rewards is more wide-ranging. Through observing our actions others learn not only how, but what to do; they benefit from our successes. Bandura (1986, p. 285) asserts that, 'If a person experiences consequences in a group setting, the observed outcomes can affect the behaviour of the group as a whole. Even mild praise or reprimand can lead other group members to adopt praiseworthy acts and to avoid censurable ones.' The implications of this fact for professional practice are far-reaching. Turney et al. (1983) highlight the difficulty of a teacher, in a large and busy classroom, providing reinforcement, on an individual basis, for appropriate behaviour and accomplishments. Under these circumstances, an appreciation of how vicarious reinforcement can be put to good use is particularly valuable.

In relation to management, the maxim of 'praise publicly–punish privately', cited by Prue and Fairbank (1981), articulates the potential vicarious benefits of bestowing rewards in the presence of others. This practice was put to good use by O'Reilly and Puffer (1989), to enhance expressed motivation, satisfaction and productivity among a group of retail sales clerks, when the basis of allocation was seen to be fair. On a more cautionary note, however, it should be recognised that, firstly, praising in public can cause embarrassment and, if so, will probably produce negative rather than positive effects (Giacolone and Rosenfeld, 1987). Secondly, watching others persistently rewarded for something that the observer has done equally competently may cause resentment and demotivation. The latter has been referred to as the implicit effects of observed consequences and distinguished from vicarious facets by Bandura (1986).

Rewards, vicariously experienced, can influence learning, motivation and emotions. In respect of learning, greater heed will probably be paid to what others do, and it will be remembered for longer, when it is seen to succeed in gaining something desired. Indeed when such learning is highly cognitively taxing, being freed from the behavioural reproduction and recognition of consequences elements, which are part-and-parcel of direct reinforcement, is often a distinct advantage as far as the acquisition process is concerned. When it comes to regulating behaviour in the longer term, direct incentives are more powerful (Bandura, 1977). Watching others rewarded can act as a strong inducement for the observer to do likewise when it is inferred that similar outcomes will accrue. Furthermore, when the consequences of actions are socially mediated, a basis is established for reassessing the attractiveness of experienced outcomes through witnessing what happens to others under comparable conditions. Receiving recognition from a supervisor will probably mean much more once it is realised, from observations of interactions with others, that this person rarely acknowledges effort. Receiving rewards and punishments is associated with the creation of pleasant and unpleasant emotional states. Awareness of these states and circumstances in other people can be emotionally arousing and this facility is believed, by Bandura (1986), to account for empathic responsivity to them. The ability to engage empathically with others is, of course, fundamental to effective counselling (Egan, 1986).

Expectancy

The concept of expectancy is centrally important, in social learning theory terms, to the explanation and prediction of behaviour. Acting on the basis of judgements formed as to the likely outcome has been alluded to in much of what has already been mentioned. For Rotter (1966), expectancy is a personal probability entertained by the individual as to the likely attainment of a given reward or set of rewards for engaging in a specific activity. The subjectivity of these anticipations should not be overlooked. What counts is the individual's beliefs about possible relationships rather than the actual contingencies to which they are exposed. While the latter are not inconsequential, there are other factors to be taken into account including past experiences of reinforcement in this type of situation, generalised expectancies from other related settings, instructions and directions as to what to do to achieve certain goals, and observational learning (Mischel, 1973). One such generalised expectancy already encountered is *locus of control* which, it will be recalled, differentiates individuals who hold that little they do makes much of a difference to what happens to them, from those who are more internally oriented operating on the basis of reaching projected goals through personal skill and tenacity, thereby actively eliciting rewarding experiences. (This topic will be returned to in Chapter Seven.)

A further differentiation within the multi-faceted concept of expectancy is relevant. Mischel (1973) mentions that although an activity may be performed in anticipation of certain results, it is unlikely to be pursued unless the individual feels able to carry it out with some minimum standard of competency. *Expectations of self-efficacy* are, therefore, important. The motivational implications of this construct, the factors that shape it, and how it determines performance have been widely researched by Bandura (1989). A history of past success is one of the most significant determinants of a belief in one's ability to pursue a course of action. However, and especially in situations where the extent to which goals have been attained may be unclear, the encouragement, affirmation and support of others also contribute. In an experiment conducted by Baron (1988) with undergraduates, for instance, critical comment on work which they undertook subsequently led to diminished goals and reduced feelings of self-efficacy.

Reinforcement value

This notion complements that of expectancy in accounting for those enterprises that are liable to be implemented. The fact that two individuals are similar in respect of their estimations of the probability of an activity leading to some outcome and feelings of competency in prosecuting that action, does not necessarily entail that both will be equally committed to commensurate behaviour. For one the anticipated consequence may be highly esteemed, for the other of little import.

Reinforcement value can be regarded, in large measure, as the degree of preference for one of a number of alternative external rewards to occur, given that all are equally probable (Rotter, 1982). Several facets of the concept should be noted. In the first case, it is independent of expectancy. It often happens, of course, that something is desired but with little optimism that it will be obtained. Secondly, the relativity and subjectivity of the force of incentives is assumed. As previously expressed in relation to the work of Premack, the value of an outcome is always relative to what else is available – there are no absolutes.

Before leaving the topic, attention should perhaps be drawn to a range of *Expectancy-value theories* that attempt to variously construe motivation by making use of these basic processes of the anticipation of outcomes together with the value bestowed upon them. (For a review, see Feather, 1982.) Some of these have been applied quite widely to professional practice in areas including personnel management and health care.

By way of concluding, we have seen in this part of the chapter a greater focus on those aspects of rewards and rewarding that are more recognizably personal and social. Their manner of operation in both directly influencing what people do, and indirectly how they learn from observing others in interpersonal settings, has been outlined. Additionally, social learning theorists have accentuated the incentive effect of positive outcomes, be they experienced at first-hand or vicariously. People engage in those pursuits that are expected to lead to subjectively valued results, given a belief in their ability to do so. Feelings of self-efficacy are enhanced, in turn, through rewarding experiences in the past.

EFFECTS OF REWARDS ON PERSONALITY AND SELF-CONCEPT

So far the underlying focus of our examination of the impact that positive responding can exercise on others has been largely restricted to behavioural acquisition and control, however the mechanisms responsible are construed. But the potential sphere of influence is more expansive. Evidence has been produced implicating parental styles of discipline in the types of personality trait subsequently manifested by offspring. While account has to be taken of the fact that some of this work is based upon recollections of childhood treatment, it seems that excessively negative and punishing parental practices may be associated with depression, hostility, anxiety and a poor self-image and self-esteem in later life (Bryan and Freed, 1982). Rewarding regimes, especially maternal use of verbal rewards, may lead, on the other hand, to feelings of general well-being and a positive outlook on life (Gussman and Harder, 1990).

In this section we will consider the views of several authors which, while differing on many accounts, have in common a commitment to the social derivation of the formulation and affirmation of the individual's personality and self-concept together with the determination of these structures on patterns of relating to others. The diversity of theoretical perspectives reflected makes the process of categorisation less straightforward than in preceding sections. At the risk of over-extending their normal usage, perhaps humanistic and cognitive social psychology would be the most appropriate paradigmatic labels.

Transactional Analysis and recognition need

A concept which, although broader, is similar in many respects to that of positive responding and rewardingness explored in this book, is the notion of *stroking* espoused by adherents of *Transactional Analysis*. Simply put, Transactional Analysis is a theory of personality which has at its centre the identification and articulation of the types of interpersonal transaction which people execute. Personality is held to be shaped in important ways, especially in the formative years, by a social world peopled by significant others including parents.

According to Eric Berne, the founding father of this approach, a persistent and enduring characteristic of interpersonal contact, and one of the primary motivating forces which impels it, is the quest for strokes from other people. From birth, it is postulated, in addition to food and warmth, there is a hunger for physical contact with another human being. To develop and thrive not only psychologically and emotionally but also physically, babies must be cuddled and caressed. Gradually, as the infant matures, this stimulus hunger becomes sublimated and transformed into recognition hunger which expresses a need to be acknowledged by others as a person in one's own right (Berne, 1964). Any interchange that results in the individual being literally or metaphorically 'stroked' will serve this end. A greater reliance is placed on the latter, however, as childhood years are left behind with a corresponding reduction in the incidence of physical contact.

Strokes are interpersonal acts that imply the affirmation of another as a social being. The form taken can be enormously varied, ranging from a casual word of acknowledgement to the most intimate declarations of love and adoration. Between these extremes we can think of obvious examples such as praising, approving and complimenting, already identified as instances of social reward. Harris and Harris (1986) list some that are less conspicuous, including both verbal and nonverbal modes of communication. Foremost among these are eye contact, listening, displaying interest by asking relevant questions, and using humour.

Strokes can be positive or negative; conditional or unconditional. We have concentrated mainly on the positive variant, but some people survive on a diet which consists mainly of negative strokes, including ridicule, threat and blame. These can have a powerful and enduring effect especially if encountered early in life. They are to be preferred, however, to being discounted. 'Any stroke is better than no stroke', in the words of Stewart (1989, p. 20).

A discount is the opposite of a stroke and implies that the recipient is of no consequence – a non-person. Being so defined must be avoided at all costs, a sentiment shared by the nineteenth-century psychologist, William James, in the graphic lines, ' no more fiendish punishment could be devised were such a thing possible, than that one should be turned loose in society and remain absolutely unnoticed by all the members thereof' (James, 1890, p. 293). The admonishments of teachers and reprimands of parents, if they are the only strokes available, are unquestionably preferred, in the eyes of a child, to being totally ignored. Children will misbehave to elicit such negative reactions if they believe that there is no other strategy for gaining recognition. Here we see how, far from acting as punishments, these negative responses by teachers and parents can actually serve to reinforce undesirable conduct (Stewart, 1989). Such a regime, however, can be the source of personal and interpersonal difficulties in later years. Strokes can, therefore, be helpful, enhancing emotional growth and well-being, or, while still desired, unhelpful, constricting and ultimately destructive.

Conditional strokes are withheld and only given if certain criteria are satisfied. They have to be earned; something has to be done in order for them to be proffered. Society, as we have seen, utilises what is here called the *stroke economy* to shape and mould as part of the process of socialisation (Steiner, 1974). Most of what has been said so far in this chapter about rewards and positive responding has depicted this sort of predication. Indeed, construed as reinforcers, one of the fundamental behaviourist principles underlying their effective implementation in controlling performance emphasises administration contingent upon the targeted response. But strokes can also be unconditional, e.g. 'I love you', 'You are really special', 'Stupid child!', etc. This issue of conditionality will be taken up later.

There are considerable qualitative and quantitative variations in the strokes enjoyed by different people. If we are highly esteemed and respected by an individual, the strokes that we provide, especially if we have not been particularly lavish in the past, will have tremendous value attached. They must also, of course, be perceived as authentic. Additional to source, their timing and intensity have an enormous impact upon the recipient, as outlined by Pitman (1984), who discusses the implications as they apply to counselling and social work practice.

Not all recipients, as intimated, are capable of accepting strokes as intended, due to early experiences which shape personalities in dysfunctional ways. Views of self, others, the world and how it works, once formed, tend to be reacted to in such a way as to validate and strengthen these initial impressions. This comes about quite early in childhood when, based on the history of stroking to which she has been exposed, the child begins to make decisions about herself and where she stands in relation to the world and other people. For a number of reasons, including lack of cognitive maturity, these judgements may be rationally flawed. Nevertheless they define the only reality that the child can envisage at that time and the one which is duly reacted to in accordance with a self-determined *script*. A script can be thought of as a preconscious life-plan which stipulates how life should be led and recognition obtained in the future. It represents a compromise of spontaneity, awareness and intimacy in the interests of coping with the immediate circumstances of obtaining acceptance from those who matter, and its consequences are far-reaching. Adults may lead their lives being 'compliant children', based on the assumption that this is how strokes are procured. Such modes of social interaction can be accentuated during encounters with more powerful, higher status professionals like doctors and lawyers, when a submissive eagerness to please may be especially marked.

Early oppressive experiences may set in place particularly fixed routines and stereotyped patterns of engaging with others, which tend to be repeated in a succession of encounters as maladaptive attempts to access, in the same ways, those strokes to which that person had previously become accustomed. Certain people, likely situations, and preferred modes of approaching and transacting with others will be chosen on the strength of their probability of affording strokes commensurate with the script being adhered to.

Acknowledgements that are forthcoming may also be denied, refused or distorted in order to make them palatable. Perhaps praise will simply not be heard, regarded as unwarranted, or interpreted as insincerely expressed if that person does not regard himself as praiseworthy (Pitman, 1984). To be successful, stroking must therefore be individualised. This has been expressed aphoristically as, 'Different strokes for different folks'.

Beliefs formed about self and the social world have a bearing that goes much beyond the mere *receipt* of recognition. According to Steiner (1974), parental influences will determine to what extent people feel happy giving, soliciting and rejecting strokes, as well as being prepared to give strokes to themselves. When early experiences have been essentially constructive, individuals are generally comfortable accepting positive recognition that they believe to be accurate, asking for it when it is deserved but not forthcoming, rejecting it when unwanted, and giving themselves and others helpful strokes generously and appropriately.

To sum up, in keeping with Transactional Analysis, people have an implacable need to be recognised by others as individuals in their own right. Early experiences of being reacted to by parents and significant others lead to the establishment of a personal frame of reference which, in turn, governs the ongoing and often maladaptive quest for further strokes. In so doing, a personality is formed which shapes social bearing and is further affirmed through it. Implications for professional interaction are evident and multi-faceted including both the professional's ability to readily provide strokes of a particular type, and that of the other to receive them as intended.

Person-Centred theory and the need for positive regard

The faith of Eric Berne in the potential residing in human nature for growth and personal development was shared by Carl Rogers, the founder of Person-Centred theory and one of the foremost figures of the humanistic movement in psychology. Instead of a need for recognition, however, Rogers believed that much of what people do is intended to win *positive regard* from those with whom they mix. This is an overwhelming need acquired early in infancy to perceive that one has been experienced by another in such a way as to produce feelings in that other of warmth, liking, and respect towards oneself. Put more simply, it is a desire for approval and acceptance which plays a central part in the formation of the self-concept (Rogers, 1959). In order to fully appreciate how this comes about, it is necessary to grasp several of the key notions at the core of Rogers' thinking including the organismic self, actualising tendency, conditions of worth, and locus of evaluation.

A useful starting point is with the differentiation made by Rogers between the organismic self and the self-concept. The former, psychologically speaking, is at the heart of all experience and is a totally organised system comprising physical, cognitive, affective and behavioural facets of the individual. It is energised by a single and immensely powerful motivating force, the actualising tendency. This is a positive vector towards growth and development. It also makes possible a flexible system for attaching value to experiences thereby enabling conduct to be assessed and directed. Opportunities for maintaining, enhancing and promoting the organismic self are good and should be pursued; those that fail in this capacity are bad and to be avoided (Rogers, 1964). In either case, the locus of evaluation is completely internal. Were it the only source, the outcome would be what Rogers referred to as fully functioning people maximising their potential and enjoying fulfilled, harmonious and integrated lives. The fact that so few achieve this happy state of being is due, not to a labile actualising tendency, but to the frustrating and distorting of this energy by societal influences.

While the organismic self can be looked upon as the genuine, underlying self, the self-concept is the individual's view of himself, together with an evaluation of it, which gradually develops over time. Incongruities typically emerge between the two. Significant others, including parents, have a key role to play in this, on account of the demand for positive regard from them.

The need to gain acceptance, approval, respect and esteem is deep-felt. But positive regard is not, as a rule, offered unconditionally. Rather certain *conditions of worth* frequently obtain – the child comes to appreciate that behaviour of a particular type has to be displayed to win the approval so badly sought. This constitutes an alternative, external system of values according to which things should be done, not because they feel intuitively right as they contribute to the well-being of the organismic self, but because they are positively sanctioned by others whose reactions matter. The compromises engendered by trying to satisfy both valuing systems inevitably become untenable. Experiences that are dependent upon the values of others rather than those of the organism may be introjected to become part of the self-concept. By the same token, self-experiences which, although organismically valid, fail to elicit positive regard tend to become disso- ciated from conceptions of self which thereby gradually becomes detached from the 'real self'.

Rogers believed that there are few of us who don't carry the psychological scars of estrangement from our deeper selves caused by a dependence upon positive regard. These scars are particularly marked among people unfortunate enough to have been subjected to the harsh and unremitting censorship of excessively judgemental but highly pertinent associates. The sense of self to emerge from such a social background, together with the value bestowed upon it, is fated to reflect the conditions of worth experienced. Having introjected a fixed set of standards from these others, the adoption and operationalisation of an external *locus of evaluation* is highly probable. The appropriateness of what is said, felt, thought or done derives from this source and is essentially designed to evoke positive respon- ses from those who count. Any sense of personal freedom and autonomy suffers as these people lose sight of their ability to think their own thoughts, make their own decisions, and order their own existences. This orientation is an extreme characterisation of what Riesman (1952) called 'other-directedness' and can be thought to reflect a high need for approval (Crowne and Marlowe, 1964). The British therapist George Lyward regarded those who conduct their affairs in this way as leading what he called 'usurped lives' (Thorne, 1990).

Unconditional positive regard engenders feelings of affirmative self-regard – when others value us unreservedly we are more inclined to look upon ourselves in a similar manner. The ultimate victim of conditions of worth is therefore the esteem with which the person holds himself. Rogers postulated that these unfortunate consequences could be avoided or ameliorated by entering into a relationship characterised by, firstly, an awareness of positive regard or acceptance being given unconditionally because people are who they are rather than on account of what they do; secondly, genuineness or congruence so that members feel safe to reveal their true selves and behave in accordance; and, thirdly, empathic understanding or a commitment to understand the other and his experiences from his frame of reference (Rogers, 1961). These attributes are indispensable for effective counsel- ling and helping to be provided. (More will be said about these concepts in Chapter Five.)

In drawing together some of these propositions, we see that Rogers, like Berne, recognised a primitive and extremely vibrant need to be reacted to in a particular way by others and that personalities, including constructions and evaluations of the self, are formed (or malformed) as a result. The potential for social rewards or reinforcers to shape and control are therefore readily recognised. Unlike behaviourist counterparts, Transactional Analysts and particularly Person-Centred theorists are quick to accentuate the psychological and emotional damage which can be wrought by being so seduced (Carver and Scheier, 1988). It is especially important for those who deal with young children such as nursery and primary school teachers, even paediatric nurses, to be aware of this possible misuse of positive responding. We can react so as to encourage, affirm, support and guide or, on the other hand, to constrain, undermine and subjugate.

It must be recognised, nevertheless, that there are contextually defined normative expectations that, if we are to be social beings, must be acknowledged and complied with. In discussing parenting skills, Herbert (1989) seems to disagree that permitting the untrammelled exercise of what Rogers termed the organismic valuing system whereby the child gets to do exactly as he wants results in a happy child, never mind a fully functioning adult. Training and discipline are crucial; children must be taught socially acceptable conduct which will not otherwise be acquired. What Rogers referred to as the introjection of the values of others, Herbert equates with the formation of a conscience which makes it possible for the child to exercise control over his own actions and practise self-restraint. Herbert, however, stresses the importance of providing praise, together with alternative forms of discipline, within a relationship of mutual respect and affection so that the child is aware of the nature of the discipline and why it is being administered. If applied in such a manner and to such an extent that those exposed come to believe that they are valued by significant others *solely* on the basis of what they do, and if they become convinced not only that behaving in a particular manner is appreciated but also that failing to do so renders them worthless, then social rewards can scarcely be regarded as having been utilised in a professionally skilled fashion.

Cognitive social psychology and the self-concept

The last decade has seen a resurgence of interest in the self among those working in what could loosely be termed the domain of cognitive social psychology. Berkowitz (1988) describes 'the rapidly burgeoning literature', documenting a plethora of research findings and accompanying theorisations in areas such as the various sources of information that are drawn on as people come to recognise themselves as particular types of individual; the nature, structure and dynamics of these self-representations; and their capacity to regulate action. Little more can be attempted here than a brief overview of several of the salient issues addressed.

The starting point of this tradition is commonly located in the seminal work of William James, who believed that a central component of our experience of ourselves is largely socially determined (James, 1890). Charles Cooley was even more adamant that a sense of personal identity presupposes interaction with others (Cooley, 1902). For him the self, far from being the product of individual personal maturation, has its origins in, and couldn't exist outwith, the social milieu. It is essentially a reflection of the reactions to us of others with whom we engage. He wrote, 'A social self might be called the reflected or looking-glass self.

> Each to each a looking glass
> Reflects the other that doth pass

The self that is most important is a reflection, largely, from the minds of others' (Cooley, 1902, pp. 183–4).

This idea of the 'looking-glass self' is one of Cooley's most influential contributions to the literature (Swensen, 1973). It incorporates an imagination of how we appear to another, an impression of that other's judgement based upon what he perceives, and corresponding feeling on our part which could include pride or shame.

A somewhat more sophisticated version of this notion was espoused by Herbert Mead. Rather than relying on inferences from the self-relevant information furnished by a partner, the self-concept is forged in the ongoing mutual interdependency of interaction with a plurality of others (Mead, 1934). This suggests the possibility of a multiplicity of personal representations corresponding to each relationship: we may be different selves to different people. But there is also an underlying unifying concept defined by the '*generalised other*': we have an idea of what others, as a collective, think of us. Indeed research evidence suggests that the formation of impressions of self gleaned from perceptions of the assessments of others is best thought of in terms of judgements of how one is regarded in a global sense (DePaulo *et al.*, 1987), and that accuracy in arriving at specific predictions may be poor (Felson, 1989).

This line of thought espousing self-identity on the basis of the experienced reactions of others during social contact is also recognisable in what has been called the interpersonal theory of psychiatry associated with Harry Stack Sullivan. At the forefront of this movement is the realisation that we are born into a social world and immersed, from the first days of life, in a continual stream of interpersonal encounters in the course of which a constant exposure to '*reflected appraisals*' is experienced from those who relate to us (Sullivan, 1955). Based upon these reactions, self-attitudes and expectations begin to become established. In so far as these appraisals are negative and disapproving, the individual is likely to have a poor view of self and low self-esteem. If they are largely positive and supporting, corresponding self-images will be healthy and constructive.

Here again we encounter the view that accepting others and being approving of them can have a positive effect on how they come to think of and prize themselves. The self, being fundamentally a product of social construction, is highly attuned to the self-relevant positivity or negativity sensed in the interpersonal environment. But the reflected appraisals we make available to those with whom we engage is only one of a number of possible interactive mechanisms whereby they can come to formulate or reassess their self-views. The expectations we entertain of them and the creation of self-fulfilling prophecies have been discussed in this regard (Backman, 1988; Markus and Cross, 1990). (Mention of *social comparison* as an alternative interactive procedure whereby others are utilised to provide self-relevant information, will be left until Chapter Eight.)

What determines the extent to which our reactions to those with whom we interact will make an important contribution to how they regard themselves? Significant factors can be categorised as pertaining to, firstly, the attribute in question; secondly, the target of the attribution; and thirdly, the other who is the source of this information (Markus and Cross, 1990). Beginning with the recipient, age is a crucial consideration, with susceptibility to self-defining opinions and judgements of partners appearing to peak in early adolescence (Elkind, 1967). As people grow older they generally tend to be less amenable to this source of influence and better able to disavow self-discrepant attitudes which may be intimated. Resistance is enhanced when age is coupled with an existing firmly established self-concept, low levels of self-monitoring, and high self-esteem (Snyder, 1987).

A second set of circumstances encompasses the source of the self-involving information. Some of these factors are dependent upon the stage of social development of the recipient. Thus, parents have been found to be the major influencing factor in childhood, whereas the views of peers become of greater salience in adolescence (Harter, 1990). More generally, the value, prestige and credibility bestowed upon the source with regard to the aspect of self-concept under consideration, is highly pertinent. This effect is further strengthened when consistent opinions are expressed by a plurality of others.

Finally, the nature of the attributed quality or characteristic must not be ignored. When people are unsure as to where they stand in relation to the attribute at issue, the chances are that the opinions of partners will have a greater impact on decisions taken. This is especially so with qualities like attractiveness that are essentially socially rather than 'objectively' defined (Felson, 1985). Again, positively valued characteristics that are consistent with extant self-judgements are more inclined to be assimilated into the self-concept (Markus and Cross, 1990).

It would be a mistake to assume that people are passively at the mercy of the views and attitudes formed of them, or that they play no active role in the construction of self. Nothing could be further removed from the complexity of the process as explicated by, for instance, Backman (1988). Individuals seek out company thought likely to furnish the sort of feedback desired. Constructive steps are taken to maximise this likelihood. *Self-presentation* is one such strategy whereby a certain face calculated to elicit sought-after social reactions is publicly displayed. Backman also acknowledges how such a presentation can have additional effects on self-concept by enabling behaviour to be entered into which is consonant with some aspect of self not yet well stabilised. Acting in a manner which is consistent with a particular attribute makes it easier to accept that the attribute is indeed possessed (Bem, 1972). By means of *altercasting* further attempts can be made to regulate the responses of partners in favourable directions. This involves behaving so as to affirm and maintain those traits and dispositions in the other associated with the receipt of rewards from them. Simply telling the person concerned how wonderfully generous they are may be an obvious approach. However, normative constraints together with the risk of accusations of *ingratiation* increase the likelihood of more subtle tactics being employed (Backman, 1988). (These notions will be expanded upon in Chapter Eight in relation to power and social influence.)

But what, in fact, is the object of these manoeuvres? What sorts of reactions are being sought? According to Tesser (1988), interactors seek to preserve a positive evaluation of self and to be looked upon favourably. (This view is consonant with that of Emmons (1989), presented in the preceding chapter, on the motivational basis of goal formation.) The attention, approval, praise and various other social rewards already mentioned are valued affirmatively on these grounds. Commensurate with an extrapolation of this theory proposing that these self-enhancement needs are most keenly felt by those with low self-esteem, Smith and Smoll (1990) discovered that children so disposed responded much more positively to sports coaches who were reinforcing and encouraging when compared to coaches with less supportive styles.

While agreeing that all people share a strong need for attention and approval, Cheek and Hogan (1983) nevertheless caution that individual differences exist in estimating the social desirability of different images and attributes. They also draw attention to the possibility of *negative* images of self being projected on occasion. Some believe that this may be done in the interests of self-verification, based on the assumption that people prefer to be considered in a manner that confirms their self-views, even when these views may be negative (Swann *et al.*, 1990). (There are interesting parallels of thought here with those writing in Transactional Analysis terms on the pursuit of negative strokes. Different underlying processes are, of course, presupposed to be at work.) A further perspective is contributed by Steele (1988). While stressing the infrequency of self-deprecation, Steele proposes that, when it is indulged in, it represents the subordination of the common need for self-affirmation in the interests of something more basic that has to do with the confirmation of self as adaptively in control of personal circumstances in a morally adequate fashion. For the most part, both needs are largely conflated.

Finally, the subtleties of the mainly indirect modes by which interpersonal responses can affect self-definition and evaluation should not conceal the much more direct impact of interaction within the context of social structures in the negotiation of the roles that members come to adopt. Backman (1988) sketches the processes through which roles are taken on and abided with as a consequence of the explicit contingencies provided by others. Performing in accordance with the normative expectations which members have for institutional roles will be rewarded and violations negatively sanctioned. Role identities, be they of teacher, father, son, husband or whatever, are, of course, relevant to the impressions we form of who and what we are. Indeed, on occasion, they can become completely merged with a sense of personhood so that the individual 'becomes the role' (Turner, 1968). Positive reactions extended to those with whom we mix as co-members of social institutions and structures can, therefore, make a further and more direct difference to their personality and sense of self.

In sum, it would seem that the positive reactions of others are an important basis upon which affirmative views of self are formed. Is this invariably so? Does praise, for example, always carry desirable implications for the self-concept of the person receiving it and serve to enhance self-esteem? Perhaps surprisingly, in view of what has been said, the responses to these questions cannot be an unqualified 'Yes'. There is some evidence, to be taken up in Chapter Seven, that receiving praise from another can, on occasion, lead to the inference that one's ability at that sort of task must be low.

CONCLUSION

We have covered a lot of ground in this chapter in considering rewards and rewarding from a number of quite varied points of view, each with radically different underlying assumptions not only about these phenomena, but also about people generally and how they operate. Perhaps the most basic commonality identified is the agreement that our positive (and negative) reactions to those with whom we interact in the social milieu can have profound effects on them. Beyond this, contrasting theoretical stand-points tend to concentrate upon the illumination of different classes of outcome including the things people do, the ways they conduct themselves as social partners, and/or personalities which are formed and how they come to regard themselves as individuals. We have also seen that different accounts have been offered as to the mechanisms responsible, with some theorists accentuating the rational processing of the informational content of rewarding episodes leading to the formulation of decisions in respect of goals and the adoption of courses of action in their prosecution, while others have stressed mainly motivational effects. For a further group, rewards as reinforcers are held to function in a largely automatic manner to mould behaviour through the positive impact of its consequences.

Nor is it the case that only those consequences that are directly experienced count. Social learning theorists have outlined the processes involved in observational learning enabling the wider application of rewards through vicarious reinforcement procedures.

Although it is readily accepted that rewards lead to the behaviour that produced them being performed more often under similar circumstances, this may not invariably be the case. There is some evidence associated with tasks that are found to have intrinsic appeal, that extrinsic incentives may have the opposite effect although this is less likely to happen with social than material inducements. Still, when the proffering of rewards is interpreted as an attempt at control rather than the provision of information on personal accomplishments, the recipient may well resist and cease to oblige by refraining from those activities on the basis of which extrinsic positive outcomes were made contingent.

A further point stemming from this is that the rewardingness of any event is relative; its reward value must ultimately be adduced by the recipient. This sentiment has been echoed at different points throughout the chapter, in the notion of reinforcement value, for instance, and in the realisation that under certain circumstances individuals may seek out, in the form of negative strokes, what could be regarded as punishment by an onlooker.

The sorts of images that some individuals form of themselves and the self-esteem which results are based, in part, on the regimes of rewards and punishments to which they have been exposed. Here self-concept can be thought to mediate the effects of reinforcement on behaviour such that individuals strive to act in a manner which sustains an acceptable self-image. On a cautionary note, Rogers points up the potentiality for psychological damage stemming from not only punishment, but also the conditionality of interpersonal reactions in the form of positive regard. It is therefore important that the professional, when using social rewards in a skilled manner, avoids creating the impression that the other is defined solely in terms of targeted behaviours or that conditions of worth are fixed on that basis. As expressed by Stewart (1989, p. 1), 'At times I may not esteem or accept what a person does. But always I esteem and accept what he or she is.' This sentiment, of course, is consonant with many codes of professional practice and coincidentally portrays an underlying relationship with the client, patient or pupil within which the skilled use of positive responding can operate to best effect. More will be said about ethical considerations surrounding these issues in the final chapter.

Chapter 3

Verbal facets of social reward

INTRODUCTION

The preceding chapter can be typified, in the main, as offering a response to the question of why interpersonal rewards are such a potent force in bringing about changes as outlined in learning, behaviour, personality and attitudes. Alternative explanations emanating from contrasting theoretical points of view were considered. In this chapter and the one to follow, the locus of concern will switch from exploring underlying mechanisms to look more closely at the communicative modes through which rewards operate and the corresponding forms which they take. The concern will be with attempting to specify what it is that people do in reacting rewardingly to those with whom they associate, to influence them in some of the ways that we have seen.

It will be recalled from earlier in the book that a fundamental distinction can be drawn between verbal and nonverbal aspects of communication. This differentiation will be made use of in structuring the contents of this and the next chapters. Here we will concentrate on a range of verbal elements that have been associated with positive responding in a variety of professional settings, while in the succeeding chapter attention will shift to nonverbal characteristics. The fact that nonverbal cues are heavily implicated in the formation and transmission of interpersonal attitudes and affect (Argyle, 1988a) is suggestive of strong rewarding possibilities. Even under circumstances where linguistic codes are dominant, nonverbal accompaniments, by providing a communicative context for what is said, can alter the interpretation of the spoken word, and consequently its reinforcing impetus.

Two points are worth restating before going further. The first has to do with the nature of the relationship between these two channels of communication – the verbal and the nonverbal. Although it is relatively easy to conceptually prise them apart, their close functional interrelationship in the ongoing conversational stream makes the task of isolating respective contributions to the global message much more difficult in practice – a sentiment expressed by Burgoon (1985, p. 347), when she wrote that, 'verbal and nonverbal channels are inextricably intertwined in the communication of the total meaning of an interpersonal exchange.' This relationship should not be overlooked despite the fact that we have chosen to illuminate verbal and nonverbal features in separate chapters. Further, as will be seen, many of the earlier studies which investigated the rewarding effects of various types of utterance failed to fully acknowledge the part played by concurrent nonverbals in leading to observed outcomes (Dickson, 1981).

The second point that should be appreciated reiterates the fact that the rewarding values of different social actions are essentially relative and conditional. Despite outlining in these two chapters various verbal and nonverbal behaviours that have been identified as reinforcers and researched in that regard, it should not be inferred that these behaviours have any absolute and immutable powers in this respect according to which they must always, with everyone, under all circumstances, produce desired effects. Having said that, however, it does seem that there are certain ways of relating that, under recognisable sets of conditions, are often found rewarding and responded to accordingly. These will be described and their application examined in professional domains including education, health care, management and sport, drawing upon relevant research findings in these areas.

Focusing on the verbal dimension, many of the things said to pupils, patients, employees and participants provide feedback on the extent to which goals have been reached in keeping with personal standards, and an external evaluation of these achievements. Furthermore, as already mentioned, when this leads to the validation and strengthening of the recipient's feelings of self-esteem and worth it is likely to be particularly positively valued. Much of the experimental work undertaken in this area has, however, been carried out within an operant conditioning framework with different types of verbalisation cast as social reinforcers. The extent to which these are capable of producing increases in designated courses of action have been investigated in keeping with this tradition. Verbal components of reinforcement range in complexity from simple single-word expressions of affirmation to more elaborate reactions relating to some aspect of the functioning of the other.

Given that in principle any utterance could act as a verbal reinforcer if the conditions permit, the introduction of a classification system must be somewhat arbitrary. Still, three broad categories have been proposed by Hargie *et al.* (1987), and will be adopted in structuring the remainder of the chapter. They are, firstly, acknowledgement/confirmation; secondly, praise/support; and thirdly, response development.

ACKNOWLEDGEMENT/CONFIRMATION

Here we have expressions, words and phrases which seem essentially to acknowledge, confirm or agree with what has been said or done. Examples include verbalisations such as 'OK', 'Yes', 'Right', 'Fine', 'I see', 'That's it', as well as nonlexical vocalisations like 'mm-hmm'. (Strictly speaking the latter would be more appropriately listed under the nonverbal heading but, since they have often been grouped for research purposes along with the other verbal utterances exemplified, it is more convenient to include them here.) These listener responses are a common feature of conversations, being particularly noticeable when, for example, people talk over the telephone. It seems, in part, that they signal to the speaker that the message sent has been successfully received and understood, and that the listener is paying close attention (Rosenfeld, 1987). As put by Poyatos (1983, p. 243), they 'serve to communicate about the speaker's performance and the listener's response to it'. Poyatos also suggests that audience attention is one of the first reactions that a speaker looks for whether it be in formal or informal encounters, private dyadic conversations, or public addresses.

From a counselling perspective, Ivey and Authier (1978) referred to these limited listener responses as 'minimal encourages to talk' and, as part of a complex of basic attending skills which the counsellor should manifest, emphasised their role in helping the client to continue exploring areas of personal concern during the interview. These subtle vocalisations have also been implicated in the regulation and orchestration of conversation. By engaging in such 'back-channel' communication, the listener reaffirms her role as listener and that of the other as speaker; there is no attempt by the listener at that juncture to made a bid to take over the floor and become speaker (Duncan, 1972). Lang and van der Molen (1990) summarise the central functions of minimal encourages as showing interest in what is being said, thereby reassuring the speaker that she is being listened to and inviting her to continue in this line of conversation. There is also some limited research evidence, produced by Bennett and Jarvis (1991), indicating that, at least for a third party, these listener expressions may be interpreted as agreement with, rather than merely listening closely to the other.

The reinforcing consequences of these attending utterances have been revealed in a number of experimental investigations, one of the most widely reported of which was that conducted by Greenspoon (1955), and referred to in the last chapter. This researcher simply asked subjects to produce as many individual words as they could think of. It will be recalled that by responding with 'mm-hmm', each time a subject gave a plural noun, and ignoring all other types of words, the number of plural nouns mentioned increased considerably over the course of the experiment. A comparable finding was reported by Reece and Whitman (1962), who also selected plural nouns as the target response.

In a recent study, Donohue and Tryon (1985) demonstrated that simply being privy to the minimal encourages received by others can have vicariously reinforcing consequences. The high school students who participated were led to believe that the study had to do with their vocabulary, linguistic and pronunciation skills. Each was instructed to write down any twelve separate words from their vocabulary in a two minute period. Two additional lists were obtained in the same way to provide a preconditioning measure of present participles (words ending in -ing), which was the class of word selected. For those allocated to the experimental condition, there then followed a number of vicarious reinforcement trials during which an accomplice in the group was asked to come up to the front and read her lists to the rest of the class. Every list contained three present participles and after each the experimenter said 'mm-hmm', ignoring all other responses. Six of these conditioning trials were held interspersed with further completions of lists by the class-members. Compared to the control group which did not take part in the vicarious reinforcing procedure, those students who had witnessed the acknowledgement of present participles by the experimenter furnished significantly more words of that sort over the course of the experiment.

But some of these research set-ups may be looked upon as rather uncommon and contrived. What about the influence of minimal encourages in the sort of ongoing interaction more redolent of an interview or indeed an ordinary conversation? Again conditioning effects with a variety of dependent measures have been found. In another frequently cited piece of research, reported by Matarazzo and Wiens (1972), the vocalisation 'mm-hmm' was one of several interviewer variables isolated in a research programme designed to establish the extent to which the duration of interviewee utterances was modifiable through natural interviewer manipulation, and the means by which this might be accomplished. In an original investigation and its subsequent replication, twenty applicants each underwent a forty-five minute selection interview. Unknown to the interviewees, interviews were divided into three segments of fifteen minutes each. The first segment enabled baseline assessments of response duration to be taken, the experimental manipulation was administered during the second, and subsequently withdrawn in the third. Throughout the second period, the interviewer went 'mm-hmm', whenever the interviewees began to talk and also periodically while they were doing so. Attempts were made to control for other contaminating sources of influence such as length of interviewer utterance and areas of interview content. The results revealed that the use of the minimal encourager by the interviewer led to marked increases in the average length of the speech-turns taken by the interviewees. O'Brien and Holborn (1979) also increased the verbal contributions of interviewees in this manner.

While one of the objectives of an interviewer may well be to get the interviewee to talk freely, in many situations directing contributions to relevant and appropriate topics for discussion is also important. One such topic which has legitimacy across different interviewing settings centres on personal details of the interviewee. Different types of respondent self-referenced statement have, therefore, been selected by researchers as responses to be modified through operant techniques. Salzinger and Pisoni (1960), for instance, encouraged patients hospitalised for physical ailments to talk about their affective state by selectively attending to statements of this sort. This was done by the interviewer providing minimal encouragements, including 'mm-hmm', 'Uh-huh', 'I see', 'Yeah', etc., whenever patients began to describe or evaluate their condition or circumstances. The result was that this conversational theme was more likely to be sustained. Health workers have often been faulted for failing to recognise and cater for the psychosocial needs of patients on the ward to the detriment of overall levels of care proffered (Dickson, 1989). The Salzinger and Pisoni study demonstrates a quite simple and non-threatening technique that practitioners can consider employing when chatting to patients to enable them, should they so wish, to begin to discuss the fears, doubts, uncertainties and anxieties that, when ignored and left to be brooded upon, can not only cause anguish and heighten stress but also stand in the way of a speedy recovery.

Self-talk can lead to the disclosure of both positive and negative information. In general it is held to be much easier to talk about ourselves in positive terms, although this varies depending upon the nature and circumstances of the interaction and the self-concept of the speaker, as we have seen. Indeed we often present ourselves so as to create a desired social image and promote ourselves positively (Jones, 1990). To what extent is it therefore possible to increase negative self-statements through the contingent use of minimal encourages? In a study conducted by Rogers (1960), it emerged that subjects exposed to such a conditioning regime displayed significantly more negative self-statements over the course of six sessions than comparable groups which either were reinforced for positive self-references or acted as controls.

This finding, however, was not corroborated by Weight (1974), who discovered that while minimal encouragers could be used to promote positive self-talk, there was little evidence that negative revelations could be likewise elicited. Possible reasons for this lack of consistency include the fact that Rogers' subjects took part in a clinical-type interview and may therefore have had a different perception of the appropriateness of such talk. Again subjects in the Weight experiment were interviewed only once, unlike their counterparts who participated in six sessions organised by Rogers. From what we know of the psychology of self-disclosure (Derlega and Berg, 1987), this heightened familiarity may have made it easier to mention less desirable qualities. Neither researcher attempted to assess the contribution which subjects' self-concepts may have made to the outcomes. It will be remembered from the last chapter that those with a poor view of themselves are believed by some to find it easier to make known negative personal detail consistent with their self-image (Swann et al., 1990).

Attending behaviour of the type featured in this section has also been found to enhance requests by interviewees for information during educational–vocational counselling sessions, together subsequently with actual information-seeking activities outside of the interview setting (Samaan, 1971). Still in the area of vocational guidance and counselling, Oliver (1974) discovered that the career choices of male undergraduates could be steered in more realistic directions by selectively reinforcing, in a laboratory context, those choices that were in keeping with their occupational type, as determined by the Vocational Preference Inventory.

Not all investigations have produced such positive outcome. A study carried out by Siegman (1973), for instance, failed to corroborate the effects of a minimal encourager, such as 'mm-hmm', on increased respondent verbal productivity as documented by researchers like Matarazzo and Wiens (1972) and O'Brien and Holborn (1979), as mentioned above. Rosenfeld (1987) suggests that this failure may be accounted for by the fact that Siegman administered social reinforcers on a non-contingent basis (subjects were exposed to them regardless of whether they were engaging in lengthy speech turns); nonverbal cues were minimised; and subjects were permitted to state when utterances were completed. Incidentally, the lack of contingent application was also one of the reasons offered by Nelson-Gray *et al.* (1989) in explaining why no discernible increase in interviewee problem-related statements was brought about, in their experimental investigation, by increasing the frequency of interviewer minimal encourages.

Commenting further on the limitations of this form of influence, Rosenfeld (1987) cautions that it is unlikely to effectively change normal use of well-established communicative practices. People probably won't be conditioned to say things that are entirely out of character, believed to be contextually inappropriate or personally meaningless. On the other hand, according to Pope (1979), interactive encounters with a high degree of ambiguity, where respondents are somewhat unsure of the expectations placed on them and the rules of procedure, are particularly conducive to verbal conditioning effects. Presumably these subtle verbal cues given by the interviewer are highly informative under such circumstances. By helping to reduce uncertainty and doubt they may also be associated, of course, with the removal of unpleasant affective states.

PRAISE/SUPPORT

Unlike the previous category, here listener reactions go beyond the simple acknowledgement, confirmation or agreement with what has been said or done to express praise or support. Someone who praises makes an evaluative statement on the extent to which a performance has matched or is matching particular standards, together with a pronouncement of appreciation, approval, perhaps even admiration for the other and actions carried out by them. In praising the successful efforts of a patient struggling to give up smoking, the health worker indicates, at least, an appreciation of the difficulties involved and the degree of success attained, and also bestows positive value upon the enterprise. Hence in praising, one is doing much more than acknowledging the occurrence of an event.

Expressions of support are slightly different. There may be no evaluation of achievement in terms of the degree to which standards have been satisfied (apart from the implication that the notional goal being pursued has yet to be reached). On the other hand the person who offers support not only is in agreement with what is being done but also makes a commitment to help the other, even if only verbally. As with praise, there is also an implicit request for that course of action to be continued (Hargie *et al.*, 1987).

Instances of this category of verbal reward range from one-word utterances, e.g. 'Good!', 'Excellent!' (and various other superlatives), through phrases like 'Well done!', 'How interesting!' and 'Keep it up!', to more elaborate avowals of appreciation, as circumstances warrant. These are commonly employed by a broad spectrum of professionals and paraprofessionals when interacting with those to whom a service is offered. When appropriately administered, reinforcing consequences can be achieved. Professional domains where such effects have been examined are as diverse as organisational management, interviewing and coaching. But probably the most extensively researched area of application is in teaching.

Teaching

Teaching is an activity where opportunities abound for putting praise and approval
to good use in rewarding effort and accomplishment in the classroom. Educationalists are generally agreed that reinforcing appropriate pupil behaviour in this way
is one of the hallmarks of effective teaching (Perrott, 1982). Teachers should adopt
a positive style of reacting favourably to what pupils do that is right and proper,
and desist from the alternative habit of only intervening to disapprove when
mistakes are made or misbehaviour occurs. (Others would recommend the judicious use of both positive and negative consequences – praise and reprimands
(Acker and O'Leary, 1987).) Children in elementary class seem to value such social
rewards to the extent of even expressing a preference for them over tangible, edible
or activity alternatives when given a choice (Fantuzzo *et al.*, 1991). Reinforcement
is, therefore, regarded as one of the core skills of teaching and features prominently
in teacher training programmes (Turney *et al.*, 1983).

Is there any evidence that teacher praise and approval makes a difference to the
quality of pupils' education? A number of reviews of research carried out over the
years have featured this aspect of classroom interaction (Kennedy and Willcutt,
1964; Lysakowski and Walberg, 1981; Brophy, 1981; Cairns, 1986; Wheldall and
Glynn, 1989). The general consensus would seem to be that significant and
beneficial changes can indeed be brought about. Firstly, by rewarding on-task
behaviour, pupils are encouraged to spend more of their time in class doing the
sorts of things that teachers expect, and less in irrelevant, unproductive or indeed
disruptive activities. Secondly, pupils can have their motivation to learn strengthened when what they do evokes a positive teacher response. Thirdly, and perhaps
most importantly, levels of academic achievement may actually be elevated when
teachers reinforce improving standards of work. Finally, it would appear that
students who are receptive to teacher approval given for acceptable accomplishments in the classroom often experience greater feelings of self-esteem.

Kennedy and Willcutt (1964) summarised the early studies that they scrutinised
by declaring that, 'Praise has been found generally to have a facilitating effect on
the performance of school children' (p. 331). Some recent reviewers, in contrast,
tend to be more qualified in the conclusions arrived at (Brophy, 1981). While not
disputing the reinforcing potential of praise and approval, Brophy questioned the
extent to which these techniques are a prominent feature of the day-to-day classroom discourse of teachers. In many cases it would appear that a reliance is placed
on challenging poor performance with the result that instances of praise given are
grossly outweighed by those of disapproval and admonishment (Heller and White,
1975). Even researchers who have chronicled less depressing findings are in
agreement that, 'teachers can be positive, encouraging, and supportive of pupils'
academic efforts, but when it comes to their classroom behaviour the emphasis
appears to be almost overwhelmingly negative' (Wheldall and Glynn, 1989, p. 87).
The important distinction here is between academic work and social behaviour in

class, with the former being controlled through positive responding, the latter by means of punishment.

Furthermore, when it comes to the distribution of praise and approval, disproportionately less attention is paid, by teachers, to the weaker sections of the class that arguably have a greater need of it, than to the brightest and the best (Russell and Lin, 1977). Could it be, as suggested by Cooper (1977), that able pupils are often more rewarding to work with, and teachers may be acting in this way to maximise the social reinforcement that they (i.e. the teachers) receive from the class? Since the brightest children are probably in a position to derive considerable intrinsic reward through success at their work, praise and approval from the teacher may be less crucial to their achievement than it is to that of the less able.

Even in situations where praise and approval is provided in class and properly distributed, Brophy (1981) argues that it cannot be automatically assumed, due to the circumstances of its utilisation, that effective reinforcement is taking place. This will depend upon a number of qualifying variables such as features of the pupils including reinforcement history, the type of the task, the nature of the praise, and the manner in which it is administered, together with characteristics of the source. O'Leary and O'Leary (1977) suggest that its success as a reinforcer can be increased by ensuring that, firstly, it is contingently applied; secondly, it specifies the particular behaviour being reinforced; and thirdly, it is credible, varied according to the context, and sounds sincere. Brophy (1981) develops this list by advocating that it be restricted to those students who respond best to it. Not all do, of course, with some finding it perhaps patronising or embarrassing when delivered in the presence of peers.

The influence of such factors as race, gender, age and socioeconomic status on children's susceptibility to reinforcers has been the subject of concerted inquiry. Socioeconomic status has attracted the attention of many researchers, leading Russell (1971, p. 39) to conclude that, 'One of the most consistent findings is that there is a social class difference in response to reinforcement.' Middle-class children have been held to respond better to less tangible reinforcers, including praise and approval, when compared with their lower-class compatriots. The latter, it is assumed, are less likely to be exposed to this type of reinforcement, especially for academic achievement, and are therefore unlikely to attach much value to it, favouring instead tangible rewards like money, food or toys. However, Schultz and Sherman (1976), having undertaken a comprehensive review of the area, were quite adamant that this view was ill-founded. They concluded that, 'social class differences in reinforcer effectiveness cannot be assumed in spite of our predispositions to do so' (p. 52). Cairns (1986), who also addresses this issue, concurs with the stance taken by these reviewers.

Relationships between these variables, if they do exist, are likely to be much more convoluted than those intimated by Russell. Miller and Eller (1985), for instance, reported significant increases in subsequent intelligence test scores among lower- and middle-class white children following the praising of initial test performance, but gender differences played a part as well. Thus middle-class white females were more susceptible than their male counterparts. Praise also improved the performance of lower-class white males but not females. Furthermore, as far as Marisi and Helmy (1984) are concerned, age differences are likely to play an important part in determining how praise is reacted to. Comparing the effects of this incentive on performances of six-year-old boys with those of eleven and seventeen years on a motor task, they discovered that it was only with the youngest group that this form of reward proved beneficial.

On the other hand, Wheldall and Glynn (1989) have shown that the behaviour of adolescents in class can be effectively managed by the teacher praising acceptable conduct in keeping with rules previously agreed by members, and largely ignoring minor infringements. Here, however, praise was contingently administered, unlike the procedure followed by Marisi and Helmy. Differences in the nature of the behaviour focused upon should also be appreciated. The boys in the study by Marisi and Helmy were engaged in the acquisition of a motor skill. Baumeister et al. (1990) point out that with certain skilled tasks, praise may not lead to improvements in performance through the operation of such mechanisms as success feedback, personal expectations for continued success, heightened feelings of self-efficacy, increased intrinsic motivation, or self-attributions of high levels of ability, as is often assumed. Instead it can have the opposite effect of impairing skilled output. The most probable explanation offered by Baumeister and his colleagues is that intervening in this way engenders dysfunctional levels of generalised self-consciousness capable of interfering with the levels of attention and control called for in producing an accomplished outcome.

Other factors which have been found to mediate the reinforcing impact of praise and support include pupils' locus of control (Kennelly and Mount, 1985). As previously mentioned, people who are essentially internally set hold a belief in their own ability to extract reinforcers from the environment, whereas externals are inclined to put rewards that do come their way down to chance or luck. While an external orientation has been associated with receptivity to verbal reinforcement (Baron et al., 1974; Henry et al., 1979), internality of control and an appreciation of the contingency of teacher rewards were predictive of good academic achievement and teacher ratings of pupil competence in an investigation by Kennelly and Mount (1985).

A concept related to locus of control is that of attribution. Pupils' understanding of the reason for praise being given will determine what they make of it. So far we have assumed that praise, among other things, strengthens belief in ability and promotes self-esteem. Meyer et al. (1986) argued that just the opposite may sometimes occur, and showed that those subjects praised for success at an easy task and not blamed for failure at a difficult task inferred that their ability for that type of work was low, when they had few other cues for basing judgements on. When praise for success at the easy task was withheld and failure at the difficult task blamed, subjects assessed their ability as being much higher. Praise does not always carry positive messages, therefore, as far as inferences about ability levels are concerned. This topic will be returned to in Chapter Seven where a much more critical look will be taken at the effects of teacher praise.

Turning attention to characteristics of the reinforcing agent, Stock (1978) revealed that praise from the experimenter, compared to that given by a peer in the person of a student who assisted with the experiment, was much more influential in raising both quality and quantity of work carried out on the set task. This finding was in keeping with an earlier piece of research by Catano (1976) demonstrating the importance of the perceived expertness of the source. Thus praise from a peer looked upon as having relevant expertise was much more telling than that from an inexperienced colleague or no praise at all. According to results reported by Henry *et al.* (1979), boys were more responsive to peer feedback while, for girls, praise given by adults led to faster problem-solving and greater perceptions of agent helpfulness. McGrade (1966) has also speculated that the socioeconomic status of the person praising may make a difference to reinforcing outcomes. More generally evidence has been forthcoming that people have a greater susceptibility to being conditioned by those reinforcing agents that they find personally attractive (Sapolsky, 1960). Presumably attraction enhances their overall potential as sources of reward.

Still on the theme of factors that help determine the effects of praise and support, there is good reason to believe, at least with older individuals, that personality may play a salient role. In particular it seems that extroverts may be more receptive to the effects of praise while for introverts the punishment of inappropriate responses can produce better results in terms of verbal operant conditioning (Boddy *et al.*, 1986; Gupta and Shukla, 1989). Susceptibility to the reinforcing influences of others seems to be strengthened among those who display a heightened need for approval and therefore have a predilection to act in ways that will increase the chances of others reacting favourably towards them (Crowne and Marlowe, 1964). Individuals also differ in the extent to which they monitor their social performances. Those scoring high on this factor show a greater inclination to compromise beliefs and present aspects of themselves that are in keeping with the demands of the situation (Snyder, 1987). In so doing, they may be predisposed to greater sensitivity to the availability of sources of social reward.

Interviewing

The interview has been defined in general terms, and quite simply, as a conversation with a purpose (Cannell and Kahn, 1968). When cast as widely as this, we recognise an activity which has been entered into by practically everyone. In more formal and specialised quarters, interviewing forms an element of the work load of a diversity of professionals. Among these, Breakwell (1990) specifies educationalists, health care providers, social and public service personnel, and managers in industry and commerce. No doubt the list could be extended. While all interview, not all do so for the same reasons nor do they abide by the same sets of rules and procedures.

Interviewing refers to a family of interactive activities the members of which, while sharing fundamental commonalities, have unique qualities. According to Bingham *et al.* (1959), interviews can serve three main purposes: they can be used, firstly, to obtain information; secondly, to engineer changes in the attitudes, emotions and/or behaviour of interviewees; and thirdly, to give information. The first two of these contexts have been more intensively researched than the third and, since they have greater centrality to the theme of this chapter, will be concentrated upon.

Praising is readily associated with teaching and what takes place in the classroom; it is probably less thought of as part of the business of interviewing. Nevertheless, if interjections such as 'Good', 'Well done', etc. can be interpreted in this manner, even if offering only limited commendation, then this, together with approval and support, is a recognisable form of reward which interviewers can make available for what interviewees may reveal and the efforts and commitments required of them to do so (Millar *et al.*, 1992).

We have already seen how verbal conditioning procedures have been put to use in establishing the reinforcing capabilities of acknowledging and confirmatory utterances. Other interviewer reactions that can more properly be labelled as instances of praise, approval and support have also been researched. Much of this early work, particularly as it relates to the clinical interview, is reviewed by Kanfer (1968) and Pope (1979).

The conditioning effects of interviewer utterances like 'Good' have been confirmed by a number of researchers. In a laboratory-based procedure devised by Taffel (1955), subjects were presented with a number of plain cards on each of which was written six different pronouns, followed by a verb. Instructions were to select a card, choose any one of the pronouns, and construct a sentence incorporating the verb. The task of the experimenter was to increase the frequency of selection of sentences commencing with the first-person pronoun by responding with 'Good', whenever an instance was presented. As hypothesised, over the duration of the experiment, subjects exposed to conditioning generated significantly greater numbers of first-person pronoun sentences than those in the control group.

A replication and extension of this experiment carried out by Arenson (1978) revealed not only that conditioning effects were restricted to those individuals who became aware of the contingent relationship between the targeted response and the experimenter's reaction, but also that females were much more susceptible to this influence than were males who took part. Differences in individual responsiveness to social reinforcers of this type have already been stressed in this and the last chapters. Using Taffel's experimental protocol, Spielberger *et al.* (1962) attempted to assess the value which subjects attached to receiving the experimenter's endorsement of their choices, expressed by 'Good'. They found that conditioning was restricted to subjects for whom this response was looked upon positively and sought after. It should be realised, however, that attitudes towards the reinforcer were gauged *after* the experiment and no attempt at independent verification was reported.

Do these effects still hold in extended exchanges bearing greater similarity to the normal interviewing process? This was the question which Hildum and Brown (1956) attempted to answer through conducting a telephone survey. Respondents were invited to give their reactions to a fifteen-item questionnaire designed to ascertain attitudes to an educational topic considered to be largely emotionally neutral. Each item had four possible responses ranging from strongly agree to strongly disagree. One group contacted had negative responses systematically reinforced using 'Good' while, for a second, only positive reactions were treated in this way. In line with expectations, the expressed attitudes of respondents reinforced for responding negatively were markedly less favourable when compared to those influenced in the opposite direction. Incidentally, no evidence was reported that the interviewer could produce the same effect by going 'mm-hmm'. Perhaps the elimination of all but the vocal elements of nonverbal communication, since the conversations were telephone-mediated, is significant in this regard. Goldman (1980) also demonstrated that attitudes elicited during survey interviews could be manipulated in this fashion by the interviewer. In this case face-to-face interviews were conducted and attitudes had to do with intercollegiate athletic competition.

The content and type of speech have also been examined and proven malleable when subjected to this type of interviewer affirmation. Thus Stewart and Patterson (1973) illustrated how people's constructions of imprecise, abstract representations of events can be readily coloured depending upon how these are received. Subjects were presented with Thematic Apperception Test (TAT) cards which depict ambiguous pictures of a scene involving people. Individuals are thought to reveal aspects of their personality in the sorts of imaginative stories that they make up in response. By reinforcing thematic responses using 'Good', these researchers reported a significant increase in the number of instances of this class of response for each card viewed, in contrast to a non-reinforced control group.

It may be wondered if these findings would still hold in situations where the individuals involved are dealing with real concerns and could therefore have, it might be argued, a greater commitment to, and investment in, what takes place, together with outcomes that might accrue. It seems that this may well be so. McBee and Justice (1977) investigated clinical interviews in which patients under treatment for mental illness were assessed using the twenty-two-item Mental Health Inventory. They showed that interviewers could substantially increase the number of symptoms reported if contingent verbal reinforcement was made available. Marquis (1970), in an earlier study, disclosed that increased health reporting in household surveys could be brought about in a similar way.

Bizarre and delusional speech is characteristic of some forms of mental illness including schizophrenia. According to a social learning approach to psychiatric management, staff should be appreciative of the consequences that may help to keep such behaviour in place (Poole *et al.*, 1981). In many cases an important source of such consequences is the reactions of other staff. By verbally reinforcing non-delusional and ignoring delusional talk, Rickard *et al.* (1960) showed how incidence of the latter could be reduced. But patients also interact with each other. Based upon an observation study of an acute admission ward of a psychiatric hospital, Positano *et al.* (1990) concluded that both nursing staff and patients tended to reinforce appropriate behaviour. However, other patients were also much more likely than nurses to reinforce bizarre occurrences. Again, over the course of therapy, patients have been found to reveal a growing independence in their line of conversation. Having analysed a number of psychotherapy interviews, Murray (1956) discovered an association between this change and approval by the therapist for talk along these lines, together with disapproval of expressions of independence anxiety.

In a further and particularly interesting piece of research within the health (but not mental health) field, White and Sanders (1986) interviewed patients suffering from chronic pain. They found that, over the course of several conversations, the 'pain talk' or 'well talk' of patients could be selectively modified by 'verbal attention, praise and sympathy' (p. 156). Not only that but also, according to ratings of pain intensity given by patients over the seven days of the investigation, spending less time talking of pain was positively correlated with actual reductions in experienced severity.

In summing up this sub-section, it is evident that there are many interviewing settings where professionals of different sorts can make positive and constructive use of praise, approval and support, at least of the limited type noted. It should also be appreciated, of course, that unskilled use by an interviewer who is unaware of the likely influence being wrought is also possible. Cannell *et al.* (1977), investigating the performance of survey interviewers, discovered that adequate or appropriate responses received proportionately less positive interviewer reinforcement than did those deemed to be less desirable. Refusal to respond, the least desirable response, received proportionately the highest levels of reinforcement! The results of this misuse of the technique may be unfortunate if it leads to insufficient or inaccurate information being obtained. Brenner (1985) warned those conducting research interviews of these dangers of bias. In other settings the outcome could be more seriously damaging and destructive of individuals and families (i.e. the social worker, perhaps, who has a child taken into care on the strength of an assessment interview during which the child was systematically led in its disclosure by the worker). The vulnerability of children to adult influence and suggestion was highlighted in evidence given during the inquiry into child abuse in Cleveland (Butler-Sloss, 1988). The biasing use of selective social reinforcement is one of a range of interviewing malpractices which should be guarded against under such circumstances.

Management

Arguably one of the most important but demanding responsibilities that besets any manager whether working in industry and commerce, or in the public services sector, is what has been called 'man management'. It has to do with managing the human resource of the organisation in such a way as to maximise the contribution of each member of staff in a quest for ever higher levels of efficient productivity. As a measure of the challenge which this task presents, over fifty per cent of wage earners admitted in response to a questionnaire some years ago that they could achieve much more on a daily basis at their jobs if they really wanted to (Luthans and Kreitner, 1975). Both employers and social scientists have been searching for ways of actualising this latent potential in the work force.

One approach which has been widely researched over the past two decades relies upon the application of operant conditioning techniques and is called *Organisational Behaviour Modification*. The key sequential procedures, as outlined by Komaki (1982), encompass, firstly, analysing the overall work environment within which the aspect of performance to be targeted is embedded; secondly, clarifying expectations and specifying requisite standards of operation; thirdly, establishing practices for the accurate but sensitive measurement of the targeted behaviour; fourthly, administering appropriate reinforcers in accordance with behavioural principles of contingent control; and finally, evaluating the impact of the intervention according to pre-specified criteria. Reviews of investigations conducted in a multiplicity of settings have concluded that OBM can reduce absenteeism, increase productivity and performance, heighten motivation and feelings of job satisfaction, and lead to better relationships between management and staff (Davey, 1981; Frederiksen and Johnson, 1981; Rapp *et al.*, 1983).

Makin *et al.* (1989) have suggested that many work-based interventions reflect a recent and powerful combination of OBM procedures and *Management by Objectives* (Drucker, 1954), or *Goal Setting* (Locke and Latham, 1984). The latter advocate the establishment of goals or objectives in relation to organisational change and the provision of feedback on how these are being met. This feedback is typically a factual record of accomplishments, unlike OBM programmes which incorporate explicit rewards for achievement. While distinguishing between informational feedback and tangible reinforcers is relatively easy, this task is not nearly so straightforward, as we have already seen, with social rewards like praise. Indeed, Kopelman (1983) readily acknowledges that feedback works in motivational as well as strictly informational terms.

When we think of rewards for working, money naturally springs to mind. But pay, while obviously important, is not the only source of reward at the disposal of management. Other possibilities, identified by Komaki (1982), include activity reinforcers, such as time off, extra work-breaks, etc., and organisational changes including promotion, job assignments, and training opportunities, together with feedback on performance and social recognition. Recognition of their role in the organisation and praise for the contribution which they make to its success is an important element in the creation of a well-motivated and satisfied work force which feels valued by the employer. Among the additional practical advantages of the programmed use of social rewards, Prue and Fairbank (1981) discuss cost-effectiveness, placing an emphasis upon positive practice, simplicity of administration, and the side-stepping of union problems than can beset attempts to introduce wage-based productivity-enhancement schemes.

Many of the OBM interventions incorporating the systematic praising and approving of aspects of work practice have combined these rewards with other types of reinforcer making it difficult to identify their relative contributions to the end result. Several studies where the sources of effects are easier to locate will, however, be briefly mentioned. Perhaps one of the best known is that implemented at Emery Air Freight (At Emery Air Freight, 1973). This company relied heavily upon large freight containers for transporting goods. An audit revealed the marked under-utilisation of these containers and identified this as the single most signifi-cant factor in depressing profits. A scheme was set in place to increase the use of empty container space. Warehousemen who had the responsibility for this task were given daily feedback on their performance. Warehouse managers were also trained to praise and compliment the achievement of set targets. Workbooks given to managers suggested a huge variety of specific ways in which this might be put into practice, from a smile and nod of encouragement through to detailed praise for a job well done. As a result the company flew fewer containers that were less than half full, made a savings of some $520,000 in the first year, and increased this to $2 million over a period of three years.

Similar procedures were also found, by Wikoff et al. (1982), to enhance worker efficiency across seven departments in a furniture manufacturing plant and, by Silva et al. (1982), to reduce absenteeism among staff in an insurance company. In the latter case, the manager praised staff for good attendance during routine visits within the department. One of the interesting features of this investigation was ensuring that the manager made use of praise as directed. One method found effective was for the experimenter to praise the manager when the manager reinforced appropriately!

Praise featured prominently in the procedures employed by both Komaki et al. (1980) and Crowell et al. (1988) to increase the quality of customer service through improving the interpersonal skills of employees. Personnel serving in a fast-food outlet were trained to be more friendly to customers by Komaki et al. (1980). Employees were made aware of how often, for instance, they smiled at the customer when greeting, taking an order, or giving change. When they did so it was recognised and praised by the manager. The authors also speculate that once staff adopt this type of friendly approach it may well be maintained through the naturally occurring and positive consequences which it evokes in customers.

The programme implemented by Crowell et al. (1988) was much more elabor-ate. Bank tellers were encouraged to execute transactions with customers in accordance with eleven behaviourally defined categories selected on the basis of extensive observation and analysis of teller–customer interactions. Although initial clarification of the categories together with performance feedback was sufficient to produce noticeable improvements, it was only with the introduction of verbal praise for targeted levels of achievement that overall category scores reached the criterion set for acceptability. During the period of the investigation, the branch recorded an increase in deposits from $24 million to $42 million. Although it is not possible to state categorically that this upturn was the direct result of improvements in tellers' interpersonal skills, this rate of growth was unprecedented for either that branch or the bank as a whole and is highly suggestive of this causal relationship.

Other programmes of this type have been set in place in the public sector. Brown *et al.* (1981), for example, increased the proportion of task-related activities undertaken by staff in a residential facility for retarded people with multiple handicaps. Daily records were kept on the amount of time that staff spent in, firstly, social interaction with residents; secondly, direct care work; or thirdly, off-task activities not related to resident or unit welfare. Making verbal feedback available resulted in reductions in off-task behaviour. Only when it was combined with supervisor praise and approval directed at individual members of staff who engaged in the targeted behaviour, however, was a change noticed in positive practices, such as devoting more attention to interacting with residents. In a comparable intervention, Montegar *et al.* (1977) increased staff–resident interactions by up to fifty per cent attributable to the contingent use of supervisor praise. Having conducted a wide-ranging review of research in this setting, Reid and Whitman (1983) concluded that explicit praise and approval of specific residential staff behaviour was an effective mechanism for changing work habits.

Despite the potency of social reinforcers, and praise in particular, in the organisational setting, Makin *et al.* (1989) discovered that it is often decidedly underused by those in positions of control. As a consequence a number of large corporations, including Xerox, have instituted training programmes to improve managers' use of this skill.

Coaching

Sport is a form of recreation which many people take part in and enjoy. In doing so, and depending upon the particular sport, they may well expend energy to the point of exhaustion, tolerate impossible environmental conditions, endure all sorts of hardships, accept physical and psychological pain, and even risk injury or death. Were these circumstances to be encountered in the work context, the same individual would predictably seek a massive wage increase or resign! Yet in the name of sport other sacrifices will be made to accommodate them. With top-class performers sport is highly lucrative and, at the same time, provides an avenue for public recognition and acclaim. But what about ordinary Saturday morning competitors, why do they do it? The question defies an easy answer; reasons are probably many and complex. Nevertheless it would seem that there must be rewards that outweigh the various 'costs' which we have identified. Thus, Lees and Dygdon (1988) have sketched a learning theory model to account for initiation into and maintenance in exercise programmes. They speculate on the contribution of social reinforcement from significant others, in the form of praise and admiration, as one category of reinforcer in a multi-source conditioning process. Apart from operating directly on the activity of exercising, it can also have an indirect influence stemming from subsequent alterations to physical appearance. The latter may make available additional social rewards. Some evidence for these speculations was provided by Brown *et al.* (1989), who discovered that the support and encouragement received from parents and peers of both sexes was a major predictor of whether adolescent girls continued their participation in sport or dropped out.

Coaches and those working closely with participants should also be aware of the significance of maximising opportunities for responding positively. Smith and Smoll (1990), having analysed a large number of coaching episodes, identified a general tendency to be supportive as a central factor in terms of which coaches differed. Those scoring highly were inclined to be seen as more attractive by the children with whom they worked. Coaches' use of praise and encouragement can also play an important role in enhancing performance and maximising effort (Martin and Hrycaiko, 1983); increasing motivation, including intrinsic motivation (Weinberg, 1984); and improving participants' attitudes and feelings towards the sporting environment (Dodds, 1983). Hence, 'When the coach considers himself or herself to be a valuable source of reinforcement he/she should attempt to concentrate on and maximise this form of behaviour because it is the most important coaching behaviour although one of the least emphasized' (Rushall, 1983, p. 90).

As far as improving performance is concerned, Anderson *et al.* (1988) instituted a training intervention which relied, in part, on getting the coach to use praise more frequently and effectively to increase the rate of legal body checking (hit rate) among members of a university ice-hockey team which had a poor record of winning. Not only was the rate increased in consequence, but also it was paralleled by an upturn in the fortunes of the team. The experiences of these authors also underscore the fact that simply mouthing platitudes is entirely ineffectual. The programme was initially introduced before the coach had been properly trained in the technique. In consequence, praise tended to be administered in a very mechanical, rote fashion. It was only when the coach began to be perceived as sincere in what he said and did that behavioural changes took place. Similarly, praise and recognition, combined with performance feedback, have been employed by coaches of American football to promote instances of correct play by members of the offensive backfield (Komaki and Barnett, 1977); in swimming to improve attendance at training and the number of lengths swum (McKenzie and Rushall, 1974); and, as part of a behavioural approach to coaching devised by Allison and Ayllon (1980), to improve the correct execution of skills in American football, tennis and gymnastics. (These findings would seem, at face value, to be at variance with those of Baumeister *et al.* (1990), mentioned earlier. The latter researchers discovered that praise had a detrimental effect on skill acquisition. This was thought to be due to interference with attention and control mechanisms. Significant differences, however, exist between the circumstances of this and the previous work on sports skills. The former was conducted in a laboratory-based experimental setting, the praise was administered by an experimenter rather than a coach, and the type of skill being practised likely required higher levels of fine eye–hand coordination and concentration than that focused upon in the sports studies.)

As with teachers and managers, it should not be assumed that coaches naturally made good use of this form of reward. Martin *et al.* (1983) suggest that the opposite may often be the case in swimming. Poor practice includes an inclination to give instructions rather than praise, ignoring participants when swimming well, and dispensing reinforcement on the basis of favouritism rather than accomplishment. Adding to this list, Rushall (1983) accuses coaches, when they do praise, of doing so in a quite invariant fashion, relying upon the same few expressions.

Some of the recommendations offered to coaches by the likes of Martin and Hrycaiko (1983), Rushall (1983), and Martin *et al.* (1983) include to:

   (i) make more frequent use of praise and encouragement (assuming that these have been established beforehand as valued by the individual athlete). Weinberg (1984) suggests that this may be particularly appreciated by those who seldom win races, swim fastest times, or get in the first team and for whom other sources of reward are therefore denied.

  (ii) individualise reinforcement.

 (iii) make it contingent upon performance.

 (iv) apply it immediately after the behaviour to be promoted.

  (v) specify the aspect of the overall activity to which it applies. Indeed the incorporation of an element of performance feedback has been recommended.

 (vi) ensure that praise is sincerely given and appropriately varied. Rushall and Smith (1979) describe a training procedure designed to improve this aspect of coaching.

(vii) use shaping techniques to gradually reach the final desired level of performance while exposing the participant to a regime of essentially positive and successful experiences throughout.

(viii) maximise alternative sources of social reinforcement, particularly team members. This is important since it may be difficult for the coach to give individual attention to a large number of athletes during training. Nevertheless, and bearing in mind what was said earlier about the effectiveness of peer praise, impact will probably be determined by the credibility and esteem with which the particular team member is held, together with the degree of cohesion and morale which exists in the group.

 (ix) encourage participants to indulge in self-reinforcement.

  (x) administer this form of external reinforcement in such a way that it does not get in the way of, or detract from natural reinforcers in the situation. Indeed, 'to use positive reinforcement and extinction effectively, coaches should deliberately reinforce desirable skills and behaviors or insure that they come under the influence of natural reinforcers' (Martin and Hrycaiko, 1983, p. 40). These include the normal consequences of executing the skill successfully, winning being, perhaps, the ultimate example. It is possible, nevertheless, for coaches to place too much emphasis on winning as a reward for skill and effort. Bearing in mind that there can be only one winner, the rest, as losers, can quickly become discouraged and drop out.

RESPONSE DEVELOPMENT

There is, in a sense, a progressive sequence of increasing involvement and acceptance which commences with the mere acknowledgement of a response, continues with the positive evaluation of it through praise, for example, and proceeds to the further exploration and development of the content. Having an idea or action form, in this way, part of the agenda for the ongoing discourse may, perhaps, be looked upon as the highest form of praise! It is quite easy for a teacher, manager, interviewer or coach to express a few perfunctory words of acknowledgement or commendation before continuing on a completely different tack, but the development of a response indicates, firstly, that the listener must have been carefully attending and, secondly, that the content must have been considered worthy of the listener's time and effort to make it part of 'the talk'.

A response can be developed in a number of ways. In the classroom, Perrott (1982) mentions how teachers may respond to pupil contributions, 'by accepting them, summarising them, applying them, building on them or asking questions based on them' (p. 97). Here is a powerful means of providing reinforcement during a lesson, even if it is less frequently used than alternatives already considered. On the other hand, a teacher may develop a pupil's contribution by elaborating upon it herself. The potential reward for pupils of having their ideas form part of the lesson will be readily appreciated. In a group, members may be asked to contribute their suggestions and be reinforced by having their responses further explored by other members. In a coaching context, certain individuals can be selected to demonstrate a skill or technique to the other participants for them to work further on. If tactfully handled this form of response development can again be highly motivating and positively valued.

Perrott (1982) claims that pupils who have their ideas and efforts rewarded through elaboration in this fashion are more inclined to want to participate in the lesson and have a constructive attitude towards what they do during it. Does achievement benefit as a result? A limited number of studies have addressed the relationship between teachers' use of pupil ideas and subsequent achievement levels. Rosenshine (1971) reviewed a total of nine of these and found a consistent positive correlation recorded by eight of them, although these results failed to reach an acceptable level of statistical significance. This somewhat disappointing finding could be explained by the rather loose definition of 'use of pupil ideas', adopted in the majority of the studies. Further research is evidently required to demonstrate a more convincing relationship between these variables.

In general, research concerning the reinforcing effects of response development is less prevalent than that involving reinforcers included in the previous two categories. Bandura *et al.* (1960) examined the outcome of an interviewer's approaching or avoiding client responses which expressed hostility. 'Approach' by the interviewer was defined to include labelling the client feeling as hostile and demonstrating interest in it by exploring it further. When a hostile statement was reacted to in this manner, rather than being avoided, the probability that the client pursued that theme in his next speech turn was significantly increased. In a comparative study of a group of experienced psychiatric interviewers and a group of inexperienced medical students, the latter were found to be less likely to develop topics introduced by the client (Dudley and Blanchard, 1976). Such lack of development tends to contribute to feelings of not being engaged with fully (Geller *et al.*, 1974).

We have considered several methods by which a response can be developed thereby constituting a positive, rewarding experience for the contributor. Another approach still to be mentioned is through providing reflective statements. Reflection of feeling and Paraphrasing were examples cited in Chapter One. These are statements which distil the essence of the interviewee's previous message and represent it in the words of the interviewer. Rewarding possibilities are evident from the functional analysis sketched by Dillon (1990, p. 186), as follows:

> A reflective restatement permits the speaker (and other partners) to infer, rightly, that what he thinks and says *matters*. It confirms the speaker in his effort to contribute. It helps him to express thoughts gradually more clearly and fully. It assures him of understanding. And it makes a public possession of a private meaning. The result is to encourage participation, both speaking and listening, and to facilitate relevant discussion of actual rather than imaginary meanings.

In certain cases the reinforcing prowess of reflections has been compared with that of various expressions of praise, encouragement and acknowledgement (e.g. Powell, 1968). It is interesting to note that these studies have largely found the use of reflections to be more effective in promoting the interviewee response focused upon. (Reflection of feeling, as an expression of empathic responding, will be returned to in Chapter Five.)

Many of the above studies featured interviewee self-disclosure as the outcome measure on the basis of which the influence of reflections could be established. In some investigations *interviewer* self-disclosure was also incorporated as an alternative experimental treatment due to the fact that this kind of talk is often reciprocated in conversations (Tubbs and Baird, 1976). In other words if we want someone to tell us something of themselves a sensible way to go about it is to reveal something of ourselves to them. Hargie (1986) proposes that, under appropriate conditions, professionals can make good use of this tendency when dealing with clients. If we define reinforcers as consequent events that operate to increase the occurrence of the preceding response upon which they were made contingent, then it would appear that we have a *prima facie* case for considering self-disclosures in this category. Vondracek (1969) and Beharry (1976) looked at the effects of this variable on the amount and degree of intimacy of the detail that subjects revealed about themselves. In both studies, interviewer self-disclosure was considered to be as successful as a contrasting reflective style. A comparable result was reported by Mills (1983) in relation to rates rather than quality of self-revelations, while Powell (1968) showed that subjects could be influenced to disclose negative as well as positive personal detail under these circumstances. Less impressive results were, however, documented by McBee and Justice (1977). Of course not all instances of interviewer self-disclosure are equally attractive. There are a complex of factors, some of which are posited by Derlega and Berg (1987), which specify the propriety of this form of interaction and hence its probable rewardingness. (The role of self-disclosure in relationship work will be taken up in Chapter Nine.)

CONCLUSION

This chapter has concentrated upon examining some of the ways in which we can reward others through the sorts of things we say to them. While the focus has been very much on the verbal domain, practical difficulties in differentiating between verbal and nonverbal effects in naturally occurring conversation were stressed and should be taken into account in reaching conclusions about effectiveness. Verbal rewards of three broad types were isolated for consideration: acknowledging and confirmatory utterances, praise and support, and response development including the use of reflective and self-disclosing statements. From reviewing some of the research carried out, mostly within an operant conditioning framework, there is ample evidence that predictable outcomes can be achieved through the promotion of selected aspects of functioning. In teaching, one of the most widely investigated professional domains, teacher social rewards have been associated with improved classroom behaviour, motivation and achievement; in interviewing with increasing the amount and intimacy of information revealed; in management with reducing absenteeism and promoting productivity and profits; and in coaching with increasing levels of participation, skill and sporting attainment.

Having said this, it appears that these potential effects are not straightforward, nor are they guaranteed. A complex of factors, the effects of some of which are more clearly specified than others, seem capable of playing a mediating role. These include, for instance, the gender, age, status, personality and socioeconomic background of both parties; the relationship which they share; the task to be completed; the way in which social rewards are bestowed; and the interpretation placed upon what is taking place by the recipient.

A further conclusion worth drawing would appear to be that, from the evidence available, professionals frequently do not make best use of verbal sources of reward when dealing with those with whom they interact. In consequence training programmes have been instituted for teachers, managers and coaches to bring about improvements in their use of this skill.

Chapter 4

Nonverbal facets of social reward

INTRODUCTION

During the last twenty years increasing attention has been devoted to the nonverbal aspects of human communication. The result has been a burgeoning literature, notably by Birdwhistell (1970), Knapp (1972), Argyle (1975), Scherer and Ekman (1982), Bull (1983), and more recently Siegman and Feldstein (1987). A great deal of this literature has focused specifically on the supposition that social rewards are conveyed in large measure via the nonverbal channel of communication. Thus we can learn that someone is interested in us, impressed by us, in agreement with us, or even sexually attracted to us by observing a range of nonverbal cues such as gestures, eye contact, facial expressions, or interpersonal distance. These are only a few of the vast range of cues available.

Not all the information we receive from and about others comes directly from what they tell us. Information reflecting a person's feelings, emotions or attitudes, for instance, is often inferred from unspoken language, or the language of nonverbal communication. Indeed we can like the manner of a person viewed only at the other side of a crowded room and at the same time form an instant dislike of someone who has not even spoken a word to us. This nonverbal channel which embraces all forms of communication apart from the purely verbal message contains powerful cues which can indicate liking and approval or disliking and disapproval. The remainder of this chapter will examine in more detail the effects which a variety of cues, ranging from the use of touch to the use of space, can have on the behaviour patterns of others.

FUNCTIONS OF NONVERBAL COMMUNICATION

Nonverbal communication serves a number of functions depending upon the context in which it is employed. The rewarding effects of some of these are more directly evident than others. Perhaps the most obvious function is that nonverbal communication can totally replace speech. There are a number of situations where persons rely solely on a sign language. At one extreme there are those who are deaf and dumb. Others may only be temporarily cut off from language communication such as deep sea divers, race course touts, police on traffic duty, etc. However, in less extreme contexts a meaningful glance, a caring touch, a forward lean can convey a message more effectively than any word. Kurth (1970) notes that we use mostly nonverbal signals such as smiling, gaze and eye contact to indirectly indicate liking, without expressing it verbally, when we initiate and develop relationships with others. He argues that it is too risky to say 'I love you' or 'I think you're terrific' for fear of non-reciprocation or even rejection.

Nonverbal behaviour is also used to complement the spoken word. More particularly, specific nonverbal acts give the listener some idea of the affective state of the speaker (Siegman and Feldstein, 1987). That is, words uttered by individuals experiencing some kind of emotional state, such as anxiety, depression, love, frustration or anger, are accompanied by the appropriate actions. We grin broadly when we are pleased, gasp when surprised, and pat someone on the head when warmly praising their efforts.

So far we have examined the consistency of verbal and nonverbal messages but they can also be contradictory and cut across each other. For example, one can say nice things and smile – or one can say nice things and frown. How are such inconsistencies interpreted? Where this contradiction exists it is generally thought that listeners place more credence on nonverbal behaviours as they are considered harder to falsify (Shapiro, 1968). Young children have particular difficulty with inconsistent messages and tend to treat all such messages as if they were negative whichever communication channel conveyed the negativity (Bugental *et al.*, 1970).

The flow of communication between listener and speaker is regulated by distinct aspects of nonverbal behaviour in addition to those verbal mechanisms mentioned in the preceding chapter. Hence when two or more persons are engaged in conversation the major issue of conversational management relates to the control of turn-taking. We do not verbally state, 'I am finished. Go on, its your turn to speak.' Instead, the speaker indicates this nonverbally by using a range of cues. Duncan and Fiske (1977) have identified a number of nonverbal cues which offer a speaking turn to the other person. These are a rise or fall in pitch at the end of a phrase, a drop in voice volume, a drawl on the final syllable, a direct look at the listener, and termination of hand gestures. In addition, it was found that if a speaker continued to use gestures, such as hand gesticulations, it essentially eliminated attempts by the listener to take over the turn.

Nonverbal behaviour can help to define relationships between individuals without explicitly stating what those relationships are. An interesting study carried out by Royce and Weiss (1975) into married couples' relationships revealed that couples who were perceived as having greater marital satisfaction displayed more smiling, laughing, mutual attention, and positive physical contact than those perceived as dissatisfied. Interestingly, the actual martial satisfaction of the mutually rewarding couples was also positively correlated with these behaviours.

When individuals are negotiating and sustaining personal relationships it could be too disturbing for one to state openly that he did not like the other very much, or indeed that he thought he was more important than the other. Yet nonverbal cues can be emitted regarding these states and rewards exchanged accordingly. Mehrabian (1969) conducted a series of experiments in which body movements were measured as participants role-played various status positions. A sample of college students was instructed to approach an imaginary person who was of high status for some of them and of low status for others. Students raised their heads more, gave more eye contact, and faced more directly when approaching a person of high status. In addition, initial relationships can change over time so that, for example, an original dominant–submissive relationship can become one more equal in nature. Change would not come about as readily, if at all, if persons had verbally stated at the outset how they felt towards each other.

Finally, nonverbal behaviour can help to define acceptable routines of behaviour in a variety of social and professional contexts. All settings from the informal, such as the office party or a visit to the local pub, to more formal contexts, such as a funeral or a job interview, carry with them appropriate codes of behaviour. If one departs from these acceptable patterns it may be construed as deviant, thereby demanding some kind of explanation (Goffman, 1972).

It should be noted that all of these previously stated functions have a bearing on the rewarding process. Thus, when we want to show liking for someone, we may convey this state nonverbally; when we wish to display a welcoming approach we arrange a comfortable environment; a smile and a pat on the back often conveys reward for effort; and positive relationships between people can be clearly observed through posture, orientation and interpersonal distance. The remainder of this chapter will analyse and interpret how these above functions can be achieved by implementing and co-ordinating a range of nonverbal behaviours.

TOUCH CONTACT

This category of nonverbal behaviour has been included first since, as Major and Heslin (1982) note, 'It [touch] is the most basic sensory process and the earliest and most elemental form of communication' (p. 148). Our first contact with the outside world and whether it is a friendly or a hostile place comes through tactile experiences. We can think of the doctor's or midwife's hands as a baby is delivered and, more importantly, the parent's hands which feed, bathe, cradle, nurse and comfort the infant through its waking hours. These early touch contacts appear to be of crucial importance to subsequent healthy behavioural and emotional development of young adults (Montagu, 1971). The views of Eric Berne on this matter have already been encountered in Chapter Two, of course.

With young children, touch can be very reassuring and rewarding. Wheldall *et al.* (1986) carried out a number of studies on infant classes in the West Midlands of England. Their aim was to examine the effect of positive contingent teacher touch on the classroom behaviour of these mixed-gender infant-class children. Each of four teachers and their classes was observed for ten thirty-minute sessions using a touch category schedule. The results showed that 'good' on-task behaviour increased substantially by an average of 20 per cent, following the inclusion of touch, and rates of disruptive behaviour fell markedly. These researchers concluded that by using contingent, positive touch in association with verbal approval, children experienced more forcefully the reinforcing effects of teacher praise.

However, as children grow up, touching is an area of behaviour that is susceptible to multiple interpretations. This susceptibility is noted by Heslin and Alper (1983), who state that, 'It [touch] is complicated by social norms regarding who has permission to touch whom and what is considered to be an appropriate context for such behaviour' (p. 47). For instance, Major and Heslin (1982), using a complex model of touch, found that it can simultaneously communicate both warmth and status. More specifically, males were more attuned to the status and dominance cues of touch, whereas women were more attuned to warmth cues and correspondingly tended to perceive this form of behaviour as a warm and friendly gesture. These differences are further highlighted by Dickson (1985), who noted that touching between women and men and also between women commonly communicates warmth/friendship while touch among men is frequently construed as regulating dominance/assertiveness.

Touching can be categorised according to its function (Heslin, 1974). Social/polite touching, for example, (especially handshaking) is an act that attempts to equalise status by signalling that the interactors are intending to acknowledge the 'human element' of the interaction as opposed to status differences. Friendship/warmth touch contacts, such as a friendly pat, arm-linking, or a comforting touch on the arm aimed at establishing friendly relationships with others, can be very rewarding to individuals in terms of giving encouragement, expressing care and concern, and showing emotional support and understanding. Functional/professional touch contacts are made by a range of professionals in the normal course of their work: nurses, dentists, doctors, physiotherapists, teachers and counsellors to name but a few. While touch in this category is seen as a necessary function of a particular job, there are opportunities to employ friendship/warmth touch contacts when patients and clients experience stress or emotional trauma. For instance, Mason and Pratt (1980) suggest that when a patient is semi-conscious, withdrawn or perhaps unable to communicate, touch is a powerful means of bringing them back to reality.

Other research into the positive influence which touch can have on individuals shows that touching can help recipients talk to others, especially about themselves and their problems (Pattison, 1973). Reactions of encounter group members were compared in groups that did exercises involving touching and in groups that did not engage in this behaviour (Dies and Greenberg, 1976). Group members who had the experience of touching rated one another more favourably and expressed greater willingness to share closeness and express personal feelings.

While touch can undoubtedly communicate warmth and caring, it can also encourage the recipient to have a more positive attitude to the toucher as well as the physical context in which the touch contact took place. In an interesting study by Fisher et al. (1975) it was found that, when library clerks in a university briefly touched the hand of a reader while retrieving an identification card, this half-second contact caused the readers to like not only the librarian but also the library better than did those who were not touched. However, positive reactions to touch were stronger for female than for male readers.

Finally, it is important to be aware that there are groups within the community who very rarely have the opportunity to employ touch contacts; elderly people with no close relatives and widowed people whose family have long since dispersed receive little or no touch contacts designed to cater for their emotional needs. Professional helpers such as social workers, health visitors, and community nurses, aware of this void, could employ appropriate touch contacts to redress this imbalance.

PROXIMITY AND ORIENTATION

Proximity can also serve as a form of reward in that we tend to stand or sit closer to people we like and want to be involved with and to sit closer to those we like more. If individuals have freedom of choice regarding the position they adopt during interaction, it can convey information relating to the nature of that relationship. Thus a reduction of distance indicates a desire to achieve a greater degree of intimacy, and by deposition the increasing of distance may be perceived as unreceptive and aloof (hence the expression 'He is stand-offish!').

It should also be noted, however, that a person who approaches too closely may be regarded as over-familiar, dominant or even threatening. A study carried out by Baxter and Rozelle (1975) focused on a simulated police–citizen interview where the distances were varied systematically between the participants.

Briefly, it was found that when interpersonal distance was decreased to within two feet of the interactors, the citizen displayed a range of stress-related behaviour (speech dysfluency, increased gaze avoidance, more head rotation movements, and sweating). Interestingly, these same behaviours were cited by the police officers as describing guilt, suspicion and deception-related behaviours. Thus it is important to be aware that the initiator can influence the other person's behaviour and totally misinterpret the resulting consequences.

Other evidence of 'crowding' or coming too close is provided by Goldman (1980), who noted that interviewers could more successfully modify the attitudes of their interviewees by means of verbal reinforcers when the interviewer stood at a moderate (4–5 feet) rather than a close (2–3 feet) interpersonal distance.

Observations of interaction distances between people have indicated differential relationships (Hall, 1966). There are also sex differences to be found. Women maintain closer interaction distances with other women friends and with friends of the opposite sex than men do with male friends (Heshka and Nelson, 1972). These findings throw further light on Hall's personal zone category in which he states those who have a close personal relationship with other individuals will take up a distance of 18 inches to 4 feet. Women interact with each other and with men towards the 18 inches end of the continuum while men interact with each other towards the 4 foot end.

Interpersonal distance is also linked to an 'attractiveness' factor. For instance,

Burgoon and Jones (1976), reviewing a number of studies of liking and proxemics, came to the conclusion that attractive people are more liked, more persuasive, and better understood if they came closer than the normal distance (4–5 feet). On the other hand, Kleck (1969) and Barrios *et al.* (1976), among others, have shown that people with physical disabilities, such as missing limbs, facial birth marks, and even blindness, suffer not only the disability, but also the avoidance of others with whom they come in contact.

Distance also has an effect on the punishment process. It has been found that those who give out negative feedback will be better liked if they increase interpersonal distance (Burgoon and Aho, 1982).

The rewarding potential of interpersonal distance, therefore, is affected by a number of factors including the nature of the relationship, the sex of the participants, the task being undertaken, and the attractiveness rating of the interactants. With these conditions in mind, a purposeful reduction in proximity can signal a willingness to become more closely involved in the interaction and thus serve as a possible reinforcer (Rierdan and Brooks, 1978).

Orientation refers to the position of the body and should be considered along with proximity when observing relationships between interactants. It has been found, for instance, that a direct face-to-face orientation is linked to greater distance, while a sideways orientation is linked to closer distance. Cappella (1981), reviewing a number of studies designed to analyse the relationship between proximity and body angle, found that increased proximity by one member of a pair led the other to reintroduce normal social distance, to adopt a more oblique body orientation, to move more, to have faster reactions, and to speak less.

These studies of proxemics and orientation have obvious implications for professional interviewers or chairpersons. For instance, counsellors or health professionals need to be aware that adopting both an appropriate distance and angle from their client can improve the effectiveness of the interaction process. A study by Greene (1977) showed that proxemics are important in the effectiveness of positive verbal versus neutral verbal feedback on the part of the counsellor in a diet clinic. Clients complied with the counsellor's recommendations to diet for five weeks to a greater degree when positive verbal feedback was given in close proximity; neutral feedback in close proximity resulted in a tendency to non-compliance. Progressive job selection interviewers adopting a 90-degree-angle body orientation with the interviewees can also effect a more conversational as opposed to a competitive approach and so increase the likely effectiveness of the interview. Dickson *et al.* (1989), referring to the spatial position which people take up in relation to each other, suggest that a 90 degree angle is more appropriate for a doctor–patient consultation since it is friendlier and less formal than a 180 degree (face-to-face) angle, which may be regarded as possibly intimidating by patients.

POSTURE

While the posture we adopt when standing or sitting can convey information about our attitudes, emotions and status it can also have a rewarding effect in that it can convey interest in, and acceptance of the other person (Mehrabian, 1969). Words and phrases commonly used in our language indicate the deep links between posture and communication in expressions such as, 'You're all wrapped up in yourself', 'I won't take this lying down', and 'Don't be so uptight'.

Some earlier studies of the relationship of bodily postures to affiliation, carried out by Mehrabian and his associates, showed that individuals, both male and female, who adopted a seated backward-leaning angle when conversing with others were significantly less liked than those who adopted a forward or sideways-leaning angle (Mehrabian and Friar, 1969). It must be noted that Mehrabian's studies were based on a role-play procedure for determining encoding and have been criticised on these grounds. However, live observation studies carried out by Washburn and Hakel (1973) substantiated Mehrabian's original findings. They found that persons who adopted more upright postural positions or 'reduced reclining angles', along with intensity of voice and increased head-nodding, had a persuasive and influential impact on others.

In a counselling context, Siegal (1980) established that clients' perceptions of counsellors were most favourable when the latter adopted forward-leaning positions. Further evidence of this relationship between posture and attitude is provided by Larsen and Smith (1981), who noted that a forward-leaning posture adopted by doctors, as opposed to a backward-lean with the head tilted back, was found to be associated with higher patient satisfaction.

Other aspects of posture, with potential implications for social rewarding, can be located within the open/closed dimension. In a study by Smith-Hanen (1977), college students were instructed to observe and evaluate videotapes of male counsellors displaying different arm and leg positions. Results showed that those counsellors who sat with their hands on the arms of the chair or with hands in their laps were seen as being warmest and most empathic, and coldest and least empathic when their arms were crossed over their chest in a closed manner. More recently, Egan's (1986) observations of skilled helpers reveal that a closed posture with arms and/or legs crossed often signals that the person is defensive or does not wish to become too involved in an interaction, whereas an open posture with hands and legs uncrossed tends to be interpreted as a signal of warmth, acceptance and a willingness to participate.

The relaxed/tense continuum is a further feature of posture which can have a strong influence on the tenor or climate of an interaction. Selection interviewers, for example, who adopt an informal or relaxed posture (sitting back in the chair with arms by the side) can help to relax interviewees and so help them to perform better in the stressed situation of the job interview. In fact, Keenan (1976), in a study of the interviewer's behaviour on candidates' performance, found that when interviewers adopted a relaxed open posture, candidates became more friendly and relaxed and so created a good impression. This concept of posture mirroring or postural congruence was first identified by Scheflen (1964), who argued that it indicated similarity of views or roles among interacting individuals. A number of studies set up to test Scheflen's hypothesis concerning postural congruence have revealed that mirror-congruent postures significantly increased rapport and relatedness (Charny, 1966; La France 1979; Trout and Rosenfeld, 1980). However, McHenry (1981) warns that the opposite can also happen so interviewers should be vigilant in case it is they who initiate the interviewee's tense posture.

GESTURES

Kendon (1983) made the distinction between gestures which totally replace speech (gestural autonomy) and gestures which complement and enhance speech (illustrators). Autonomous gestures or emblems have a communicative function and constitute a form of nonverbal communication of which people have explicit awareness. Examples of reinforcing gestures commonly found are handclapping to show approval and a 'thumbs up' signal to indicate a successful outcome. It is interesting to note that forms of autonomous gesture tend to be different from one culture to another (Kendon, 1981), and that the cultures of the Mediterranean region appear to be far richer in such gestural forms than those of northern Europe (Morris *et al.*, 1979). For instance, a gesture named the ring, where the hand is held up with the palm facing away from the presenter, thumb and forefinger touching to form a circle, means in Great Britain something is good, in parts of France something is worthless, while in Sardinia it is a sexual insult! Once again it should be remembered that what is regarded as a social reward is dependent upon the cultural context of the interaction.

Head

The reinforcing effects of the head-nodding gesture have been well documented and its frequent use can be seen during almost all social and professional encounters, being commonly used to indicate listening, attentiveness and agreement (Forbes and Jackson, 1980; Rosenfeld and Hancks, 1980). Before examining this behaviour in more detail, it is important to note that the majority of research studies which have investigated its rewarding effects have been in combination with a variety of other nonverbal and verbal reinforcements. For instance, Clore *et al.* (1975) asked college students to rate more than one hundred nonverbal behaviours in terms of how much liking or disliking they communicated. Nodding one's head was ranked high up on the liking category and shaking one's head ranked high up on the disliking category.

Apart from likeability/dislikeability being related to head-nodding and head-shaking respectively, judgements of interpersonal competency can also be accrued. Dickson (1981), in a study of careers officers undergoing a microcounselling training course, found that interviewers' use of head-nods was a significant predictor of their interviewing competence as rated by experienced judges.

In terms of displaying interest or attentive listening towards a speaker, Ekman and Oster (1979) suggest that tilting the head to one side is a strong indicator. Bull

(1978), on the other hand, investigating male and female student head positions while listening to talks, found that extracts judged to be 'boring' by the students were associated with lowering the head, tilting it to one side, turning the head away from the speaker and supporting the head on one hand. In addition, head-nodding is a signal to others that you wish them to continue talking and it is widely used by professionals to encourage and motivate their clients to self-disclose at length. Duncan (1972) identified five cues – namely sentence completions, requests for clarification, brief phrases such as 'uh-huh', 'yeah' and 'right', head-nods and head-shakes – which indicated continuous attentiveness towards the speaker. Similarly, Matarazzo and Wiens (1972), examining the interactive processes inherent in an interview, found that the use of head-nodding by the interviewer increased the average duration of utterance produced by the interviewee. More recently, Scofield (1977) noted that head-nodding by the listener increased the total verbal output of speakers. In addition, there was also a higher number of self-referenced statements following contingent application of interviewer head-nods when combined with a paraphrase, restatement or verbal encouragement.

Finally, head-nodding plays a prominent role in leave-taking where the function is to convey inaccessibility and supportiveness in the relationship. Knapp *et al.* (1973) set up an experiment in which they examined the behaviour of interacting pairs up to 45 seconds before they prepared to leave the room. The behaviours which signalled future inaccessibility were the breaking of eye contact and pointing the legs and feet away from the other and towards the door. Other behaviours conveyed supportiveness such as leaning forward and head-nodding, although the authors point out that these might also convey future inaccessibility. Hence the task of leave-taking is to communicate that the interaction is terminated but the relationship continues, a situation most professional interactors would wish to achieve.

FACIAL EXPRESSIONS

One facial expression that has received much attention in research into the communicative function of nonverbal behaviour is smiling. Smiling is usually interpreted as a positive expression of warmth and liking. For example, studies have shown that children laugh and smile more when they play with friends than with strangers (Foot *et al.*, 1977); college students assess each other as being normal, more empathetic, and more understanding when they smile occasionally while listening to someone self-disclose (D'Augelli, 1974); and listeners use smiles to enhance a conversation by communicating that they are interested in what the speaker is saying (Brunner, 1979).

Many studies have combined smiling with other nonverbal and verbal reinforcers. For example, Argyle *et al.* (1972) carried out research in which verbal and nonverbal signals for friendliness and hostility were compared. Subjects were asked to rate videotapes of a female reading friendly, neutral and hostile statements in a friendly, neutral or hostile nonverbal style. The speaker used a warm, soft tone of voice, open smile, and relaxed posture to convey friendliness; a harsh voice, a frown with teeth bared, and a tense posture to convey hostility; and an expressionless voice and blank face to convey a neutral attitude. Results revealed that while speech content and nonverbal styles were judged approximately equal on friendliness and hostility when rated independently of each other, when judged in combination, nonverbal cues accounted for nearly thirteen times as much of the variance in the perceived messages as speech content. On the basis of this evidence it would seem that nonverbal cues are of considerable importance when evaluating friendliness or unfriendliness.

Waldron (1975) investigated the relative importance of facial expression and body posture in judging likeability and found that significant effects on judgements of liking were found for both, but that facial expressions were judged to be the more important of the two cues. A significant statistical interaction revealed that smiling combined with a more relaxed posture was judged as conveying more liking than smiling with a closed, tense posture. When such inconsistent messages to do with interpersonal attitude are emitted, it would appear that facial messages are the more powerful component. We tend to assume that the facial expression indicates the speaker's true evaluation of the listener. 'Well done' said with scorn, for instance, may indicate grudging praise for someone who is disliked. In addition conflicting messages in which the speaker smiled while making a critical statement were interpreted more negatively by children than adults (Bugental et al., 1970). Those who deal regularly with young children such as doctors, dentists, teachers, etc. need to employ consistent verbal and nonverbal expressions if they wish to demonstrate a warm friendly approach.

Finally, it should be noted that although smiling is generally interpreted as suggesting warmth and friendliness, it can also convey insincerity, scorn and even contempt. Research carried out by Tankard et al. (1977) into the effects of smiling and no smiling at the end of brief news reports by newscasters when being videotaped showed that newscasters were evaluated as being slightly more pleased and dominant when they smiled. Thus the context in which smiling occurs has a strong influence on its meaningfulness to the observer. The constant use of an isolated smile by an interviewer, for example, would undoubtedly be interpreted as rather odd and unnatural to an interviewee and, most likely, fail to serve as a social reinforcer.

GAZE

People have always been fascinated with the potent effects of communication through the eyes. Indeed, the direction and intensity of gaze from one person to another is closely related to feelings as diverse as love, hostility, threat and dominance. Analysed as a social reward, continued use of eye gaze usually indicates attention, interest and involvement. Kleinke (1975), in an interview-type experimental situation, instructed interviewers to (1) look at the interviewee constantly, (2) look at the interviewee intermittently, or (3) refrain from looking.

Results revealed that interviewees in the 'no gaze' condition, compared to the other two experimental treatments, made briefer statements and talked less. Interviewers in the 'constant gaze' condition were rated by interviewees as being most attentive, while interviewers who did not look at those they were interviewing were considered to be least attentive. On the other hand, Argyle and Cook (1976), using a similar category system of constant, intermittent and no gaze, found that British students associated intermittent gaze more closely with liking than constant gaze and no gaze. In a British context, continuous gaze was associated with the potency and the power of the person who was gazing.

Gaze is an important means by which counsellors convey interest and attention to their clients. Research indicates that counsellors are viewed more favourably when they look at their clients very often rather than seldom during a counselling interview (Fretz et al., 1979; Kelly and True, 1980). In addition, counsellors who couple verbal reinforcers with eye gaze can effectively reinforce their clients to express attitudes and feelings (Goldman, 1980).

A review of research literature on eye gaze reveals that women and girls generally gaze more at others than men and boys do (Rutter et al., 1978; Cary, 1978). Two possible accounts for this phenomenon are that women display a greater need for affiliation than men and this desire for affiliation is reflected in more gazing (Argyle and Cook, 1976). Alternatively, it is contended that eye gaze is viewed as less threatening to women than men, with the result they are less likely to break eye contact than men in similar situations. Thus the use of eye contact or gaze can be reinforcing for women at levels which may act as punishment for men.

PHYSICAL APPEARANCE

Physical appearance as a potent source of social reward cannot be over-emphasised, particularly its influence in initiating some form of interpersonal contact. (Chapter Six goes into more detail than is possible here.) In Western society physical attractiveness is one of the key dimensions of appearance, although we also manipulate our appearance on some occasions to signify a particular occupation, status or personality type. A great deal of research confirms that we react more favourably to physically attractive people than we do to those less attractive, ugly or physically deformed (Berscheid, 1981; Moore et al., 1987). However, it is important to note that while physical attractiveness may have a strong influence on initial interactions, over time other factors typically become more influential in a developing relationship. Barnes and Rosenthal (1985), investigating the effects of physical attractiveness and attire in same and mixed-sex dyads, found that, 'When actual people are used instead of photographs, the strong effect of physical attractiveness may become diluted by the amount of other information available' (p. 445). Riggio and Friedman (1986) spelled out in operational terms what some of these other behaviours are likely to be. In a study designed to identify those nonverbal and verbal cues which determined likeability, confidence and competence when people were engaged in public speaking, it was found that physical attractiveness, although initially important, in the long term was less so than other social skills such as expressive facial behaviours together with speaking and gestural fluency.

In addition to evaluating attractive people more favourably than unattractive people, we also tend to behave more positively towards them. Research demonstrates that people are more willing to give assistance to someone who is attractive and also to exert more effort to win an attractive person's approval. Willingness to help attractive and unattractive people was tested in a study carried out by Stroufe et al. (1977) in which money was placed on the shelf of a public telephone booth. A female experimenter who was made up to appear either attractive or unattractive approached people in the telephone booth and asked if they had found the money which the experimenter had 'inadvertently' left there. Significant results revealed that more people returned the money when the experimenter was attractive. Similar results were found by Wilson (1978) who noted that people were also more willing to mail a letter for a woman who was made up to be attractive as opposed to unattractive.

In a counselling context, several studies have shown that the rewardingness of an attractive counsellor and its effects on client willingness to self-disclose is subject to gender differences (Brundage et al., 1977; Pellegrini et al., 1978; Kunin and Rodin, 1982). For instance, women revealed more personal information about themselves to men who were attractive but they did not disclose much about themselves to an attractive female counsellor. The reasons for this were not made clear by the research. However, it might be speculated that women do not put such a high premium on female as male physical attractiveness and are consequently less likely to be influenced by it (Reis et al., 1980). Evidence to show that men do place a high value on female attractiveness comes from an interesting study of trainee teachers by Hore (1971). He revealed that attractive female student teachers, received consistently higher grades on teaching practice than those who were considered 'unattractive'.

In a sales context, Mayfield (1972) noted that factors such as physical attractiveness and being liked were related to sales effectiveness, especially when the salespersons had similar characteristics to the customers in terms of background (e. g. education and work history) and appearance (e. g. physique).

The results from this range of studies suggest that when we take care to dress and groom ourselves so that we appear attractive to others, we may enhance our rewarding capabilities, especially in the context of more transient relationships, thereby increasing our ability to effect positive changes. Professionals, therefore, need to be alerted to the fact that patients or clients will respond more favourably to a well-presented person. While this section has focused specifically on physical attractiveness at a general level, further analyses will be made about specific aspects, such as face, body type, clothes and hair, etc., and attractiveness per se in Chapter Six.

PARALANGUAGE

Paralinguistics is commonly referred to as that which is left after subtracting the verbal content from speech. Vocal features such as rhythm of speech pattern, intonation, rate of speech, pitch, volume and even silence itself help to qualify the verbal message. Verbal praise, referred to in the previous chapter, demonstrates appreciation, approval and admiration for other people and their actions. However, unless those praiseworthy statements are accompanied by the appropriate vocal cues, they will be negated. As we have already seen, the potency of verbal praise, as a reinforcer, can be increased by ensuring that it 'sounds sincere' (O'Leary and O'Leary, 1977).

More specific evidence of sincerity or genuineness can be found in the investigations of Tepper and Haase (1978) and Kleinke and Tully (1979). The former two researchers examined tape recordings of therapy interviews that had been judged by experts as successful or unsuccessful. During successful interviews the voices of therapists had a medium or normal amount of intensity and stress and a soft, warm, relaxed tone. In the unsuccessful sessions the therapists invariably sounded dull or monotonous and they uttered more 'uhs' and 'uhms' during speech turns. The latter investigators corroborated these findings by noting that vocal concern was characterised by soft low voice tones and slow speech rhythms. Vocal indifference was expressed with harsh, high-pitched voice tones and rapid speech. It has also been found that interviewees can give longer answers to interview questions when the interviewer adopts a non-threatening manner that is attentive and uses a soft warm tone of voice (Kleinke, 1975).

One more predominant vocal cue which increases the length of utterance of the respondent is that of pausing. Much of the evidence for this occurrence comes from research into teaching and learning. Results indicate that by pausing after a pupil's responses, teachers can increase the level of participation in classroom lessons (Hargie, 1980). Whether such pauses serve as reinforcers, however, is open to question. In operant conditioning terms, it seems probable that pausing by teachers in this context serves as a discriminative stimulus.

In addition it has been found that the teacher's use of pausing during one-to-one oral reading can promote different child behaviours. Clay (1969) identified self-correction of errors as an important predictor of good progress in learning to read. McNaughton and Glynn (1981) subsequently found that self-corrections occurred less frequently when teachers responded immediately to errors. When the teacher waited for a period of up to five seconds (or when children reached the end of a sentence), it resulted in increased self-correction of errors and in increased reading accuracy. The delaying of teachers' comments appeared to provide an appropriate climate in which children could detect and attempt to correct their own errors. Unfortunately, later research carried out by McNaughton et al. (1987) and Wheldall et al. (1988) revealed that attending immediately to errors is what teachers tend to do when they hear children read, particularly those diagnosed as low-progress readers. In effect, teachers are thus denying this group of learners the opportunity to self-correct and more worryingly encouraging their perceptions that they need the 'teacher's help'.

Hart and Risley (1980) have also shown that in the field of language teaching it is important that teachers pause, allow the learner to make the first move, and respond appropriately to that initiation instead of prompting, questioning or giving instructions as a means of promoting language use.

Finally, frequent changes in a speaker's vocal pattern can be useful in gaining and maintaining the attention of others. We have all borne witness to the 'boring speaker' who speaks in such a dreary monotone that even the most interesting material can seem humdrum and prosaic. Conversely, quite boring material can become interesting if delivered in a stimulating way by varying the pitch, tone, speed and volume of vocal pattern. Politicians and good public and after-dinner speakers use these vocal techniques in order to emphasise points, stimulate feelings, and generally obtain and sustain the interest of their audiences (Watzlawick, 1978).

ENVIRONMENTAL FACTORS

The environment (or setting) within which social interaction takes place can be highly suggestive of the kinds of transactions that are likely to be conducted therein. As such it can have a significant impact upon the perception and interpretation of cues and their chances of being used in a rewarding capacity. For instance, when an individual enters a room for the first time, he will receive information concerning the layout of tables and chairs and other furnishings such as carpets, curtains, pictures, plants and lights, and so on. Porteous (1977) identified the social skill of 'environmental competence', which was defined as the ability to use your environment constructively to achieve particular outcomes or goals. Both environmental design and seating arrangements are two of the principal ways 'environmental competence' can be exercised.

Perhaps one of the first points to make regarding environment is who controls the physical and social setting. Any setting has associated norms and rules which are culture bound. If these conventions are transgressed an unfavourable perception of the other party usually results. Evidence to support this claim comes from a series of studies into sales encounters (Woodside and Davenport, 1974; Busch and Wilson, 1976). Professionals need to be aware of these cultural norms when visiting clients 'on their patch'.

The environment can also affect our positive and negative moods. An early study by Maslow and Mintz (1956) asked students to rate a series of photographs of faces while they were seated in a 'beautiful' room (complete with carpet and curtains, etc.), an 'ugly' room (store room in a dishevelled state), and an 'average' room (professor's office). Results showed that subjects in the beautiful room gave significantly more favourable ratings to the faces than did participants in the ugly room. Interestingly, experimenters and subjects alike engaged in various escape behaviours to avoid the ugly room. In real life, situations which are not usually relished are visits to the dentist or doctor. Such visits are not made more palatable by the nature of the waiting rooms in these establishments (bleak furniture, hard-backed chairs, drab colours, strip lighting, etc.). Yet a very different effect could be produced for patients if easy-chairs coupled with appropriate lighting and soft music were introduced. While such changes may not completely allay the fears of patients, they would certainly make the waiting time more acceptable and less stressful. The relationship between moods and room temperature has also been investigated. Griffitt (1970) placed research participants in rooms that were either uncomfortably hot or mildly comfortable. Results showed that subjects significantly displayed more negative moods in the hot room and additionally their primary goal was to get out of the room as quickly as possible. Thus it is important to carry out social interactions in room conditions which can be altered according to the prevailing climatic conditions.

The effects of seating arrangements on social interactions are well documented in the literature. By altering the position of the seating arrangements within a room it is possible to increase or decrease the amount of social exchanges between individuals. For instance, Holahan (1972) studied the effects of modified seating arrangements in the dayroom of a psychiatric hospital, and noted that when the chairs were arranged around tables there was more rapport between patients and greater patient satisfaction than when the seats were placed against the wall. Similar results were found within a student population when Holahan (1977) partitioned one large dining hall for 800 students into a number of attractive smaller eating areas. These changes in room design resulted in a significant increase in social exchange and student satisfaction.

Sommer's (1969) studies of seating behaviour in North America, replicated by Cook (1970) in the UK, point to some interesting differences in seating arrangements when individuals are given a choice of where to sit in different situations. A cooperative seating arrangement is more likely to be diagonal or side by side, while sitting face-to-face across a table, for example, is likely to be perceived as a competitive situation. Most competitive games, in fact, are played face-to-face. Thus as Duck (1986) states, 'We find it more appropriate to sit opposite people with whom we will have an argument and to sit next to people with whom we agree' (p. 44). More recently, Wheldall and Lam (1987) carried out a detailed study of seating arrangements in a special school for children with learning and behavioural problems. The two seating arrangements used were with the children seated in rows or grouped round tables. Results dramatically concluded that on-task behaviour doubled during rows seating (from 35 per cent to 70 per cent) and fell back during tables seating conditions. Similarly, rate of disruption trebled during tables seating and fell during rows seating.

Changes in teacher behaviour were also observed. Positive comments consistently went up during rows conditions while negative comments decreased. The authors concluded that teachers apparently found it easier to praise and to refrain from disapproval when the class was seated in rows. Reasons for these findings, they suggest, are that table arrangements enhance social interaction by facilitating eye contact, a prime means of initiating social encounters. This type of seating arrangement would obviously be advantageous if the teacher's goal was to promote small group discussion in a lesson.

In a professional context a desk can act as a barrier to increasing social contact. According to Korda (1976), most offices have two distinct areas within: the zone around the desk he calls the 'pressure area'; the semi-social area is away from the desk and usually contains armchairs and a coffee table. He suggests that effective businesses use the latter area to encourage clients to talk freely. Goss (1984) investigated the effects of a male therapist's seating arrangements on observers' ratings of attractiveness, expertise and trustworthiness during an initial pre-therapy interview. The therapist was judged most attractive when not seated behind a desk. All of these studies cited across a range of situations can be viewed as instructive because they show how environmental factors are crucially important forces in the determination of interpersonal rewards and the outcomes of behaviour.

CONCLUSION

This chapter has focused upon a number of nonverbal behaviours which have a considerable bearing on the process of social rewarding which individuals utilise in most social and professional encounters. The majority of cues used to communicate positive responding such as liking, approval and attention range from touch contact to posture, from appearance to facial expressions, and from paralinguistic features of speech to the environment itself. Indeed, so powerful is this nonverbal channel of communication that where a contradiction exists between the verbal and nonverbal message being conveyed, it is generally accepted that listeners place more credence on the nonverbal behaviours as they are considered harder to falsify (Shapiro, 1968). The potency of the nonverbal aspects of rewarding behaviour should not be underestimated by professionals since they form the foundations of the interpersonal ambience they are creating, the impressions they are conveying, and the relationships they are attempting to establish or maintain with their clients.

Chapter 5

Positive dimensions of interpersonal interaction

Warmth and empathy

INTRODUCTION

In most people's everyday activities and interactions with others, considerable use is made of words and phrases which describe the behaviour of the other in global or generic terms. For example, Sam, meeting someone for the first time at a formal function, may be overheard whispering to a friend later that the person he had been introduced to was 'very warm and friendly'. At school, teenager Janet, after requesting a meeting with her teacher because she is experiencing considerable difficulty in completing her homework, may remark to her best friend later that, 'Mr Stevens showed a genuine interest in my problem!' And, at work, employees often recognise the 'caring' approach adopted by the management. Each of these brief examples could be said to illustrate the daily use being made, in natural communication settings, of broad dimensions of interaction which have rewarding implications. While Chapters Three and Four focused separately on specific verbal and nonverbal behavioural elements of social reward, this chapter will, at a more molar level and in keeping with everyday observation and parlance, consider such behaviours as they contribute to perceptions of personal qualities such as warmth and empathy. These in turn can have rewarding capabilities.

The concept of dimensions of interpersonal interaction has received reasonably wide coverage in the literature and is referred to in a number of professional contexts such as education, counselling, psychotherapy, mass media, and group therapy. This chapter presents two core dimensions, namely warmth and empathy along with their verbal and nonverbal correlates which emerge as important determinants of social reward. In addition, since space limitations will not permit an exhaustive review of all the available literature, brief research evidence will be cited which appears to confirm the rewarding effects of warmth and empathy on client outcomes. As a first step, however, the term 'dimension' needs to be clarified and discussed in relation to the concept of social skill.

CLARIFYING THE CONCEPT

In the literature there seems to be some semantic confusion in the use of the terms 'skill' and 'dimension'. Ivey and Authier (1978), when referring to the microtraining process, claim that,

> Microtraining is centrally a quantitative factual approach to counsellor training (skill training). Clearly some attention should be paid to the more subjective qualitative dimensions of helping.... Central attention will be given to the dimensions of empathy.
>
> (p. 128)

Dimensions are perceived as including skill determinants. On the other hand, for Egan (1982) the relationship between these levels is completely reversed. He contends that,

> The kinds of skills (helping) discussed here have three components or dimensions. First is awareness. Every helping skill has an awareness dimension.
>
> (p. 84)

Zimmer and Park (1967) and Zimmer and Anderson (1968) also talk about factor analysing counsellor communication in an attempt to isolate 'dimensions' of empathy. It would appear that they too are referring to dimensions as actual skill behaviours. For the purposes of this chapter, the terminology which will be adopted is that of Authier (1986), who identifies those verbal and nonverbal skills which convey warmth and as such can be utilised to establish a positive relationship with others. Trower and Dryden (1981) adopt this usage of terms when they state that,

> In the search for effective therapist skills, investigators have been attracted to several comparatively global variables such as the warmth–empathy–genuineness triad.
>
> (p. 91)

This derivation of terms is also utilised by Griffiths (1973) when discussing the future developments of microteaching. He recommends the introduction of more 'global' teaching skills like 'empathising' and 'respecting' which would build upon smaller teaching behaviours such as reinforcing. Hargie and Maidment (1979), encompassing this rationale, put forward a method of building up the teaching act with actual operational skill behaviours at the bottom and global teaching approaches at the top. In operational terms they:

> Divide the teaching dimension of warmth into subdimensions of encouraging, stimulating and relaxing. These are then further divided into skill areas such as positive reinforcement; which are in turn presented in terms of sub-skills such as nonverbal reinforcement. Finally these are exemplified in relation to actual observable behaviours, which occur in the classroom.
>
> (p. 99)

It is this relationship of skills to dimensions which will be adhered to in this chapter. A second problem which arises when the literature is perused concerns the means of acquiring or displaying these dimensions or qualities of warmth and empathy, when interacting with others.

Traditionally, research into counselling has been concerned with the problem of identifying, defining and disseminating Rogers' (1957) core conditions or dimensions of empathy, warmth and genuineness. This research has invariably been linked to the extraordinary growth in both demand for and provision of counselling training programmes in the last ten to twenty years (Jacobs, 1990). During this period of intense research activity there has been a move away from a learner-centred approach to counsellor training to one which is skill-centred (Kurtz *et al.*, 1985). Proponents of this trend assert that effective counselling performance may be broken down into identifiable skills or behaviours which can be learned by trainees. This technique has become known as microcounselling (Ivey and Authier, 1978). As a result of this move towards microcounselling, research has concentrated on identifying those behaviours which might best communicate attitudes of empathy, acceptance, positive regard, genuineness, and so on (Bayes, 1972; Smith-Hanen, 1977; Hermansson *et al.*, 1988). For example, the relationship between nonverbal behaviours and empathy was investigated by Haase and Tepper (1972), and Uhlemann *et al.* (1976) related empathy to the skill of reflection of feeling. Further research evidence linking verbal and nonverbal behaviours to global dimensions will be examined in more depth later in the chapter.

However, before moving on to more fully explore this relationship of skills to the two core dimensions of warmth and empathy, it should be noted that there are those who claim, from a humanistic perspective, that these qualities or dimensions are not circumscribed complexes of behaviours which can be acquired in short skill-based programmes (Mahon and Altmann, 1977), but rather attitudes that are developed and fostered within the individual through personal growth and maturity (Thorne, 1984; Patterson, 1984; Tamase, 1989). Egan (1990), on the other hand, warns that many helper training programmes are still overly cognitive, and that trainees have difficulty in translating their own feelings or attitudes into effective helping. Egan (1982) goes on to claim that,

> Skill- or competency-based training in counsellor education programs makes a great deal of sense. In fact, Hatcher, Brooks and Associates (1977) reported that of over 400 counsellor education programs surveyed in 1977, 76.1% of those responding reported a commitment to competency-based training.
>
> (p. 10)

In the field of psychotherapy, Matarazzo (1978) points to the trend away from a person-centred approach to focusing upon specific helping skills and techniques. However, he acknowledges that:

> Although subsequent research has taken the bloom of the original optimism (of client-centred training) those training programmes led the way in formalizing the need for rigorous specification of skills.
>
> (p. 103)

There seems little doubt that at present a skill-based approach to helping or counselling is proving more fruitful.

Lest it be thought that core interpersonal dimensions of warmth and empathy are the sole prerogative of psychotherapists or professional helpers, it should be remembered that all of us within the context of living and working are called upon at some time to help a family member, friend or colleague manage more effectively a problem they are temporarily experiencing. Indeed most professionals carry out a counselling role as part of their overall interactions with customers, patients, clients or students. College lecturers, for example, while being principally concerned with teaching a specific subject area to students, are also given a pastoral role in that they are required to counsel students who are experiencing particular difficulties affecting their studies. In summing up this section, it would appear to be productive to expose the rewarding potential of what we have identified as core conditions of social involvement, warmth and empathy, together with those skills and sub-skills which seem to comprise them. The remainder of this chapter therefore will be devoted to this task.

WARMTH AND EMPATHY?

Can we make a distinction between warmth and empathy, since, in common parlance, these terms seem so general, even vague, that they are sometimes used interchangeably? When an attempt is made to define these concepts it is difficult to define one without giving some consideration to the other. For instance, in order to display empathic understanding to another person, warmth is often present and, conversely, conveying genuine warmth subsumes a certain degree of empathy. However, one level of distinction that can be made between them acknowledges the traditional 'fact versus feeling' differentiation. Thus warmth can be evinced towards a person or group of individuals while merely considering the factual content of their problematic situation, whilst empathy concentrates more particularly on the feeling component inherent in such a problem. As mentioned in Chapter One, Ivey and Authier (1978) refer to the factual and affective aspects of the skill of reflection as 'reflecting of feeling' in which selective attention is paid to the feeling or emotional component of a person's expressions, and 'paraphrasing' in which selective attention to the objective verbal content of a problem is made. However, these authors make the further point that reflection of feeling entails some articulation of content, and paraphrasing entails some recognition of the other person's feeling. The primary distinction between the two key expressions is one of emphasis.

Following a description of the general differentiation that can be made between warmth and empathy, it is expedient to define warmth more specifically. Rogers (1961) refers to it as an 'Attitude of deep respect and full acceptance for the client as he is' (p. 74) and goes on to suggest that warmth is an attitude of acceptance in which the most profound type of liking and affection is portrayed. Certain dissatisfactions have recently been expressed concerning the global nature of Rogers' original definition (Lambert *et al.*, 1978; Mitchell *et al.*, 1977). These authors conclude that a better way to unravel the complexities of portraying warmth and empathy, for instance, is to take a more molecular approach; that is, to examine the elements of verbal and nonverbal behaviour and try to relate these more precisely defined variables to perceived client satisfaction or therapeutic outcome. Authier (1986) sums up this need to define warmth in behavioural terms when he states that,

> Warmth is basically a valuing of the other person and a communication of that attitude both verbally and nonverbally such that a genuine interest in him/her as a person and his/her problem has been conveyed.

(p. 441)

As previously stated in Chapter Two, when this communication of warmth leads to an increase in the receiver's feelings of self-esteem and worth, it can become positively valued thus leading to reinforcing possibilities.

RESEARCH INTO THE REWARDING EFFECTS OF WARMTH

Before moving on to examine some of the recently identified behavioural correlates of warmth, it would be useful to review earlier research into the positive effects of 'molar' warmth on client or patient outcomes. Truax and Carkhuff (1967) cite a range of studies which present evidence that non-possessive warmth is related to constructive changes in patients. Two researchers, notably Whitehorn and Betz at the Johns Hopkins Hospital (Whitehorn and Betz, 1954; Betz, 1963; Whitehorn, 1964), were early pioneers into the effects of different styles of therapy on patient outcomes. In a now classic investigation, Betz (1963) analysed the effects which fourteen psychiatrists had on their schizophrenic patients. Results showed that seven psychiatrists had an improvement rate of 75 per cent, as contrasted with seven other psychiatrists of similar training but with an improvement rate of only 27 per cent. Their evidence indicated that the patients counselled by the two sets of therapists did not differ in any systematic way that favoured one group over the other, and yet they showed this striking contrast in success rates. For instance, both groups of therapists worked with talkative and quiet, passive and active, extroverted and introverted clients. The therapists themselves included both bright and dull conversationalists. The differences appeared to lie in their attitudinal approach to the helping relationship. The successful therapists were warm and attempted to respond to the patient in a personal, immediate and friendly way; by contrast, the less successful therapists tended to relate to the patient in a more impersonal manner, focusing upon psychopathology. Expressions of warmth by the therapists would seem to have a facilitating effect upon the performance of the clients. Subsequent studies into the effects of psychotherapy on hospitalised schizophrenic patients have yielded similar results (Truax, 1963; Strupp *et al.*, 1964; Lorr and McNair, 1966).

The effects of warmth have also been examined within a framework of teaching and learning. Weiss *et al.* (1960) reported data showing that a hostile experimenter (not warm) decreased the number of verbal responses elicited, while an experimenter who showered assent and attention upon college student subjects (i.e. were warm and supportive) produced an increase in the amount and frequency of self-references. One very intriguing aspect of this particular study was the finding of greater emotional disturbance in the subjects during extinction (a period of non-reinforcement for performance) with the experimenter who had previously showered attention and agreement on them. Perhaps the extinction period under these conditions introduced a certain incongruence or artifice to the situation which caused subjects to be upset. Heightened emotionality during extinction is quite common and has been commented upon by Lieberman (1990) among others.

Literature on the parent–child relationship also produces evidence consistent with the notion that warmth is characteristic of human encounters within which personal changes for the better can take place. Several studies, notably Frazee (1953), Lidtz *et al.* (1957), and Baxter *et al.* (1963), have found that an inordinate degree of interpersonal conflict (lack of warmth) exists in the homes of schizophrenic patients. Even studies of so-called 'normal' children reveal that warm paternal attitudes are positively related to less hostility in their children. Typical of such findings is a study by Schulman *et al.* (1962) of forty-one boys aged between eight and twelve, and their parents. Analysis of data based upon observations made during an experimental period showed that parents of children with conduct problems were more hostile and rejecting towards their children than were parents of the control group. The report concluded that children of mothers who responded warmly and with approval had significantly more favourable social behaviours than the control group. However, these studies fail to make explicit whether or not the warmth displayed by the parents was contingent upon the pro-social behaviour of their offspring.

Still on the topic of warmth and change, a number of early studies of mass communications and public opinion (Winthrop, 1958; Gompertz, 1960; Zimbardo, 1960; Sargent, 1965) indicate that the higher the level of personal attentiveness given to the receiver by the communicator, the greater the degree of opinion change in the receiver. Findings showed that this was the case even when it entailed the recipient of the communication changing to a position she had previously described as unreasonable and indefensible. These studies emphasise the facilitation that occurs in opinion changes if warmth or friendship exists between communicator and recipient. This finding surely has implications for a range of health professionals, including doctors, dentists, health visitors, etc., who are attempting to redirect patients to a healthier life-style.

Turning back to the issue of defining warmth, two authors subscribe to the reinforcing effects which warmth conveys in a relationship. An early definition by White (1948) claims that,

> The therapist is an expert.... the therapist is permissive, the therapist is 'interested' and 'friendly' communicating in this way a certain 'warmth' that makes

the relationship more personal than is ordinarily the case.... the therapist is a source of encouragement.

(p. 45)

The concept of encouragement is discussed in Chapter Three and a range of relevant research into the use of 'minimal encourages' is presented. Rotter (1964) also notes the crucial role of reinforcement in the dimension of warmth. He states that,

[The therapist is] more active in making interpretations to the patient and directly reinforcing or rewarding particular kinds of optimal behaviour, and in helping the patient find new alternatives to deal with problems. In order to do this successfully it is necessary that the patient 'trust' him and accept his objectivity in the situation. Consequently, the good therapist is 'warm' and communicates to his patients his concern and interest in them.

(p. 86)

Egan (1990), however, warns that if counsellors crank out unconditional reinforcers continuously they may be viewed as 'warmth machines' issuing responses such as 'Oh, that's all right' that are phony and unhelpful. Consider the following example.

Client: I don't seem to care about what I do or even how I look these days. As you can probably see I've let myself go. I'm out of condition and two stones overweight. I've no interests. And now I'm even arguing and falling out with people at work.

Counsellor: First of all, John, around about forty most men start to let themselves go a bit. You look OK to me. I think you're being overly hard on yourself.

In this scenario the counsellor translates warmth into glibly reassuring the client; indeed he even goes further in positively reinforcing a lowering of the client's standards and there is an inappropriate use of warmth as a social reinforcer. On the other hand, appropriate use of reinforcers can help clients to explore and express problematic situations. Consider the following example.

Client: I haven't taken drugs all week. This is the first time this has happened since as long as I can remember.

Counsellor: So this is something new and you're feeling pretty good about it.

If the counsellor had issued a response such as 'OK, let's see if you can repeat this next week!', the client could have interpreted this negatively in that it does not recognise his or her accomplishment. Instead of recognition there is a demand for more effort. However, when the counsellor reinforces what the client has achieved in this way he is conveying warmth and understanding. In addition, helpers show respect and warmth when they reinforce all constructive action on the part of the client: for instance, when clients work at self-exploration or when they take tentative steps in the direction of constructive behavioural change. Cormier and

Cormier (1979) substantiate the use of social reinforcers by claiming that punishment and the denial of rewards tend to inhibit self-exploration while appropriately administered positive reinforcers assist this process. But how they are used, when they are used, and which type is used must be given careful consideration by the counsellor.

VERBAL AND NONVERBAL COMPONENTS OF WARMTH

So far, warmth has been described in such a way that the reader may still be entitled to ask, 'But what exactly is it? How can I convey it to my patient, client or student as a positive response?' By the late 1960s there was a need to operationalise the characteristics of warmth since counsellor training courses featuring it were burgeoning. One of the first studies, by Zimmer and Park (1967), used factor analytical procedures to extract the main factors which differentiated effective from ineffective counsellors along a warm–cold dimension. A total of one hundred and fifteen seventeen-year-old high school students, enrolled on a counselling course, were requested to evaluate two taped counselling sessions using a five-point scale ranging from coldness to warmth. Results showed that reflection of feeling, minimal encouragers, and supportive statements were the main factors to emerge. (See Chapter Three for further details regarding these verbal behaviours.) While this was of considerable interest, it must be added that the emphasis in this investigation was solely on the verbal utterances which the counsellor emitted. At that point in time, research principally focused on the verbal dimensions (Carkhuff and Berenson, 1967; Truax and Carkhuff, 1967).

Following this, a large number of studies showed a growing trend to investigate counsellor warmth and empathy levels through nonverbal channels (D'Augelli, 1974; Kelly and True, 1980; Siegman, 1985). One study, carried out by Strong *et al.* (1971), asked the question, 'What impact do counsellors' gestures and postures have on how clients perceive them?' Eighty-six college coeds were asked to observe two videotaped counsellors who emitted either high or low frequencies of postural and gestural movements in a standard interview segment. Following their viewing, each student was requested to describe the counsellor using a twenty-seven item checklist. Results showed that adjectives such as warm, friendly, casual and carefree were correlated with high levels of movement, while precise, reserved and thoughtful were linked to low levels of movement activity. The authors conclude that there is little doubt that a counsellor's gestural, postural and other nonverbal movements have an impact on how he is perceived and described by observers. Since most counsellors would probably desire to be seen positively by their clients, these results suggest that clients have greater attraction towards more active counsellors.

Building upon the work of Strong, Smith-Hanen (1977) was interested to focus more precisely on arm and leg positions in relation to a counsellor's display of warmth. Forty students in their early twenties were asked to rate counsellors on this dimension after viewing each of forty-eight video-segments incorporating all or no limb movements, four different arm positions, and six different leg positions. Unlike Strong's findings, the researcher did not find a significant difference in the subjects' perceptions of the counsellors' warmth although arms crossed was judged the coldest of the arm positions. This result finds support in Spiegal and Machotka's (1974) conclusion that figures with closed arm positions are judged as cold, rejecting, shy and passive. The leg position described as one leg crossed over the other such that the ankle is resting on the other knee was judged as the coldest leg position. However, the author points out that the effects of the matrix of variables studied were quite complex and that more research is needed before these results can be regarded unreservedly.

Still on the topic of nonverbal behaviours suggestive of warmth, Hermansson *et al.* (1988) examined the relationship between counsellor deliberate postural lean and the communication of non-possesive warmth. Twelve male counsellors, acting as their own controls, under three postural lean conditions (forward, backward and counsellor's own choice position) conducted small-scale counselling sequences with female student social workers. That there were no significant differences between the experimental postures themselves (either forward or backward) suggests that for male counsellors, working with female clients, adopting a particular postural lean *per se* has no significant effect on the communication of warmth. The process of making a *deliberate* postural lean, however, does seem to make some difference. Results revealed that levels of communicated warmth were significantly heightened in association with a decisive backward lean. Nevertheless, it should be noted that greatest effects were in connection with movements away from clients only when counsellors who preferred a forward lean were assessed by the clients as being more effective. A possible explanation for this finding takes into account Patterson's (1976) model of interpersonal intimacy. This model suggests that responding to adjustments in intimacy depends on whether there has been a breach in the individual's arousal threshold. If so, the counsellor should be sensitive to these cues and make a response based upon that negative or positive feedback. Forward and backward leans, per se, are not the telling factor. Rather, by being responsive to the actions and perceived feelings of the client, the counsellor heightens his communication of warmth. In addition, if a forward leaning posture is adopted too early in an interaction or in too arbitrary a fashion (i.e. not necessarily contingent on the clients' responses), it may be construed negatively by clients so necessitating a compensatory adjustment (e.g. a backward lean). It would appear that for counsellors to effectively convey warmth, subtle adjustments of postural leans need to be made in order to maintain an equilibrium of involvement appropriate to the situation and phase of interaction.

One other nonverbal factor worthy of comment emanates from the work of Siegman, who has spent more than twenty years investigating the effects of paralinguistic features on interpersonal interaction. Siegman (1987) was interested to test the notion that people are likely to feel more relaxed with warm rather than cold interviewers and, therefore, will adopt a less formal style manifested in a less 'elaborated code' of language, to use Bernstein's (1961) terminology. One hypothesis to be tested was that interviewees would be more fluent, that is, exhibit fewer and shorter silent pauses when addressing a warm as opposed to a cold interviewer. In a series of interesting experiments (Siegman, 1979; Siegman and Crown, 1980), in which interviewees' attraction scores were correlated with the use of pausing (intra- and inter-utterance), it was concluded that interviewer warmth (as measured by the attraction score) was associated with a faster pacing of speech demonstrated by shorter and fewer pauses. The authors go on to suggest that this finding has implications for those social psychologists concerned with unearthing the determinants of interpersonal attraction. However, more research into the relationship between the temporal pacing of speech and subjects' mutual liking for each other needs to be conducted.

In summing up this section it seems appropriate to refer to the writings of Ivey and Authier (1978), who contend that warmth consists of skills such as attending behaviour, minimal encourages, open questions, and paraphrasing which are utilised in order to demonstrate a willingness to listen, respect an individual's worth, and help someone to tell her own story. Authier (1986) suggests that respect can be principally communicated by using positive statements and minimal encourages regarding a person's abilities and actions. Indeed, even the simple response of using a person's name in appropriate circumstances is seen as entirely consistent with social rewarding behaviour. Getting a client to articulate or disclose a problem requires the listener to contingently use, for instance, minimal encouragers, reflections and open questions. By judiciously utilising both verbal and nonverbal cues at the appropriate juncture in any interaction, a person is more likely to convey warmth which in turn will be positively received and responded to by the other.

EMPATHY

It was emphasised earlier in this chapter that a person's ability to convey warmth is an essential first stage towards portraying a feeling of empathy. While empathy involves attending and listening accurately to a person which is also part of responding with warmth, it goes further. In addition, it indicates what Egan (1982) calls 'know-how' and assertiveness; that is the ability to,

> communicate an understanding of both the affect and the content of the client's message in a way that makes sense to him or her.... [going on to suggest that assertiveness is a] need to engage the client in dialogue, the kind of dialogue that leads to developing a working relationship and to clarifying the problem situation.
>
> (p. 92)

Ivey and Authier (1978), in more specific terms, also stress a three step structure for enacting empathy, namely: attending accurately to the client; using the skills of directing and self-disclosure to develop an understanding of the client's problem; and then checking out the accuracy of the feelings/facts gathered. These authors contend that this latter step allows room for mutual growth and understanding.

Brammer (1973) emphasises the same point of checking for accuracy of perceptions by suggesting that counsellors should solicit the clients' reactions to their own interpretations. The affective/cognitive components of empathy are given further credence by Aspy (1975), who defines empathy as:

the ability to understand and to communicate to another, your understanding of both his feeling and the reasons for his feelings.

(p. 11)

Perhaps a good example of this empathetic approach is demonstrated in the following brief interactive sequence:

Client: I feel very alone.
Counsellor: You feel sad, because it seems as though no one is with you.

In this instance, the counsellor's response reflects the feeling (sadness) and the reason for it (it seems as though no one is with you). Thus this statement contains both an affective and cognitive element as exemplified in the skill of reflecting. A number of authors (Aronfreed, 1970; Stotland, 1969; Laird, 1974) suggest that feeding back the purely affective component of a person's message is more akin to conveying sympathy as opposed to empathy. Harrigan and Rosenthal (1986) develop the notion of a conceptual difference between these two terms by suggesting that sympathy or a mere affective response to another's emotional state does not signify empathy because the element of objective understanding and the possibility of being helpful is missing. Rogers (1957) clarifies the difference between sympathy and empathy by stressing the 'as if' quality of the observer's empathetic response; that is, sensing the other's private world as if it were your own but without losing the 'as if' quality.

In summary it is clear that the skill of reflection is a core element in communicating an empathic approach.

REWARDING EFFECTS OF EMPATHY

Truax and Carkhuff (1967), in a comprehensive review of studies which examined the effects of dimensions such as empathy, warmth and genuineness on human behaviour, came to the conclusion that people exposed to interactive episodes typified by these qualities were changed for the better. Much of the research cited focused on the area of counselling and psychotherapy, although not exclusively. In particular, it is claimed that therapists high in empathy are more effective in psychotherapy because they are personally more potent sources of reward and as a result elicit a high degree of positive affect from the patient in terms of positive self-concept, increased self-exploratory behaviour, and extinction of anxiety or fear responses when relating to others. Selecting empathy as a reinforcer, Truax (1966) was interested to find out if therapists using differential degrees of empathic reinforcement could affect the level of depth of self-exploration by the patient. A group of raters, employing the Accurate Empathy Scale originally designed by

Melloh (1964), were asked to rate therapist/patient interaction sequences randomly collected from thirty patients across twenty-four group therapy sessions. To determine the degree of reinforcement employed, correlations were computed (for each of the thirty patients across samples taken from the twenty-four sessions) between the therapists' scores on the AES and the level of patient exploration. From the analyses of variance it was found that those patients receiving the highest levels of contingent empathic reinforcement showed a significantly greater capacity for self-exploration than those given low levels of reinforcement. Interestingly, though, this result held whether the data were analysed in terms of high and low reinforcement of the therapy group as a whole, or reinforcement given to individual patients.

Altmann (1973) was interested to know what the longer-term effects were when therapists used differential amounts of empathic reinforcement. Seven counsellors recorded initial interviews with nineteen clients who were first-year university students aged between eighteen and twenty-six. After completing a precounselling data sheet, all clients indicated a desire to meet with a counsellor on a weekly basis for a series of ten or more counselling sessions. Of the nineteen clients registered, eight discontinued and the remaining eleven continued. Raters, using the initial interview material recorded from the nineteen clients, found that for nine of the eleven clients who continued in counselling, counsellors provided significantly greater levels of empathy and, conversely, counsellors provided significantly less empathy for all eight clients who terminated counselling. In addition, further analysis of each interview showed that when counsellors were low in accurate empathy early in the interview, there was a tendency for this level to deteriorate further as the interview progressed. On the other hand, when empathy was at a high level early in the interview, it was maintained or increased through the rest of the session. This investigation would appear to support the notion of mutual reinforcement in that counsellors rewarded client efforts through appropriate use of empathic responding, making it more likely that those clients returned for counselling which, in turn, reinforced the counsellors' use of this technique!

Truax and Carkhuff (1967) advocate that for therapists to be successful in facilitating clients they must make the amounts and levels of warmth and empathy they offer contingent upon patients' responses in the therapy interview. This may mean, say the authors, that,

> Even negative or hostile reaction to the therapist would be met by heightened expressions of warmth and accurate empathy.... The criterion for reinforcement is gradually raised as the patient is better able to relate.
>
> (p. 152)

Encouraging the client to ventilate, albeit in a negative or aggressive manner, facilitates the therapeutic process. Regarding the administration of empathic understanding, Goodstein (1965) suggests that the value of a reward such as empathy or warmth is greatly enhanced by shortening the time interval between the termination of a client's response and the delivery of empathic reward. In the counselling process, for example, immediate empathic responding to clients describing feelings or emotions should lead to increased client ventilation and eventual facilitation.

While fewer studies have been carried out into the effects of empathy on the teaching and learning process with children, it seems that positive changes in pupils' behaviour accrue from such rewards. Truax and Tatum (1966), reviewing a group of studies which attempted to relate the level of empathy communicated to pre-school children by their teachers to their pre-school performance and social adjustment, found that higher levels of empathy were significantly related to positive changes both in the child's work rate and in their ability to cooperate with other children. Thus, even in very young children, it is possible to influence their progress by delivering appropriate amounts and levels of empathic rewards.

What about the influence of empathy on older children in terms of academic achievement? Again similar effects have been found. In another frequently recorded piece of research, Aspy and Hadlock (1966), studying the gains in third to fifth grade regarding achievement, noted that pupils taught by teachers high in accurate empathy, showed a reading achievement gain of 2.5 years during a five-month period, while pupils taught by low-conditions teachers gained only 0.7 years. Even more striking, the truancy rate in classes with low-conditional empathy was twice that in high-conditional classrooms. From a review of studies into the effectiveness of teaching across a range of age groups and subject lessons, Hawkes and Egbert (1954) concluded that empathy was found to be a significant factor in pupils' ratings of teacher competence. No doubt there is considerable anecdotal material, consistent with this research evidence, which can be recalled by most pupils about teachers who responded empathically to their problems of learning.

In summing up this section, converging research studies suggest that, whether we are focusing on changes in verbal conditioning, social development, academic learning, or social learning, an empathic communicative response is both facilitative and rewarding.

VERBAL AND NONVERBAL COMPONENTS OF EMPATHY

The construct of reflection of feeling, originally identified by Rogers (1961), is primarily considered to be one of the main verbal skills underpinning empathy. Ivey and Authier (1978) define reflection of feeling as,

> Selective attention to the feeling or emotional aspects of the client's expressions.
>
> (p. 80)

In other words, by selectively identifying, abstracting and reflecting the observed feeling states of clients, the interviewer is positively reinforcing emotional expression while at the same time possibly extinguishing factual aspects of communication by marginalising them.

The reinforcing consequences of accurate reflecting have been revealed in a wide range of experimentally designed studies particularly in the domains of counselling and psychotherapy. Several studies (Powell, 1968; Kennedy et al.,

1971; Highlen and Baccus, 1977) have attempted to correlate the effects of reflecting with interviewees' ability to increase self-disclosures or, as some investigators state, produce self-referent statements. Results from these studies conclude that significant increases in self-referent statements by interviewees were obtained when reflecting statements were contingent upon them. One study by Barnabei *et al.* (1974), however, found no significant difference in the interviewers' use of reflecting and the affective self-talk of subjects. One possible explanation for this latter finding could reside in the fact that reflections of feeling were administered in a random or non-contingent manner. Hill and Gormally (1977) also found that reflecting as a technique was largely ineffective in producing the desired increase of affective self-talk by experimental subjects. However, not only was a non-contingent procedure of application used in this investigation but also the amount of reflections employed was significantly low, thus reducing potential reinforcing effects.

A number of researchers have distinguished between the amount of self-disclosures revealed by clients and the quality or depth of such information (Vondracek, 1969; Beharry, 1976; Mills, 1983). In the main, an increased degree of intimacy contained in the subjects' self-disclosures was contingent upon interviewers' use of reflections. Results from these same studies also revealed that self-referent statements could also be increased when contingent upon interviewer probes, supportive statements, and self-disclosures. It must be noted, however, that these experiments were largely or solely male centred. One study by Feigenbaum (1977) included a gender factor when deducing the quantity and depth of subjects' self-disclosures. Interestingly, he found that while females disclosed more and at greater depths, when reflective responses were utilised, males scored significantly higher on both counts when the interviewer responded with self-disclosure as opposed to reflections. On this evidence it would appear that females are perhaps more susceptible to the effects of reflecting than their male counterparts. Further research is required before confirmation or refutation of this claim can be made.

Some of the researchers working within an operant tradition have suggested that reflections may play an essentially antecedent role, serving as discriminative rather than reinforcing stimuli (Merbaum, 1963; Kennedy *et al.*, 1971). As such, increased responding is produced by signalling the circumstances under which behaving in this manner results in subsequent but unspecified reinforcement being made available. In the continuing conversational stream, the task of locating sources of influence are fraught with difficulty. Rachlin (1976) makes the point that much instrumental behaviour, especially social behaviour, comprises chains of events with different elements acting *both* as reinforcers of preceding actions and as discriminative stimuli for the next.

Some studies have tended to focus upon the perceptions of or attitudes towards the interviewer as a result of his or her communicating accurate reflection of feelings. For instance, Ehrlich *et al.* (1979) found that interviewers who made use of affective responses (defined as statements reflecting feelings not yet identified by the interviewee) were considered by interviewees to be more expert and trustworthy. Nagata *et al.* (1983) reported similar results from analyses of counselling type interviews in that clients felt those counsellors were more effective when they were able to 'sense' their clients' unstated feelings. Further evidence of the relationship between reflections of feeling and evaluations, by trained raters, of the degree of empathic understanding conveyed by the interviewer is contained in a study by Uhlemann *et al.* (1976). Evaluations were based upon written responses in conjunction with an audio recording of an actual fifteen-minute interview for each of twenty-five male and twenty-five female psychology students who participated in the project. A major finding was that reflection of feeling accounted for a substantial amount of variance in the written expression of empathy (50 per cent) and for a smaller amount of variance in the verbal expression (22 per cent). But by concentrating on the written and verbal elements of reflecting, this study failed to take account of the paralinguistic and nonverbal accompaniments of speech which are important behaviours in the total process (Nelson-Jones, 1983; Authier, 1986; Hill and Stephany, 1990). It is to these nonverbal features of empathy that we now turn.

Previous research has suggested that empathy is communicated in an important way by nonverbal means including eye contact, forward leans, open posture, and proximity (Haase and Tepper, 1972; Toukmanian and Rennie, 1975; Smith-Hanen, 1977; Kelly and True, 1980). This communication can again be thought of as a form of reward which facilitates further interaction and invariably encourages respondents to continue in a similar way to that which pertained before the supportive response from the listener. Smith (1986) notes that this ability to empathise is an important element in effective communication for many social roles and situations and claims that empathy is fundamentally the ability to listen.

The condition of listening is a potent reinforcer in any type of social interaction sequence and plays a vital role in the establishment of a relationship. Hargie *et al.* (1987) stress that while verbal responses are the main indicators of effective empathic listening (e.g. verbal reinforcers, verbal following, and reflection of feeling) there are a number of related nonverbal behaviours associated with this skill. For instance, Rosenfeld and Hancks (1980) found that head-nods, forward leaning posture, visual attention, and eyebrow raises were associated with positive ratings of listening responsiveness. These authors also indicate that the most prevalent nonverbal listening indicator is the head-nod. Numerous other studies have justified the importance of these findings (Mehrabian, 1972; Ivey and Gluckstern, 1974; Tepper and Haase, 1978; Hermansson *et al.*, 1988).

While these nonverbal behaviours would appear to be central elements in the reinforcing effects of empathic listening, Haase and Tepper (1972) point out that they need to be combined with a positive verbal message if they are to convey a high degree of this type of understanding. Likewise they found that a positive verbal message was devalued by clients when not accompanied by the appropriate nonverbal behaviour reflecting good listening skills. Thus, the effectivenesss of empathic listening is heavily dependent on the complementary relationship between the verbal and nonverbal cues. Signals such as lack of eye contact, no smiles, inappropriate facial expressions, slouched posture and the use of distracting mannerisms such as yawning, reading while the speaker is talking, etc. are not in keeping with good listening. If these behaviours are employed clients can feel punished. Bourget (1977) also noted that the effectiveness of counsellors' verbal reinforcement was increased when accompanied by nonverbal behaviours such as smiling, gazing and pleasant tone of voice. Graves and Robinson (1976), on the other hand, found that when counsellors presented verbally and nonverbally inconsistent messages they were approached less closely and perceived to be less empathic by subjects. Therefore, for nonverbal behaviours to be rewarding they need to substantiate the positive verbal message.

Several studies have been mainly concerned with clients' ratings of counsellors based upon the latter's ability to empathise accurately. One study reported that those helpers who initiated more gestures and actively changed posture, gaze and facial expressions were judged to be more empathic, agreeable, casual and energetic than their counterparts who restrained most of their nonverbal movements (Strong *et al.*, 1971). In addition, Clairborn (1979) reported that nonverbal responsiveness (defined as paralinguistic cues, facial expressions, gaze, head-nodding and gestures) combined with verbal interpretation produced the highest client ratings of counsellor expertise, empathy, trustworthiness and attractiveness.

CONCLUSION

The focus of this chapter has been to identify some of the means by which rewards are administered at global or dimensional levels of social contact. These include being 'warm and friendly', 'caring' or 'genuinely interested' in others. The concept of dimensions of interpersonal interaction was examined, and verbal and nonverbal determinants which appear to be implicated were enunciated. Two core dimensions were selected for consideration: warmth and empathy, since both have been held to have reinforcing effects upon others.

From a review of relevant research, largely within an instrumental conditioning frame of reference, it is evident that warmth and empathy are characteristic of human encounters which change people for the better. In counselling and psychotherapy, where most research has been carried out, counsellor warmth and empathy have been associated with changes in clients in terms of increased self-exploration, positive self-concept, and ability to articulate problematic areas; in teaching and learning, with increased favourable social behaviours; and in mass communication, with an increased degree of opinion change in the receiver.

Attention was then turned to the questions, 'What are warmth and empathy?' and 'How can I convey this to my patient, client or student?' A complex matrix of verbal behaviours such as reflection of feeling, minimal encourages, and supportive statements together with nonverbal behaviours ranging from posture and gestures to facial expressions and eye contact were identified as playing a crucial role in conveying warmth and empathy which in turn tend to be positively valued by others. However, it should be pointed out that more research, particularly in naturalistic settings as opposed to experimentally designed investigations, needs to be conducted in order to benefit our understanding of these rewarding processes.

Before leaving the topic a further point is worth making in relation to warmth in particular. Much of the research cited in this chapter has assumed a reductionist stance and investigated the reinforcing effects of warmth, defined as specific instances of verbal and nonverbal behaviour, on various outcome measures. But the notion of warmth also operates at a different level as a label referring to a more enduring interpersonal quality. Here possibilities of controlled, contingent application predicated on some targeted response are less feasible. Warmth has also a much broader impact in terms of the views of unconditionality, for example, expressed by Rogers and mentioned in Chapter Two.

Chapter 6

Interpersonal attraction and reward

INTRODUCTION

We have seen how various verbal and nonverbal features of interpersonal behaviour, acting as social rewards, can have a significant impact on what the interactive partner does and, in more global terms, not only determine perceptions of warmth and empathy, but also make a beneficial contribution to outcomes in counselling, therapy and education. Additionally, the giving and receiving of rewards have also been associated with the establishment of interpersonal attraction. It is to this topic that we now turn.

Social interchange which is rewarding can have the effect of establishing positive attitudes between interactants which in turn can lead to lasting friendship and even love. We are often attracted to those who react positively to us. The first part of this chapter will examine three factors which are considered to be instrumental in attempting to explain attraction between people: physical attractiveness, attitude similarity and complementarity, and personality. In addition, it can be shown, from a review of studies devoted to the phenomenon, that, firstly, an individual deemed 'attractive' is more likely to obtain rewards from others and, secondly, that an individual's 'attractiveness' can be a source of reward to others. The remainder of the chapter focuses upon the research and application of ideas about attraction in some of the applied professions. It is important to bear in mind that the intention is not to provide a litany of research findings on the topic (see Byrne, 1971 and Berscheid, 1985 for extensive research reviews), but rather a brief account of some of the central features of it and an overview of key research findings in three distinctly different contexts, namely teaching, counselling and the law. While some reference will be made to attraction as a feature in the initial stages of forming a relationship, a more detailed consideration of relationships and the contribution of rewards to them will be left to Chapter Nine.

ATTRACTION AND ATTRACTIVENESS

It is important at the outset to enunciate the relationship between attraction and attractiveness: attractiveness is considered one of the main causes of attraction. Society and the way it is organised reduces the range of persons that are readily accessible for us to interact with. Thus there is considerable preselection of the possibilities for relationships to develop since these are mostly from our own race, religion, socioeconomic group, intelligence level, educational background, and geographical location (Woll and Cozby, 1987). Duck (1988) puts forward the notion that two possible advantages of this preselection is that communication is made easier because of sharing of common assumptions and also that similarity is more reassuring and less risky. Other factors which contribute to mutual attraction or affiliation are shared anxiety situations (Schachter, 1959), moving to a new area (Duck, 1982), and mere chance or coincidence (Perlman, 1986). Given that there are these constraints placed upon the availability of persons we would want to get to know, how can we explain attraction when face-to-face meetings take place?

EXPLANATIONS OF ATTRACTION

From a review of research a number of factors have emerged as possible explanations of attraction. The following are some of the main areas which will be examined in this section, namely, physical attractiveness, attitude similarity and complementarity, and personality.

Physical attractiveness: effects upon attributions of mood, personality and disposition

It is widely acknowledged that physically attractive individuals are at an advantage in our society and as Cialdini (1985) believes:

> We may have sorely underestimated the size and reach of that advantage.
>
> (p. 161)

Physically attractive individuals are judged more positively than unattractive counterparts on several traits, especially those, according to Dion *et al.* (1972),

> reflecting social competence and interpersonal ease.
>
> (p. 288)

The notion that physically attractive people are more socially adept appears to hold some truth. Goldman and Ewis (1977) found that physically attractive individuals were perceived to have higher social skills than less attractive individuals. There appears to be a clear consensus on what determines physical attractiveness and this uniformity may have been affected by the media's portrayal of 'the perfect person'. Hargie and Marshall (1986) make the point that:

> Cross-cultural agreement about ratings of attractiveness are [*sic*] likely to be increasingly influenced (and Westernised) by the ever-expanding role of the media (Soap-operas, world wide beauty contests and so on).
>
> (p. 49)

When a person is perceived as being attractive there are many other attributes which are automatically assigned to that person. These include being friendly, competent, trustworthy, talented, sensitive, sociable and altruistic (Dion *et al.*, 1972; Adams, 1977). These attributes contrast with those perceived of unattractive individuals who are thought to be insensitive, unsure, submissive, sad, aloof, serious, reserved and rigid (Millar, 1970).

Physical attractiveness: effects upon helping behaviour and self-disclosure

In addition to attributing favourable characteristics to attractive people we also react more positively towards them by, for instance, giving assistance when it is needed and also making every effort to win their approval. There is additional evidence to suggest that we are warmer and more sociable towards people whom we have judged to be physically attractive.

Benson *et al.* (1976) carried out an interesting experiment to test the willingness of persons to assist attractive and unattractive people. They placed stamped addressed envelopes containing graduate school applications in the telephone booths of a large airport. The applications contained photographs of both sexes previously judged as attractive or unattractive. Researchers observed those persons who found the 'lost' applications and recorded their mailing behaviour. Significantly more attractive applications were mailed than unattractive applications. The researchers concluded that people were more willing to mail applications for attractive students because they were better liked and viewed as more qualified for graduate school.

Pellegrini *et al.* (1978) were interested to find out if people would go to greater lengths to win approval from an attractive person rather than an unattractive one. Results revealed that when men and women were asked to describe themselves to a person of the opposite sex, made up to look attractive or unattractive, both men and women employed significantly more self-disclosures when interacting with the attractive person.

Warmth was measured by judges' ratings of telephone conversations between college men and women they had never met, in a study by Snyder *et al.* (1977). However, before the conversation, each man was shown false photographs of either attractive or unattractive women. The results showed that men sounded more sociable, humorous and warm when they believed the woman was attractive. Judges also rated tape recordings of the female respondents' voices and noted that they expressed more confidence, innovation, enjoyment and liking when they talked with a man who believed they were attractive, thus providing evidence of a self-fulfilling function of this attribute. It can be postulated that if we behave in a warm friendly way towards attractive people, they will respond in a similar manner and so confirm our perceptions that such people are warm and friendly in the first place.

These studies and others which will subsequently be cited are relevant to Clore and Byrne's (1974) reinforcement–affect model of attraction. The basic tenet of the reinforcement–affect model is very simple: we like those who reward us and dislike those who punish us. The reward, in whatever form it takes, albeit a smile, an acknowledgement or a 'pat on the back', is the 'reinforcement' part of the model; the 'affect' part is the feelings we associate with the reward given. One important feature of this model is that, through association, any neutral stimulus concomitant with a reward or punishment becomes similarly evaluated. Thus a neutral person in our vicinity when something pleases us will be liked, and disliked if around when something displeasing happens. Hence, in many situations it is not necessarily the traits or attributes of the other (e. g. appearance, attitudes, personality, etc.) that are important for interpersonal attraction but simply the association of positive and pleasant feelings with that person. It has long been known in the education profession, for instance, that when pupils are asked which subjects they like in the school curriculum their perceptions of subject are inextricably linked with their perceptions of the teacher of that subject (Thelen, 1967).

To test the reinforcement–affect model, Veitch and Griffith (1976) formulated a hypothesis which stated that 'something' making a person feel good would cause that person to be attracted to another more than if the person felt depressed. From a group of subjects, half listened to a radio news broadcast consisting entirely of pleasant news items, while the other half were subjected to unpleasant news events. Immediately after this listening episode, subjects were asked to rate their feelings about a stranger following interaction with him/her. As hypothesised, those subjects who heard bad news disliked the stranger, those who heard good news liked the stranger.

In general terms, the more a person or persons provide us with rewards in proportion to punishments, the more likely a relationship will develop and endure. But additional factors also seem to be implicated. It has been reported, for instance, that recipients who are forced to be obligated to agents through being placed in a position of being unable to reciprocate rewards received from them on a charitable basis, find those rewarding agents *less* attractive than others with whom reciprocation is possible (Gergen, 1969). There are a number of reasons why being obligated to another may prove unattractive, one of which is the possibility of thereby empowering that individual to exert control over us. (Power and the role of reciprocity in the exchange of rewards will be returned to in Chapter Eight.)

Bodily characteristics of physical attractiveness

The research studies examined so far have focused on physical attractiveness in a general sense rather than attempting to identify and evaluate specific physical traits or characteristics that differentiate attractive and unattractive people. In some interesting studies carried out in the early 1970s (Lerner *et al.*, 1973; Lerner and Karabenick, 1974), young adults were asked to rank those features which they considered were most important for their own physical attractiveness and their opposite sex peer. They listed, as most important, general appearance, face, weight distribution, facial complexion, and body build and, as least important, neck, hair colour, chin, ears and ankles. As a result, therefore, much of the subsequent research has concentrated on the face and body. However, in addition there is considerable literature regarding the perceptions of clothing and dress and on evaluations of personal details such as cosmetics, beards and spectacles.

One of the problems for such investigations into the separation and isolation of specific components of attractiveness, such as the face and the body, from the overall picture is that of validity of results. In other words, how meaningful are the studies which isolate one aspect or characteristic from the whole? Do people respond to any one of the physical attributes singly or do they only react to the total picture? Results from carefully formulated and rigorously executed studies suggest that despite beliefs of individual differences in opinions of beauty and the assertion that 'beauty is in the eye of the beholder' there is considerable evidence of a widespread agreement in the level of attractiveness of others (Stewart *et al.*, 1979). However, it must be borne in mind that features of the face in particular are influenced by culture and the historical period in which the investigation was carried out (Liggett, 1974).

While the previous studies have concentrated on the face in general, others have studied specific facial features in relation to attractiveness. For instance, Liggett (1974) also carried out a survey of college women's ratings of attractiveness in males and found that men were regarded as attractive when they had a firm jaw and wide chin, large or 'strong' mouth, clear eyes, facial hair, and a large or strong face. Facial features seen as attractive in women, on the other hand, included large eyes, smooth skin, full mouth, and delicate features such as a small nose, chin and ears. Evidence that these preferences of attractiveness remain relatively constant irrespective of age, socioeconomic status, geographical location, or sex of the respondent can be found in the studies of Kopera *et al.* (1971), Murstein (1977), and Cavior and Dokecki (1971).

Next to the face, physique or body shape has a strong influence on how individuals are perceived and reacted to. Franzoi and Herzog (1987) carried out a questionnaire survey of American psychology students and found that body shape as a whole was relevant to both males' and females' ratings of physical attractiveness, with upper body shape being most important in judgements about men and overall weight being most important in judgements about women. In particular, women gave greatest preference to male physiques with medium wide arms, medium wide upper trunk, medium thin lower trunk, and medium thin legs; that is they liked tapering V-shaped figures the most. Men, on the other hand, rated the underweight women as most desirable and those overweight as least desirable. These stereotypical body types, portrayed regularly in daily newspapers and magazines and on TV commercials and advertisements, help to sustain people's preferences.

Alicke *et al.* (1986) posed the question, 'Is body shape more important than facial features or vice versa when evaluating physical attractiveness?' and set up some interesting experiments to test this hypothesis. They created composite slides from faces and bodies photographed during two summers at a swimming pool, which showed persons with attractive bodies and unattractive faces, the same attractive body but with an attractive face and so on. These photographs were presented to a range of male and female subjects who rated them. Results revealed that faces affected ratings of intelligence, sociability and morality while bodies influenced ratings only of sociability and intelligence. However, it is important to note at this point that physical attractiveness is more valued by some people than others. Snyder and Smith (1986) suggest that 'high self-monitors' (that is, persons who tend to be highly conscious of their own performance in social situations) consider physical attractiveness to be more highly valued than 'low self-monitors' (those people who are unconcerned about how they appear to others) who are more interested in others' thoughts and views than in physical attractiveness. Further evidence that beauty may not always have a positive effect upon relationships is provided by Krebs and Adinolf (1975), who found that physically attractive persons are more likely than physically unattractive persons to be rejected by members of their own sex.

Considerable research has been undertaken on the effects of height on subjects' ratings of physical attractiveness (Feldman, 1971; Koulack and Tuthill, 1972; Kleinke, 1986). These studies imply that we have a tendency to judge people of high status and people we like as taller than people of low status and people we dislike. In addition, there is evidence to suggest that taller men have advantages over shorter men in terms of job opportunities. A survey of professional men showed that taller men received higher average sterling salaries and were more likely to gain promotion than shorter men (Knapp, 1978). When women were asked to give their preferences for men's height, two factors stood out as important to them. Firstly, women claimed that they liked men of average height best (five feet nine inches to five feet eleven inches) and, secondly, they preferred the man to be five to nine inches taller than themselves (Graziano *et al.*, 1978). However, while height appears to be a positive asset for men, it can be a penalty for women since one of the unstated norms in our society is that, in a dating partnership, the woman must be shorter than the man.

While clothes provide a basic function of warmth and protection, our choice of dress communicates information about ourselves leading to value judgements and differential behaviour and expectational responses on the part of the observer. Evidence of the value placed on dress comes from an early survey by Eicher and Kelley (1972) of high school girls' choice of friendships. These adolescents put dress first, then personality, followed by common interests when recording how they chose their friends. However, we can also effect differential responses in others when presenting ourselves wearing distinctly different kinds of clothes. For example, a number of studies have shown that people receive more help and more readily comply with requests when they are dressed formally and neatly than casually and untidily (Giles and Chavasse, 1975; Kleinke, 1977). This factor has obvious implications for professionals who are invariably expecting their clients to accept and carry out their professional advice.

Similarity: attraction, affect and attitudes

It has also been found that people give more help to those whose clothing indicates attitudes, tastes and beliefs similar to their own (Hensley, 1981). Indeed the notion that, aside from appearance, similar attitudes and personalities are instrumental in making us attracted and attractive to other people has been vigorously argued by Byrne, Clore and other psychologists attempting to explain the similarity–attraction effect. Byrne (1961) set up a series of experiments to manipulate the similarity levels between subjects and subsequently examine the levels of their attraction for one another. These experiments pioneered a methodology usually referred to as the 'bogus stranger' or 'hypothetical stranger' method and has been used extensively by other researchers interested in developing our understanding of interpersonal attraction. Briefly, the essentials of the method are these: subjects complete an attitude questionnaire and hand it back to the experimenter; the experimenter alleges that he is going to collect a questionnaire from a subject in the next cubicle but, in fact, constructs a profile which resembles the subject's own to an extent required by the experimental conditions (e. g. highly similar, moderately similar, or dissimilar to the subject). The bogus information is then presented to the subject as if it had been completed by a stranger (who is actually the 'bogus stranger' immortalised in the title of the method). From this information, the subject is asked to form an impression of this stranger. Results showed that attitude similarity and attraction are significantly correlated. One suggestion put forward concerning how similarity operates is that attitude similarity is an example of reinforcement or rewardingness and, as such, something attractive, desirable and positive that we like to experience. A further suggestion postulated is that the perception of similar opinions in others increases one's confidence that one's own opinions are reasonable thus making one feel more competent, satisfies one's effectance needs, and makes one feel good.

Clore (1977) notes that in attitudinal formation there is a cognitive or informational factor (own attitudes confirmed or disconfirmed by others) and an affective factor (how one feels about this information). That attitudes are learned responses and most typically occur within the context of an operant reward situation is propounded by Staats (1968). Indeed interpersonal attitudes have been the specific focus of a number of theoretical and empirical investigations on attraction which have led to the proposition that if a person is positively reinforced in the presence of another, a positive attitude towards that other will be formed (Lott and Lott, 1985).

Further studies have added to our knowledge of similarity/attraction processes. For example, Byrne and Nelson (1965) noted that the amount of attraction between individuals is directly predictable from the proportion of similar attitudes; in essence the more similar we are to others the more we like them. However, Byrne (1961) warns that once we begin to gather additional information regarding others the picture becomes more complex. In brief, it matters whether we have a positive view of the other person (e.g. the person is not alien, repulsive to us, or mentally ill – unless we are too, of course); the similar attitudes are important to us; the reason given for holding them is similar to ours; others are stating their true opinions and not attempting to ingratiate themselves with us. Those people who are in a dependent relationship with another person face what has been termed the 'ingratiator's dilemma', in that it is difficult in such a situation to present opinions and views that will be interpreted as sincere (Jones and Wortman, 1973). More recently, Lea and Duck (1982) have added to our knowledge by suggesting that uncommon similarity, or similarity on attitudes that are not regarded as widely held generally, are particularly attractive.

While these results cited have been derived experimentally, there is ample evidence outside the laboratory to substantiate these findings. For instance, Byrne (1971) found that bank managers gave bigger loans to people with similar attitudes and Start (1968), in a study of headmasters' ratings of secondary school teachers, found that the ratings made by heads were related to the similarity of their attitudes and personalities to those of the teachers. In addition, it is invariably the method used by dating agencies who match partners according to similar attitudes, values and beliefs.

While these results demonstrate that similarity can have a variety of positive consequences, exceptions can be found. If we were asked to produce an example of a situation in which dissimilarity would have a more functional value than similarity, we would surely find the task easy enough to accomplish. One study designed to test this hypothesis involved college students' attraction to their college tutors and was carried out by Grush *et al.* (1975). It was hypothesised that dissimilarity would lead to attraction on characteristics relevant to the teacher's role but not on characteristics irrelevant to teaching. Personality measures were obtained on students and teachers in ninety-three college classes. A characteristic was considered relevant if scores on it were correlated with ratings of teacher skill and irrelevant if they were not. Teachers who were high, medium and low on both the relevant and irrelevant dimensions were selected, and from their classes equal numbers of students were chosen who were either similar or dissimilar (one standard deviation or more below the teacher). The results showed that those who were similar to their teachers on relevant characteristics were less attracted than those students who were dissimilar. The students' reasoning appears to be that if teachers are expected to lead and direct the learning processes of students they ought to possess more of those characteristics which make for effective teaching. If they only possess the same amount as the student, it is felt they are less effective and therefore less rewarding. (The link between power, status and reward is dealt with more comprehensively in Chapter Eight.)

Thus the point needs to be made that both similarity and dissimilarity can lead to attraction depending on which is ultimately more rewarding for the perceiver. Although similarity would appear to be far more frequently associated with positive outcomes, nevertheless there will be situations in which dissimilarity will be more rewarding.

A concept less researched but nevertheless worthy of further investigation is

that of complementarity in attraction which is that dissimilar but congruent behaviour may produce attraction. One only needs to examine the marriage relationships
of some of our friends to find an illustration of the complementary needs in
attraction. John is untidy while Margaret is neat and highly organised in the home.
As a result Margaret is constantly clearing up books, papers, clothes and other
belongings left lying about the house in order that she lives in a neat and organised
environment. It could be postulated that such recurring scenarios could engender
a series of conflicts over neatness and so put a strain on the marriage. Instead, as
so often happens in these situations, they can jokingly relate these differences to
friends and relatives. It would appear that the attitudes of both partners can make
the conflict an inherent part of the marriage: Margaret happily playing the nurturant
role of looking after her husband, and John enjoying being looked after. This is an
example of mutual need gratification in which both interactants find the interaction
mutually or reciprocally rewarding because one's needs are expressed in behaviour
that is rewarding to the other person. In this way, each individual satisfies needs
and is in turn satisfied. Seyfried (1977) refers to these complementary needs as
falling into,

> a reinforcement model of attraction; behaviours that gratify needs are rewarding
> and rewards elicit implicit affective responses in people.
>
> (p. 184)

While the above is an example of the nurturance–succurance dimension of complementary need gratification, Winch (1967) notes that other dimensions such as
assertiveness–receptivity or achievement–*laissez-faire* could be investigated.
More research needs to be conducted in this area in order to deepen our understanding of this phenomenon.

Personality

Early research tended to focus upon the identification and matching of personality
characteristics of couples in both short- and long-term relationships (Day, 1961).
However, this has proved to be a fruitless search largely because researchers began
to realise that knowledge of a partner's personality could only be gleaned over the
development of a relationship where partners began to appreciate such aspects of
one another (Duck, 1977). Thus, studies such as Levinger and Breedlove (1966)
and La Gaipa (1982), which set out to predict the success of a relationship based
upon the personality correlates of each partner, have failed to demonstrate the
efficiency of such a procedure. These investigations were based upon the belief
that the 'true' personalities of people could be matched up from scientifically
scored measures of each individual. Interestingly, on a less scientific level, dating
agencies match partners for successful relationships on the basis of interests, values
and personality characteristics. Their view is that this matching process will get
couples off to a good start and keep the relationship running smoothly as it
develops.

However, more recent research, using more clearly defined terms of reference such as the nature of the relationship between individuals, whether initial or long-term, and using personality measures that have different functions, purposes and concerns, has shown that in the process of forming and maintaining impressions of a partner's personality, individuals will alter their focus as the relationship evolves (Van Lear and Trujillo, 1986). This point is given further credence by Burgoon and Koper (1984). In an interesting study of the nonverbal correlates of shyness, they found that shy and lonely people seem to produce behaviours that put off people who are relative strangers but once they somehow get past that barrier and become acquaintances or even friends their behaviour is reinterpreted and viewed in a more positive and attractive light. Thus personality cues which may initially appear unrewarding can be revised once more knowledge of that person is revealed. The authors suggest that actions such as showing interest in others, acting fairly and kindly, helping someone, and sharing self-disclosures carry more weight in terms of reward indices than an evaluation of personality.

INITIAL AND LONG-TERM ATTRACTIVENESS

It is contended by Murstein (1972) that:

> The process of approach (of two interactants) depends on the reward value of the meeting, the subjective estimate of the probability of success, and the cost to self-esteem of failure.
>
> (p. 116)

There is ample evidence, some of which was described previously in this chapter, to suggest that physical attractiveness has a major impact on first impressions of others. The importance of physical attractiveness resides not only in its being highly valued by society as a status-conferring asset but also in all kinds of other desirable personality, attitudinal and intellectual attributes being ascribed to the 'beautiful'. In other words, these people are viewed as:

> more sensitive, kind, interesting, strong, poised, modest, sociable, outgoing and exciting.... more sexual, warm, and responsive, than unattractive persons.
>
> (Berscheid and Walster, 1972, p. 46)

It is also worth pointing out that initial impressions are not wholly dependent on the physical characteristics of interactors. An individual's stimulus value may also include information regarding his reputation or abilities which precede him into the initial contact. Thus a teacher who has been regarded by a generation of pupils as warm, caring and good at her job may compensate for her less than glamorous appearance. It would seem that initial judgements are made on the basis of perceptions of the other and/or previous information gained about the other.

While initial attraction to strangers is the interactional starting point, we do not necessarily set up a relationship with every attractive person we meet, and indeed Duck (1986) suggests that:

long-term acquaintance is probably not caused by, say, physical attraction even if that is what interests us initially. The development of relationships is not caused by initial attraction.

(p. 79)

Long-term relationships depend more upon the selection and communication of information about ourselves so that we can negotiate and create a relationship which will endure. Thus a range of social skills – such as the use of self-disclosures and overt listening behaviours to denote interest, head-nodding and appropriate paralanguage to encourage others, the correct gestural and postural cues to show empathy and warmth, and smiling and touch contact to show support and praise (see Chapters Three and Four for a range of verbal and nonverbal rewarding behaviours) – can be regarded as the sources of ongoing attraction towards others as the relationship develops.

This is borne out by Capella (1984) who argues that:

Attraction between persons ought to be found in the interactional structures they exhibit, how they fit in with or adapt to one another's communicative styles, not just in the communicative styles that they exhibit independently.

(p. 241)

Three contexts have been selected to provide evidence that professionals can be influenced by attractiveness factors in the everyday course of their work. The three chosen for closer attention are teaching, counselling and the law.

TEACHING

Research has found that the advantages which accrue from being deemed an attractive individual begin at an early age (Dion *et al.*, 1972; Berscheid, 1981). 'An ugly baby is a very nasty object,' remarked Queen Victoria in 1839, and indeed this quotation sums up many people's assessments today. A number of studies (Dion and Berscheid, 1974; Rich, 1975) have investigated teachers' and adults' perceptions of children and how they should behave on the basis of photographs of the children along with a written report. Those rated attractive were perceived as more intelligent and more likely to succeed than unattractive children. In addition, attractive children were nominated more independent and self-sufficient than unattractive children; while unattractive children were more often nominated the aggressive, antisocial and non-conforming descriptions. More recently Herman *et al.* (1986) noted that parents,

expected their children to make behavioural attributions and social choices consistent with the 'beauty is good' stereotype.

(p. 26)

Cavior and Dokecki (1971) found that children also rated physically attractive children as more competent and their preferred friendship choice over unattractive children. Thus, as well as being judged on the basis of their attractiveness by adults, children also judge other children on this aspect from an early age. This is hardly surprising as in most fairy tales and cartoons, children are presented with stereotypical pictures of 'baddies as ugly and heroes/heroines as beautiful'.

There is also ample evidence to suggest that teachers may be affected by the attractiveness of their pupils and indeed credit them with more intelligence than unattractive pupils. Clifford and Walster (1973) carried out a study in which five hundred and four elementary school principals were asked to provide an evaluation of a fifth grader based upon the pupil's report card and a photograph. The principals were not told that the report card of the pupil remained the same but that the photograph was varied to make the pupil appear physically attractive or unattractive. Results revealed that male and female principals rated attractive pupils as more intelligent and as having more academic and social potential than unattractive pupils. A replication of this study two years later by Clifford (1975) with first grade pupils found the same results when principals evaluated report cards of attractive and unattractive pupils.

Evidence that this prejudice or bias towards physical attractiveness is not merely confined to children is provided by Hore's (1971) study, previously mentioned, of the ratings of trainee students on teaching practice in schools. Five female senior teachers rated one hundred and fifty-nine male students and five male senior teachers rated one hundred and sixty-two females on a three-point attractiveness scale (attractive 3, neutral 2, unattractive 1). This initial attractiveness assessment was made from a head-and-shoulders only photograph of all the students. When the attractiveness rating given to students was correlated with the grades these students obtained on teaching practice, there was a significant finding that attractive girls obtained higher grades. The author concluded that unconscious bias in the tutor's assessment of a lesson taught by an attractive student teacher may have been a factor in the result. Interestingly, for male students the differences were not significant. Thus female tutors appeared not to give male physical attractiveness such a high value.

As well as giving differential academic grades to attractive and unattractive students, there is evidence to suggest that the amount of blame assigned to misbehaviours of attractive and unattractive children also varies. Dion (1972) carried out an investigation in which three hundred and twenty female teachers were instructed to read a description about a seven-year-old boy or girl who had intentionally hit another child on the head with a hard snowball, so causing a deep cut. A photograph identified the child for half the sample of teachers as attractive, the other half as unattractive. Teachers significantly assigned more blame for the incident to an unattractive child and went on to suggest that such a child was more likely to commit similar anti-social acts in the future. Further evidence of this finding is provided by Rich (1975), who noted that teachers were more likely to blame unattractive boys in particular for any misbehaviours in class.

A person's name may be considered a personal characteristic in much the same way as physical appearance, clothes, speech style, and personality. On this basis, the attractiveness/unattractiveness label constituted by a name would be expected to directly influence its bearer and those who interact with him, and thus indirectly influence the reinforcement–affect model of attraction postulated by Byrne (1971). Names are a type of information exchanged early in most social relationships and as such represent an important influence on the initial stages of their development (Duck, 1977). Evidence that teachers can differentially reward those pupils with attractive Christian names can be found in a study by Erwin and Calev (1984). These researchers asked fifty trainee teachers to rate forty-five female and thirty-five male Christian names on a seven-point attractiveness scale. Six essays of approximately equal standard written by nine- to ten-year-old pupils and assigned bogus names were given to the trainee teachers to mark independently. Results revealed that the essays of unattractively named pupils received significantly lower marks than anonymously named pupils, who in turn received lower marks than attractively named pupils. One way to overcome this effect in the marking of written scripts is of course to ensure the anonymity of the author, and indeed in most formal and national examinations this procedure is adopted. However, name stereotype effects may be expected to be pervasive in face-to-face social interaction in general.

COUNSELLING

Effective counselling depends to a large extent upon the client having a trust in and positive regard towards the counsellor. A number of studies has revealed that those counsellors considered attractive by their clients were thought to be more competent than their unattractive counterparts. Cash et al. (1975) videotaped two male clinical psychologists interviewing a client in a counselling session. The first psychologist was made up to look attractive (well-dressed and hair well-groomed); the other was made up to look unattractive (unstylish clothing, padding to appear overweight, shadows made up under the eyes, and greased hair to look dirty). The question and statements spoken during the counselling session were identical. One hundred and seventy-eight college students who viewed the tapes rated the attractive counsellor as more competent, friendly, trustworthy, intelligent, warm, assertive and likeable than the unattractive counsellor. The above study was subsequently replicated using a female counsellor who was made up to appear attractive or unattractive (Lewis and Walsh, 1978). In this investigation there were gender differences in the way the female counsellors were perceived. Women rated the attractive counsellor as more competent, professional, relaxed, likeable and interesting than the unattractive counsellor, while men, on the other hand, did not significantly favour the attractive female counsellor. The authors concluded that men might have been reluctant to give unfavourable ratings to the unattractive female counsellor since there was a great deal of adverse publicity around at the time regarding male chauvinism. However, some further studies (Cash and Salzbach, 1978; Cash and Kehr, 1978; Vargas and Borkowski, 1982) confirmed the original findings in favour of the attractive counsellor. One further point that needs to be made regarding the previous studies is that the importance of physical attractiveness was probably over-emphasized because the researchers were investigating the counsellor's appearance at its extremes. Carter (1978) notes that at moderate levels of physical attractiveness it does not matter whether one counsellor is slightly more attractive than another.

One aspect of attractiveness, notably dress and appearance, can be regarded either positively or negatively in the counselling context. This treatise is given validation by a number of studies (Kaats and Davis, 1970; Mathes and Kahn, 1975; Adams, 1977) which suggest that clients' perceptions of counsellors are influenced by their dress. The general findings are that people prefer counsellors who dress formally enough to maintain an image of expertise but not so formally as to appear stuffy and aloof. Not surprisingly, counsellors come across as more competent when their clothing is in style rather than out of date.

LAW

While defence and prosecuting barristers make a serious attempt to base their cases on objective evidence, nevertheless they are also sensitive to the perceptions and emotions of the jury. Those of us who are familiar with jury trials are aware that the decision of the jury is partially subjective. Thus those people who are requested to appear in court usually know that it is worth the extra effort to dress formally and look presentable. Obviously it is difficult to study the effects of physical attractiveness on jury decisions in actual court cases, because the nature of the offence being tried and the weight of evidence produced by defendants and prosecutors cannot be equally balanced among attractive and unattractive defendants. However, Kleinke (1986) makes the point after reviewing a range of studies that:

> Simulated jury decisions are suitably controlled because participants can be given exactly the same case material, which is attached to a photograph of a defendant who is attractive or unattractive.

(p. 45)

Several studies have revealed that attractive defendants are more likely to be acquitted or given less severe sentences if found guilty than their unattractive counterparts. Palpable evidence for this assertion can be found in a study by Landy and Aronson (1960), who showed how physical attractiveness can significantly affect jurors' opinions of a defendant. In a simulated setting the researchers requested the jurors to choose a sentence for a convicted person (a normal procedure in American courts). In 50 per cent of cases, the defendant was an attractive person and the remaining defendants were unattractive. Results revealed that defendants with an attractive character and appearance were sentenced much more leniently than an unattractive defendant (even though the crime committed was exactly the same). It also revealed that when the victim was deemed attractive the defendant received a significantly more severe sentence than if perceived unattractive. This response of reacting more positively to attractive defendants by assigning less blame and awarding lighter sentences, and recommending punishment and assigning guilt when the defendant is identified as being unattractive, would appear to be the case irrespective of the gender of the defendant. For instance, Kulka and Kessler (1978) asked over a hundred subjects to take the role of the jury in a trial in which a male victim was suing a male defendant for damages in a car accident. Half of the sample of jurors were asked to make decisions about a trial in which the victim was attractive and the defendant unattractive. The other half of the jurors were given unattractive victims and attractive defendants. Results showed that jurors ruled in favour of the victim 49 per cent of the time when he was attractive and only 17 per cent of the time when viewed as unattractive. In addition, it was interesting to note in monetary reward terms that attractive victims received higher cash settlements than unattractive victims.

Soloman and Schopler (1978), carrying out an investigation on the effects of female victims' attractiveness on mock jury trials, found similar results. Research subjects were asked to recommend a jail sentence for a woman who had been found guilty of burglary. A photograph identified the guilty woman as attractive or unattractive. Results were significant. The attractive woman was given an average sentence of 2.80 years while the unattractive one was sentenced to an average of 5.20 years. However, in the same study, the investigators changed the nature of the crime to swindling. The swindle case was described as an incident in which the woman had ingratiated herself with a man and induced him to invest money in a bogus company. In this case, the attractive and unattractive women were both given five year sentences. Nevertheless, the results from these researchers suggest that physical attractiveness in a jury case is invariably an asset and rarely a liability. Unattractiveness, however, is a liability. This is borne out by two studies (Seligman et al., 1977; Deitz et al., 1984) into the attribution of responsibility for rape and the influence of a rape victim's attractiveness on observers' empathy. Research participants (more than one hundred college students) were less sympathetic to unattractive rape victims, especially when they were 'unfeminine' for instance, resisting their attacker and being generally aggressive. Unattractive women were also suspected, more than attractive women, of having provoked the attack.

CONCLUSION

The research studies summarised in this chapter show quite clearly that attractive and unattractive people are perceived and treated differently in many aspects of their social and professional lives. An examination of the explanations of attraction reveals a range of factors, notably physical appearance, attitudes and personality. While acknowledging that physically attractive individuals are at an advantage in our Western society, particularly in the initial stages of relationship development, long-term relationships depend more upon the selection and communication of information about ourselves during the interaction process.

Aside from appearance, similar attitudes and personalities are instrumental in making us attracted and attractive to other people. Thus the more similar we are to others the more we like them. Research also indicates that the concept of complementarity in a relationship can be highly rewarding; that is, behaviour which is dissimilar but congruent. In other words opposites can attract each other. Personality studies of attraction have been less conclusive in their results. It would appear that general communication skills such as showing interest in others, helping someone, and sharing disclosures are more profitable indicators of rewardingness than an evaluation of personality.

In conclusion, professionals including teachers, counsellors and jurors need to be aware of the bias towards attractiveness and, therefore, must consider carefully the basis of their judgements and perhaps prejudices towards others.

Chapter 7

Locus of control and attributional processes

INTRODUCTION

Perceptions of what is taking place when rewards are offered will largely determine how they are construed and reacted to. While so far in this book essentially constructive and beneficial effects have been espoused, we have come across at various junctures sets of circumstances under which predicted outcomes of positive reactions to the other in terms of self-beliefs, motivation and subsequent practice have failed to materialise. Here we will take a more critical look at the impact of rewards such as praise by considering the role that locus of control and attributional processes play in understanding how the individual makes sense of success and failure. The main emphasis throughout the chapter is on attribution theory as proposed by Weiner and his colleagues (Weiner, 1985, 1986), and its applications.

In the skill model of interpersonal communication outlined in Chapter One, the importance of treating the communication process as a dynamic and ongoing sequence of events that involves reciprocal determination was highlighted. Hargie and Marshall (1986) have outlined several important distinctions between early models of motor skill performance and social functioning that have important considerations for any theory of social interaction. From the standpoint of the present chapter the most significant of these is their distinction between the perception of objects and people. As we have seen, the more complex nature of person perception requires a recognition that individuals evaluate both their own and other individuals' responses and, through a process of metaperception, the overall process of perception itself. Within the skill model outlined at the beginning of the book, this facet of the communication process is recognised together with the inclusion of mediating factors that, along with situational and personal considerations, allow an explanation of interpersonal conduct in different situations to be contemplated.

One of the most fundamental aspects of interpersonal interaction that is also central to certain explanations of the role of reward is the process of attribution. *Attribution theory* is based upon the belief that people are motivated to make sense of experienced events by inferring what brought them about. Causal attributions are about the individual's search for the reasons for success and failure. In trying to answer this question people have to determine whether the results of a particular behaviour can be attributed to their effort, to their ability, or to other external factors. If we succeed in an examination we can attribute this to our own ability or to help from others. Similarly, failure could be attributed to lack of effort or lack of ability. In this sense, attribution theory has been criticised as presenting a 'common sense' view of human behaviour. While from a purely scientific viewpoint a common-sense position may hinder research (see Fletcher, 1984), the fact that some of the basic tenets of the theory correspond to commonly held views or beliefs about the social world is a positive advantage in persuading professionals to apply the theory in practical settings.

Although there are several competing conceptions of attribution, Weiner's (1985) formulation is arguably the most comprehensive account available, dealing as it does with attributional antecedents (factors that influence attributions), causal attributions themselves, and the consequences of these attributions for the individual. These different aspects of the theory will be looked at in turn along with their applications in teaching and health contexts.

EARLY THEORETICAL APPROACHES TO ATTRIBUTION: LOCUS OF CONTROL

The historical roots of attribution theory can be traced back to the work of Julian Rotter and more distantly to the Expectancy-value theory of Kurt Lewin (1938). Rotter and his associates accepted the basic premises of Expectancy-value theory as proposed by Lewin. This states, it will be recollected, that the degree of motivation to perform an action is determined by the reinforcement value of the goal involved and the individual's expectancy of attaining that goal. In a series of experimental studies investigating the determinants of expectancy of success in skill and chance tasks, Rotter was led to the conclusion that there were distinct individual differences involved in the perception of causality. As a result he constructed the Locus of Control or I-E scale (Rotter, 1966) which was designed to measure the degree to which individuals construed environmental events in terms of skill (Internal, I) or chance (External, E). This distinction between those who perceive the world as filled with personal events that occur by chance (external), and those who perceive the same events as determined by skill (internal), led to a wave of research that reported relationships between locus of control and a host of other variables.

It is important to determine clearly what is meant by the locus of control construct before examining its relationship with other psychological ideas and attempting to apply it to practical situations. Rotter (1966) defines the construct thus:

> When a reinforcement is perceived by a subject as following some action of his own but not entirely contingent upon his action, then, in our culture, it is typically perceived as the result of luck, chance, fate, as under the control of powerful others, or as unpredictable because of the great complexity of forces

surrounding him. When the event is interpreted in this way by an individual, we have labeled this a belief in **external control**. If the person perceives that the event is contingent upon his own behavior or his own relatively permanent characteristics, we have termed this a belief in **internal control**.

(p. 1)

In simple terms then locus of control refers to whether individuals believe that reinforcements or rewards follow from their actions (internal control) or are determined more by chance factors or powerful others (external control). A student who believes that she will obtain a bad exam result no matter how hard she tries, because the teacher has her pigeon-holed as a failure, is an example of external control. The student's belief that her actions do not matter as much as the actions of powerful others (in this case the teacher) in the environment lead her to expect little correspondence between her own actions and any rewarding outcomes that may take place.

LOCUS OF CONTROL AND LEARNED HELPLESSNESS

It is not surprising that the idea of locus of control is closely related to the phenomenon of learned helplessness introduced earlier. This phenomenon has its origins in a series of animal experiments carried out by Seligman and his associates in the late 1960s (Seligman and Maier, 1967; Overmeir and Seligman, 1967). In these studies, dogs were restrained and given a series of random shocks that they could neither avoid nor escape. Following this procedure, the dogs were placed in a shuttlebox that allowed them the opportunity to escape the shock by simply crossing a small barrier to a safe section. The investigators found that the dogs did not learn this simple escape response but instead came to display few signs of emotion and little attempt to move from the unsafe end of the box. This reaction in response to unavoidable shock (which animals do not display under normal conditions) was termed learned helplessness. Research into learned helplessness in humans quickly ensued. These studies followed the same basic procedures as the animal studies with subjects being exposed to bursts of noise through headphones that could or could not be controlled. The results of these studies suggested that, as with animal subjects, exposure to uncontrollable events led to a detriment in humans' performance. It quickly became clear, however, that helplessness in people was a much more complex phenomenon than in animals. Abramson *et al.* (1978) revised the theory to try to consider the cognitive capacity of human beings. While maintaining the original notion that expectation was central to producing helplessness, they postulated that the individual's interpretation of the reasons for this event had to be taken into account. In this respect, research into locus of control and learned helplessness pointed to the conclusion that a more systematic approach was required that emphasised other dimensions of causality.

Locus, stability and controllability

Whereas most psychologists recognise the pioneering work of Rotter (1966), and indeed Heider (1958) and Kelley (1967), in setting up the basic premises of Attribution theory, it is the work of Bernard Weiner and his associates (Weiner, 1985) that has arguably had the greatest influence on the theoretical development of attributional research. Weiner proposed three dimensions of causality that have been experimentally identified. The first of these, Locus, defines the location of a cause as internal or external. Characteristics of the individual, for example effort and ability, are seen as internal whereas luck and task difficulty are external. To this was added a Stability dimension, which relates to whether causes continue or vary over time. Ability, for instance, can be described as stable as it is likely to persist for any given task. Effort by contrast is unstable since it may fluctuate according to how the individual feels at a particular point. The final causal dimension is Controllability, which refers to whether the individual senses responsibility for the cause. Effort is therefore controllable since it is something for which people have direct responsibility. Ability and luck, on the other hand, are not perceived to be controlled in this way.

Table 7.1 outlines the three causal dimensions for ability and effort. Ability is classified as a cause that is internal, stable and controllable. Success due to high ability is therefore perceived as something internal to the individual, which will persist and over which little personal control can be exercised. Effort by contrast although also classified as internal to the individual changes with time and is something over which the individual has personal control.

Table 7.1   Ability and effort ascriptions related to causal dimensions

	Causes	
Causal dimensions	*Ability*	*Effort*
Locus	Internal	Internal
Stability	Stable	Unstable
Controllability	Uncontrollable	Controllable

Source: Graham, 1991, p. 8

The effects of causal attributions

The way in which the three dimensions of causality proposed by Weiner relate to how individuals think, feel and act when faced with success or failure form a central part of an attributional approach to motivation. To best understand the contribution of attribution theory, it is necessary to describe the individual's emotional reactions to failure and success as the different dimensions of causality are brought into play. Following failure, for example in an exam, a student's first emotional reaction is likely to be one of sadness or frustration. These initial reactions are generally attribution free since they relate directly to the preceding event and do not involve a search for reasons for this failure. The individual, however, is likely to require some cognitive explanation for this unsatisfactory happening that invokes a causal search for reasons. It is here that the three causal dimensions operate to provide explanations for what took place. The Locus dimension appears to be most closely linked to the individual's self-esteem. This relationship is perhaps most strongly documented in the tendency to ascribe positive outcomes to internal factors and negative outcomes to (external) others (Weary, 1978). The student who fails an exam can either attribute this to personal shortcomings leading to lowered self-esteem or blame environmental circumstances/others for the failure, thereby ensuring that self-esteem remains intact.

The Stability dimension is most closely related to future expectations. People who fail consistently may start to believe that their actions play no part in the outcome. This state of learned helplessness is hard to break out of once it has been 'learned' that personal actions do not affect environmental outcomes. This can lead to feelings of apathy and hopelessness.

The final Controllability dimension is linked to the emotions of guilt and shame. If failure is due to factors that are perceived to be under the control of the agent, then that person is likely to feel guilt. Failure due to lack of personal effort is an example of an attribution that is liable to be experienced in this way. It could be a student who has not really studied for an examination and subsequently fails it. Shame, by contrast, is associated with failure that is due to uncontrollable causes such as lack of ability. A student who tries hard but fails does not have the option of blaming failure on lack of effort; instead the student will be inclined to believe that failure is due to uncontrollable factors such as poor aptitude.

How the individual perceives failure is one of the most problematic issues facing educationalists, since the consequences can affect not just current and future educational performance but also the self-esteem of the individual. In this respect, it is much more adaptive from an attributional perspective for a student to perceive failure as a result of lack of effort rather than lack of ability. The attribution of failure to lack of ability is more likely to result in a lowering of future expectations of success. In addition, because low ability is perceived as uncontrollable it leaves the individual feeling that no personal action can alter the current undesirable state of affairs.

APPLYING ATTRIBUTION TO ACHIEVEMENT CONTEXTS

Direct information about failure or success in an examination confronts the student with straightforward causal cues. There is nothing subtle about failing couched in these terms, particularly when you are aware that others have been successful. By contrast feedback from teachers about performance, be it positive or negative, is likely to be indirect. In this section the impact of a series of actions by teachers will be examined to assess their effectiveness when viewed in attributional terms. These indirect cues include praising or blaming, displaying pity or anger, and offering help or refraining from doing so (neglect).

The use of praise or blame in teaching

Without applying attributional research it is hard to envisage that praise and the absence of blame could function in a *negative* fashion. In Chapter Three the role of praise and approval in teaching is examined in detail with a comprehensive review of this research also provided by Brophy (1981). While this research suggests that reward as praise or encouragement is indeed a powerful factor in classroom settings, it also highlights the need for teachers to be aware of the circumstances within which it is administered, and to consider possible socioeconomic and individual differences in reactions to it (Brophy, 1981). The ever-increasing list of variables that have to be considered in assessing the impact of reward in the classroom serves to challenge the traditional assumption that it will *always* and invariably have beneficial consequences for students. This is because we traditionally view these actions as providing only *positive* feedback. Indeed, one of the more common principles within educational circles is that teachers should always strive to give feedback of this type. The notion that rewarding desirable behaviour is invariably preferable to criticising that which is undesirable, and therefore should be applied whenever possible, has become almost a cultural truism within educational circles. Is such a viewpoint justifiable?

Weiner and Kukla (1970) relate praise and blame to the amount of effort that the individual invests in a task. It is held that students perceive a straightforward relationship between teacher praise and the amount of effort that they put in. A student who puts in little effort and fails is the subject of blame or punishment, whereas the successful student who has tried hard is given rewarding feedback. In this way praise and blame from teachers and significant others provide information on which to base judgements about how effort results in success or failure. Nicholls (1978) notes that among older children and adults effort can be viewed as being related to lower ability. If two students achieve similar results, it is the one who has tried harder who is perceived as being lower in ability. Indeed, we tend to go further, perceiving higher ability students as those who have to put in less effort than successful peers.

Attribution research therefore suggests that we can view praise, compared with neutral feedback, as implying high effort and higher perceived effort as reflecting lower ability. For blame or punishment the opposite holds, with blame leading to the assumption of lower effort relative to neutral feedback and lower perceived effort reflecting higher ability. These suggestions have been well supported by experiments by Meyer *et al.* (1979) and Barker and Graham (1987). In the Barker and Graham study children between the ages of four and twelve years were presented with two differing videotapes depicting students receiving feedback when doing maths problems. In one condition both students were shown as being able to solve the mathematical problems. One student received praise with comments such as 'Great job' while the other student received simply the statement 'Correct'. In a second videotape both students were depicted as failing to solve the mathematical problems. Here again the two students received varying feedback.

One student was criticised for this performance, whereas the other received feedback to the effect that the answer given was incorrect. The children in the study were then asked to rate the students' abilities and the amount of effort they felt they were putting into the problems. Analysis of these ratings revealed that, as children become older, they rate the student who was praised for success and the student who was not blamed for failure as lower in ability than counterparts receiving neutral feedback.

As with all laboratory studies of behaviour there is always the suggestion that such findings may not be replicated in classroom conditions. However, a series of studies by Parsons and her associates (Parsons *et al.*, 1982) of actual feedback given in classroom situations suggests that, while these theoretical distinctions are generally supported, the effect of the actual context within which feedback is given is likely to prove an important determinant of how praise or blame is interpreted. In their study of nineteen classroom interactions, they found that frequent criticism of the quality of students' work was related to both higher future expectations in mathematics and higher self-concepts regarding mathematical ability. Praise was, however, not found to be related to students' conceptions of mathematical ability, although lack of praise appeared to be associated with students' perceptions of higher expectations.

It would seem that the prospect of praise acting as a *low* ability cue is increased when it is offered under conditions in which the recipient has little existing appreciation of his or her ability to accomplish the set task, assumes that the evaluator has, is led to believe that the task is relatively easy, and notices, through social comparison, that others who seem to have performed equally well do not receive praise in the same way for their achievements (Meyer *et al.*, 1986). When received under such a set of circumstances, praise may well lead to a less optimistic reassessment of one's capacity to cope with that type of work.

While it is beyond the scope of the present chapter to present a discussion of the many contextual factors that affect feedback in achievement settings (see Brophy, 1981), clearly attributional approaches provide a systematic way of examining how such information may operate in learning tasks. The results so far suggest that the use of praise as a reward cannot be accepted, in unqualified terms, as an entirely desirable principle in educational contexts. As teachers move more systematically towards a reward-based approach in the classroom while also removing the notion of performance-based criticism or punishment, the child's conception of the value of praise is also likely to change. In an environment where praise and criticism are meted out in equal measure, the value of praise can be maintained by simple contrast. However, when praise dominates to such an extent that its main contrast becomes lack of praise rather than criticism, there is a clear danger that the value of praise itself as a reward will diminish. Parsons *et al.* (1982) summarise these sentiments well:

> To suggest that teachers should avoid criticism or give praise more freely overlooks the power of the context in determining the meaning of any message.

A well chosen criticism can convey as much positive information as a praise; abundant or indiscriminant praise can be meaningless; insincere praise which does not covary with the teachers' expectations for the student can have detrimental effects on many students.

(p. 336)

In conclusion, it is clear that the relationship between praise and achievement in educational contexts is likely to be much more complex than previously thought. Attributional research has done much to highlight this complexity, but research so far has tended to concentrate on rather simple tasks in laboratory as opposed to classroom settings. Given the powerful role that contextual factors are likely to play in attributing causes for success and failure in real life situations, future research that concentrates on students' reactions to praise and criticism on both complex and simple tasks in the classroom is needed.

The use of pity and anger

Of all the indirect cues used in educational contexts, the emotional reactions of teachers to pupils' performance are among the least likely cues that one might suspect of being involved in students' perceptions of their personal competence. Yet, as documented in Chapter Four, nonverbal behaviour is an important aspect of teaching performance. The affective displays that teachers evince to accompany verbal utterances may indeed carry more meaning than the actual words themselves. Given that most children are only too aware of the reinforcing role that a teacher represents within the classroom environment, it should be expected that children will pay particular attention to the nonverbal cues that emanate from this source. The two specific cues that will be considered here are pity and anger.

In an educational context, the display of pity towards a student is mostly associated with failure that is due to causes beyond the student's control such as low ability. This is a natural reaction to others who find themselves, through no fault of their own, in a disadvantaged position. Anger, on the other hand, is most likely to be exhibited when failure at a task is perceived as being due to lack of effort, something that is seen as changeable by the student. Weiner *et al.* (1982) have shown that teachers' emotional reactions of pity and anger provide students with information that they can use to determine the causes of failure. In their experiments, they presented college students and children aged both between five and nine and between nine and eleven years with a series of scenarios that depicted teachers displaying anger or pity with other emotions in response to student failure. The subjects were asked to rate four possible causes for the student's failure: low ability, lack of effort, task difficulty, and bad luck, on rating scales. The results consistently demonstrated that anger is perceived as being related to lack of effort and pity to lack of ability. Likewise, Graham (1984), in a laboratory study, looked at the effects of failure on children following a puzzle-solving task. Following failure the experimenter gave feedback to the children of one of three types: pity, anger or no emotional reaction (control condition). The children were then asked to say why they had failed in the puzzle task. The results showed that, following pity, attributions for failure were most often ascribed to low ability whereas, when anger was conveyed, failure was attributed to lack of effort. These results confirm the important part that teachers' emotional reactions to failure are likely to play in classroom contexts. It is clear that children look towards this source in order to help them judge how to interpret their successes and failures.

Providing help or neglect

As with praise or the absence of blame, it is at first hard to see how providing help to a student might serve as a cue to low ability. Here again, the positive nature of gaining attention from the teacher would at first imply that the consequences must invariably be beneficial. Schmidt and Weiner (1988), however, using an attributional analysis of helping behaviour, have shown how this can serve as a low ability cue. They argue that we are more likely to help others when we view the cause of their need as low ability, since this is something that is perceived as being due to a factor that is not under the individual's control. By contrast when we see need arising from perceived lack of effort, a controllable factor, we are less likely to offer help. If teachers' attributions determine whether they will or will not offer help to students, it is reasonable to suggest that these actions may, like praise and blame, serve on occasion as low ability cues.

Graham and Barker (1990), using a videotape methodology, have been able to demonstrate this effect in a simulated classroom context. In one videotape, a teacher is observed in a classroom moving around as two students work at a mathematics problem. The teacher in this first tape (the non-helped condition) simply stops, looks over the student's shoulder without comment, and then passes on. In a second videotape, the teacher is seen performing the same behaviour but upon stopping behind the student offers unsolicited help by saying, 'Let me give you a hint, don't forget to carry your tens.' The timing of the help intervention was designed to occur in the early stages of the problem-solving task when it was still uncertain whether the student would successfully complete the task. After viewing the two videotapes students were asked to rate the two students in terms of effort and ability. Graham and Barker found that across all age groups the student receiving help was perceived to be of lower ability. The findings of this study strongly support the assertion by Schmidt and Weiner (1988) that unsolicited help can function as a low ability cue. It has to be acknowledged, however, that this finding applies only when help is offered that provides answers as opposed to help that attempts to guide the student in an appropriate direction.

Environmental considerations

The role of situational factors in perceptions of success or failure are less clearly documented, although recent research by Jagacinski and Nicholls (1987) suggests that the environmental context can be a contributing factor. They argue that the challenge facing the student in some situations is structured so that there is clear awareness that the goal is to acquire a new skill or to complete a particular task. In other situations the student's goal is to demonstrate high ability or to conceal low ability. These two differing environmental contexts they term 'task-involving' or 'ego-involving'. Research by Jagacinski and Nicholls (1987) suggests that these contextual arrangements can also influence attributions of effort and ability. They found that, when subjects were given instructions that highlighted the intrinsic value of the task (task-oriented) and they succeeded after trying hard, this was interpreted as indicating high ability. By contrast, subjects given instructions that highlighted the need to show high ability or hide low ability (ego-involving) and who put in high effort to succeed were viewed as being of low ability in comparison to other equally successful subjects. These results suggest that the nature of the task itself can also serve to influence subjects' attributions about the relationship between ability and effort.

ATTRIBUTION AND MODELS OF HELPING IN EDUCATION AND HEALTH

In this section, differing conceptions of helping and coping are examined using an attributional analysis to highlight the differing expectations that teachers and health professionals may bring to bear upon those requiring help. If rewards are to be used successfully to help individuals, it is important to establish that the same models are being used by those individuals within interactions. In the previous sections, the unintentional effects of rewards were examined using Weiner's attributional framework; here we will explore ways in which individuals think about help and how this can be of potential benefit to professionals who are trying to assist in education and health settings.

Recovery from serious injury or illness is now recognised to be influenced as much by patients' beliefs about their responsibility for the injury and their role in its treatment as by the recovery process itself. Brickman *et al.* (1982) provide a most useful discussion of four differing models of helping and coping that draw heavily upon an attributional analysis. They argue that a distinction can be drawn between attribution of responsibility for a problem or injury (who is responsible for the past event) and attribution of responsibility for a solution (who is responsible for future events). This allows them to develop four possible models of coping based on differing combinations of past and future responsibilities. Two of the models, the moral model and the medical model, attribute responsibility for both the problem and its solution to the individual or see the individual as being responsible for neither. The other two models, the compensatory model and the enlightenment model, attribute responsibility for the solutions to problems to self and others respectively.

In what is termed the 'moral model', people are held to be responsible for both past and future events. They are conceived as having full responsibility for their current state arrived at through their past actions and for dealing with the consequences of this condition. According to this view, individuals are seen by themselves and others as not putting in enough effort. The fault and the hope for change rests firmly with the agent concerned. Help is viewed as serving to remind individuals that they must act to help themselves. The strength of this model is its ability to remind those concerned that they must take personal responsibility for their own lives and for change. If people do not like the way things are, it is their responsibility to do something about it. Problems such as alcoholism, homosexuality and mental illness which were all initially treated using a moral approach have been replaced with treatment based on the medical model (Albee, 1969). The potential disadvantage of this concepualisation is that people can take it to extremes and view even innocent victims as being responsible in some way for their problems.

The compensatory model regards individuals as responsible for future but not for past events. Here people see themselves, and are seen by others, as having to deal with difficulties which have arisen through no fault of their own but through lack of environmental resources. This approach has the advantage of focusing attention on solutions rather than dwelling upon individuals' responsibility for their current state. Help can therefore be offered in the form of resources and can be perceived as being necessary for the solution to problems rather than as making up for some personal fault or deficiency.

In the medical model, those seeking assistance are regarded as having no responsibility for either past or future events. Medical interventions can be aimed at the level of faulty organs without the necessity to treat the patient as a person. The person under this model is not viewed as being responsible for the illness or its treatment. Help is provided by experts who can determine the exact nature of the problem and who will also accept responsibility for treating it. The clear advantage of the medical model in terms of coping is that it allows individuals to divest themselves of responsibility for their difficulties without fear of punishment. Mulford and Miller (1964) found that those who viewed alcoholism as a disease rather than as a personal weakness were more likely to prefer supportive treatments. The major shortcoming with the medical model, however, is that it can lead to over-dependence upon external agents. Wack and Rodin (1978) illustrate this problem well in their discussion of the helplessness that many nursing home patients feel when treated using this approach. The realisation that even simple roles, which promote individual responsibility, can have dramatic effects on both the physical and psychological health of older patients has led to many criticisms of this approach to caring (Langer and Rodin, 1976).

The fourth model, the enlightenment model, is one in which people are assumed to be responsible for their problems but not the solutions to them. Brickman *et al.* (1982) cite Alcoholics Anonymous as one example of a successful enlightenment model. New recruits to this organisation are forced to take responsibility for their past drinking behaviour and to admit that control of this behaviour at present is impossible without external help. The enlightenment model tends to come into play when individuals are no longer able to exert control over a habitual form of behaviour such as drinking or drug taking. The most consistent shortcoming associated with it is that it can lead the individual to become overly concerned with a particular problem so that the person's whole life revolves around it (see Cummings, 1979).

The choice of models and their applications

In applying models of helping behaviour two particular issues will be addressed. The first concerns which of the models provides the best framework for successful interactions in terms of improving competence. The second addresses the problems that are associated with interactions between individuals where two different conceptions of helping are being adopted. In both cases, evidence will be assessed in health and educational settings to illustrate the potential application of adopting a model-based approach.

Brickman et al. (1982, p. 368) hypothesise that, 'models in which people are held responsible for solutions (moral and compensatory models) are more likely to increase people's competence than models in which they are not held responsible for solutions (medical and enlightenment models).' In a review of studies which examine the effects of attributing symptoms to external causes and those which attribute progress to external causes they conclude that the evidence is inconclusive. Some studies show gains when subjects are given reasons to believe that their symptoms (e.g. anxiety, insomnia) are due to external rather than internal causes (Rodin and Langer, 1980; Ross et al., 1969) while other studies have shown no such effects (Chambliss and Murray, 1979; Singerman et al., 1976). Brickman and his colleagues suggest that these contradictory results may be due to the nature of such external attributions. When an external cause is suggested as underlying an individual's symptoms, it will lead to a reduction in anxiety but will also have the effect of reducing the degree to which the individual can take credit for subsequent improvement.

Evidence for the beneficial effects of attributing responsibility for improvement to internal factors is much less ambiguous. Liberman (1978), for example, found that subjects who believed (following experimental intervention) that their improvement was due to medication were significantly less likely to maintain this improvement over time than those who believed this was due to their own efforts. It would appear that attributing responsibility for solutions to external causes leads to improvement, but that such gains may be temporary. Miller et al. (1975), in a classroom study, found that primary school children who were rewarded through persuasion by their teacher that they should keep their classroom tidy by reducing the amount of litter did so, but only for a limited time. Those children, however, who had internalised this tidiness lesson and attributed this new-found improvement to themselves maintained tidy behaviour over time. In general, it appears that individuals will tend to sustain behaviour which they attribute to internal factors better than behaviour associated with external factors (see Lepper and Greene,

1978). A similar pattern of results can be found in the attribution and helplessness literature with subjects who believe that they are in control of events, being more resilient in the face of stress and adverse conditions (Seligman, 1975; Dweck, 1975).

As children pass through the various stages of education from primary school to secondary school and in some cases college or university, they are faced with contrasting models of behaviour. It is possible to discern those that Brickman and his colleagues propose operating at differing levels of education. In primary school, learning is determined largely by the teacher using a medical model. At this stage children learn to accept and follow the instructions given by the teacher. As they progress through secondary school, they are able to accept more responsibility and adopt a compensatory model. They learn to attend class regularly and the values of turning in work on time. In college or university, students are faced with a much less structured learning environment in which they can create and define problems in their own way. There is much more emphasis on individualistic approaches with students developing an intrinsic motivation for their subject.

Evidence in favour of compensatory or moral models of student performance at present is patchy. Deci *et al.* (1981), in a survey of over thirty primary schools, found that teachers who used rewards in order to give students information, as opposed to those who used rewards to control behaviour, produced more competent and intrinsically motivated students. Similar results have also been reported by Dweck (1975) and de Charms (1976). Brickman *et al.* (1982) suggest that while in general holding pupils responsible for their learning appears to be beneficial, this conclusion needs qualification. Giving pupils too much responsibility can lead to problems in terms of lack of teacher support and discipline (Swann and Snyder, 1980). Finally, as has been reported in earlier chapters, socioeconomic status appears to be a complicating factor with some studies reporting that students do worse following such interventions (Kolb, 1965). This would suggest that different models of help may be required for particular types of student.

The application of models of helping which fail to take into account the distinction between attribution of responsibility for problems and solutions can lead to severe management difficulties for health professionals. Carers are faced with the choice of viewing patients/clients as being responsible for both their problems and their solutions and therefore be unable to offer help, or they can hold them responsible for neither and offer help which undermines the individual's sense of control. Brickman *et al.* (1982) point out that among professional helpers success may be as beneficial to the helper as the client. Therapists, they argue, are supposed to be helpful since this is perceived as their role. Continuing to apply models which are inappropriate to the client's needs not only may undermine the treatment programme itself, but also, in the long term, may lead to a loss of self-esteem and active involvement among staff. Utilising inadequate models of help over extended periods can produce burn-out (Maslach, 1978), a problem which is becoming increasingly common among nurses, teachers and other professional groups.

ATTRIBUTIONAL RETRAINING

It is now a well-established finding within attributional research that when failure is attributed to low ability, which is viewed by the individual as something stable and relatively uncontrollable, it is likely to recur in the future. If, however, failure is attributed to lack of effort, it presents the individual with a much more optimistic expectation. Attributional retraining is based on attempts to change the failing individual's attribution from one of low ability to lack of effort. Dweck (1975) reported the first such retraining scheme with primary school children who had been classified by teachers and psychologists as 'helpless'. These children were doing badly in school and were assumed to be attributing their failure in the classroom context to lack of ability. The attributional retraining consisted of a series of sessions in which they were taught to attribute failure to lack of effort, rather than lack of ability, following induced failure in a laboratory setting. After retraining, the behaviour and cognitions of the children were compared to a control group. The results of a large number of such laboratory studies suggest that attributional retraining leads to both improved attributions to lack of effort and increased achievement (Dweck, 1975; Anderson and Jennings, 1980; Zoeller *et al.*, 1983). Studies which have examined the results of retraining in classroom or college settings have demonstrated similar improvements (Borkowski *et al.*, 1988; Perry and Penner, 1990). Graham (1991), while applauding the progress made in this area, highlights the narrowness which characterises current retraining approaches. She points to the lack of attention that has been paid to emotions as motivators of achievement and the tendency to focus almost exclusively on failure. Maladaptive attributions for success are in her view equally likely to prove responsive to such retraining.

CONCLUSIONS

A number of conclusions can be drawn from current attributional research which have clear implications for those who seek to use rewards in professional contexts. The first and most dramatic of these is the realisation that rewards do not always lead to positive outcomes. This is most clearly evident in the examination of particular teacher behaviours which, although positive, serve as indirect cues to low ability. These include praise following success and pity following failure (in both cases following easy tasks) and giving help when it is not requested by the student. Such unintended effects of praise are most likely in situations where the pupil has little existing awareness of his aptitude for the task but is led to believe that the teacher has such insight, believes that the task is relatively undemanding, and notices that others do not receive praise for their comparable achievements. In addition, the application of negative behaviours such as assigning blame following failure and withholding help have been shown to have effects upon students' perceptions of their ability. Attributional research therefore provides a framework which highlights the complexity of the use of rewards and punishments in professional settings.

Some research findings in these areas suggest that the use of rewards in such contexts needs to be balanced by the use of constructive performance-linked criticism. In environments where performance-linked criticism is absent, the value of rewards such as praise is likely to be undermined. The role of environmental considerations was also highlighted through an examination of the effects that task-oriented or ego-involving circumstances have upon subjects' attributions of effort and ability. It is clear that teachers' behaviours have to be viewed within the organisational context of the task being undertaken, in order to fully understand the effects of such behaviours on children's attributions.

The role of models of helping was also highlighted in order to illustrate the value of an attributional analysis in both education and health. This demonstrates the importance of obtaining and using feedback from professional interactions in order to determine which model of help will be most successful for a particular client or student. In addition, the dangers of applying inadequate or inappropriate models over extended periods were highlighted in terms of the negative consequences that this has for both parties. Following Brickman *et al.* (1982), it was suggested that models which hold individuals responsible for solutions to problems, rather than for problems themselves, are more likely to produce better results in both education and health. Finally, the application of attributional retraining was examined in classroom settings. Despite the limited number of studies that have been carried out under classroom as opposed to laboratory conditions, the results suggest that retraining individuals to attribute failure to lack of effort as opposed to lack of ability has positive advantages in terms of students' self-esteem, motivation and effort.

In conclusion, attributional research highlights the importance of viewing rewards as useful only in so far as they achieve positive results. The utility of an attributional analysis lies in its ability to help professionals who make use of rewards in educational and health settings both to consider the model of help that they are adopting, and to more clearly appreciate how their behaviour influences those around them. Attributional retraining programmes, although still in their infancy, offer exciting possibilities for changing how individuals view both success and failure.

Chapter 8

Power, social influence and reward

INTRODUCTION

Dispensing rewards can confer a certain degree of power on the provider. Being in a position to release or withhold sought-after benefits makes possible the exercise of control over recipients. In order to be favoured in this way, they must abide by the conditions of receipt that the rewarder decides to impose. This is likely to be particularly telling when the benefit is highly desirable and alternative sources are limited. While people have a reasonable understanding of what power is and can recognise it in its most obvious forms, they are surprising ill-informed about the more subtle ways in which they can be influenced by it.

In this chapter, the importance of distinguishing power from other related concepts such as social influence and dominance is outlined. Power is conceived of as the ability to achieve goals through intentional influence, although the importance of incidental influence is acknowledged. Six different bases of power are outlined. These are legitimate, reward, coercive, expert, referent and informational, and the advantages and disadvantages that each presents are examined. The reasons why individuals are susceptible to influence from others are discussed in terms of normative and informational considerations. These explain the impact of influence through the basic needs to be liked and to have our views supported by others. The psychological importance of these processes for both the maintenance of mental health and communication with others is emphasised. The different types of social influence that can be employed are outlined, noting the inherent advantages and disadvantages of each. Illustrative examples of how these strategies can be used are described along with ways in which they can be successfully resisted. The importance of taking account of bi-directional and incidental influences in the use of power is discussed to accentuate the interactive nature of the process and to highlight the need for appropriate social skills to implement successful strategies.

DISTINGUISHING POWER FROM SOCIAL INFLUENCE AND DOMINANCE

Although most individuals have a fairly clear notion of what power is and can recognise its use in society, it has been described as one of the most difficult concepts to define adequately (see Bierstedt, 1950). Perhaps the most compelling reason for the lack of clarity surrounding it is that it has been used to explain several quite different aspects of interpersonal influence. Before considering power further therefore it is necessary to distinguish it from influence and dominance.

Social influence can be said to exist when the actions of one individual have a causal effect on the outcomes or life events of another. This is perhaps best exemplified in close relationships where the actions and events in one person's life have a consistent effect on those of the partner (e.g. marriage). When this influence is one-sided, it moves beyond influence and becomes dominance. In dominance influence is exerted so that resources, responsibilities and rights reside primarily with one individual, usually to the detriment of another.

Power, by contrast, may be defined as the capacity to alter the actions of others (Kelman, 1974), or in more specific terms as the *ability* to achieve ends through influence (Huston, 1983). It is quite possible for individuals to be influential by failing to achieve their goals, but such individuals are seldom powerful. The powerful person is therefore someone who has the ability to effect *intentional* change in others. The importance of these two aspects of power, namely viewing it as an ability and as intentional influence, also illustrates the difficulties that researchers face in this area. While theoretically it is possible to talk about and distinguish intentional and unintentional influence, in practice the two are closely interlinked. The powerful individual who is able to exert intentional influence is also likely to serve as a source of unintentional influence as well. Similarly, the notion of power as ability poses difficulties in its assessment. If power is viewed as an ability, it is something that can be either used or not used. In addition, when it is used it will not always be effective and, finally, even when it is used successfully the full extent of its effects may not be easily apparent unless it is opposed. In short, the conceptualization of power as ability is fraught with the same difficulties that have faced researchers interested in investigating other abilities.

FORMS OF POWER

It is useful to distinguish between the different bases or forms of power that are available to compare and contrast their effectiveness. In the present chapter the framework adopted by French and Raven (1959), in their classic paper on power and influence, will be used. They identified five initial sources of power: legitimate power, reward power, coercive power, expert power, and referent power to which a sixth, information power, was subsequently added (Raven, 1965). These different sources will be examined in turn with the advantages and disadvantages that each presents.

Legitimate power

Legitimate power as defined by French and Raven (1959, p. 159) is 'that power which stems from internalized values in (one individual O) which dictate that (another individual P) has a legitimate right to influence (O) and that (O) has an obligation to accept this influence'. This form of power thus rests on a social agreement that under specific circumstances one individual has the right or authority to direct the behaviour of another. Examples of legitimate power are to be found in government and in highly structured bodies such as armies where certain senior members, for example ministers or generals, have (an accepted) right to influence the behaviour of lesser employees.

The major advantage of legitimate power is that it can be invoked without the need for the powerful individual to be physically present to ensure appropriate actions are taken. This is because people in general will obey the instructions of those they believe to have legitimate authority over them. The disadvantage of this form of influence is that it is dependent upon social agreement. The demands of an individual holding legitimate authority over us will only be obeyed within the socially accepted bounds of their sphere of influence. We will obey the instructions of a car park attendant while we are in the car park, but are less likely to obey similar instructions given outside this restricted environment.

Coercive power

Coercive power is exerted when one person controls the punishments that may be applied to another. The extent of this type depends on the ability of an individual to control the occurrence of negative events that will hinder or block another's goals. Punishments that can be used range from physical and verbal abuse to more subtle forms of nonverbal behaviour such as a look of disapproval. Coercive power is exercised by letting other people know clearly what you expect from them and ensuring that they are aware of the negative consequences that will follow if they do not follow these directives. The use of coercive power, therefore, results in compliance rather than any more permanent psychological or behavioural change.

While the use of coercive power can be highly effective when used against individuals, it poses problems when used against groups. Several interesting suggestions have been forwarded by social psychologists to account for this difficulty. The first problem that has been identified is that coercion, when directed towards groups, leads to increased group cohesion and solidarity (Tedeschi, 1972). Secondly, the use of coercive power is often reciprocated by groups, leading to an escalation in the encounter with ever-increasing punishment being meted out by the two sides.

A third reason coercive power may be counterproductive is the effect it sometimes has on a group's perceptions of the value of a threatened activity. Emphasising the negative consequences that will ensue if a particular activity is continued may lead to this activity acquiring added value. Finally, coercion can produce a backlash against the coercive agent that can be out of proportion to the original coercive attempt. This appears to occur because groups feel more justified in dealing out very harsh treatment to those they perceive as threatening. This can sometimes extend to calls for the coercive individual to be removed altogether (Tedeschi *et al.*, 1974).

Expert power

This form of power is based on the attribution of special knowledge to the influencing agent. The use of 'scientists' in adverts to sell products such as washing powders is an example. We tend to assume that specialists in a particular field who have gone through extended training (e.g. a doctor), or have acquired a qualification or degree, have expertise within their areas. In this respect, expert power can be acquired by anyone who, through luck or practice, can demonstrate a competence in a particular area or activity. This can be anything from playing a musical instrument to performing a new dance move. Raven *et al.* (1975) notes that wives in Western cultures are more likely to attribute expert power to their spouses than any other particular type. However, husbands who have similar educational and occupational backgrounds to their spouses are not as readily perceived in this way. The major advantage of expert power is that it can influence individuals without the need for the type of checking that is required with coercive power. Like legitimate power it has the disadvantage that it is dependent upon social agreement that the person concerned possesses particular skills or knowledge.

Referent power

Here power is based upon identification. If someone possesses characteristics that are particularly admired by us, we are likely to look to that person as a role model. The act of identifying with another involves a marked tendency to imitate the attitudes and behaviours of that individual. Christians, for example, through identification with Christ should be more likely to copy his behaviour. This example, however, indicates the potential mediating effects of rewards and punishments on such identifications. We may admire an individual's characteristics and actions and also be aware that copying their behaviour involves costs as well as gains.

This is one of the most advantageous forms of power since it can be employed without creating any hostility in the target. Because the target desires to be similar to the referent, it is not necessary to influence the former by direct means. In addition, it requires no checks by the referent since the target is making voluntary changes in his or her attitudes and behaviour. Indeed, the referent may sometimes be completely unaware that he or she is being used as a role model. Since referent power is based upon identification, making shared similarities or characteristics known to the target is likely to heighten its effect.

Information power

As the world becomes ever more complex, the value of information increases, enabling those who hold it to maintain control over both events and people. People tend to act according to their beliefs and attitudes towards different topics, and these beliefs and attitudes are in turn dependent upon the information that they have available. It is a frightening thought that much of what we know about the world is conveyed through information that is directly controlled by others (through television, radio and newspapers) rather than through personal experience. In societies where these sources are controlled by the state, people can be given information in the form of propaganda that is supportive of a particular viewpoint. The skilful use of this form of power enables the individual or state to manipulate the attitudes and beliefs of others without them being aware of it. Information power, if used skilfully, can therefore work without arousing hostility or the need for checking since the information becomes a part of the individual's own belief structure.

Reward power

Reward power is based on one person's ability to reward another. It will be appreciated that, from our earliest moments as young children, we are responded to positively by our parents for displaying appropriate behaviour. As we get older the rewards we respond to may change, but our behaviour is still likely to be influenced in this way by others. One can acquire reward power either by being able to introduce positive events or by removing negative or unpleasant events that are blocking the goals of other individuals. Rewards can be applied directly by giving another attention, praise or material inducements, or they can be used indirectly through controlling access to positively valued resources (see Chapter Two). To exercise this type of power it is necessary for the agent to indicate how they would like the target to behave, and to promise either implicitly or explicitly that compliance with this directive will be rewarded. Since the exercise of power implies that those subjected to it may not wish to comply with such directives, reward power normally includes checking to ensure that instructions have been followed.

So far we have only dealt with reward power that is based on fairly large and clearly observable rewards or payoff. While there is little doubt that such ap- proaches are effective in producing compliance, they may have little effect on a recipient's underlying attitudes. The reason large rewards tend to lead to com- pliance but little attitude change has been explained through notions of *cognitive dissonance*. When we are given a large reward for doing something, we feel obliged to act in an appropriate manner even though we may disagree with the actions we are in effect being forced to take. The important aspect here is that we can justify our behaviour in terms of the size of the reward being offered. In this way we can avoid conflict between what we do and how we think and feel about it. When, however, the reward offered is much smaller, we experience difficulty in reconcil- ing our behaviour with our underlying beliefs, leading to the arousal of unpleasant feelings (cognitive dissonance). Festinger and Carlsmith (1959), for example, gave subjects either a small reward (one dollar) or a large reward (twenty dollars) for telling other individuals that the boring tasks that they had just performed were interesting. When they asked subjects later to rate how pleasant they actually found the tasks, those in the low payment condition rated them as significantly more pleasant than those in the high payment condition. This finding has been replicated in many subsequent experiments (Riess and Schlenker, 1977).

Due to the shortcomings inherent in the explicit use of reward power which may be cast as an attempt to control, it is often used implicitly, so that such negative effects are minimised. Given the importance of intrinsic motivation and the need for self-determination (see Chapter Two), blatantly explicit rewards for actions that would not otherwise be contemplated may trigger resentment. Rewards producing negative affect reactions towards the source are an interesting contrast to the earlier discussion of interpersonal attraction. In these circumstances, rewards which are given in smaller doses over an extended time span can lead to much more satisfactory changes in individual behaviour. The rewarded individual over time internalises the contingencies that govern the likelihood of reward and anticipates the desired actions of the one exercising reward power. In this sense rewarding events cannot be studied in isolation since they are dependent upon the overall reinforcement history of interactions between individuals. This point is perhaps best illustrated by the difficulty that observers can have in spotting the use of rewards in the later stages of this power technique.

The implicit use of reward power, involving as it does the notion of identification, highlights another important point relating to the different bases of power, namely that they are interrelated. Firstly, it is clear that these do not operate in isolation. Individuals who possess high reward power are often found to have high coercive power as well. Secondly, the use of one type of power can also have effects on other forms. The use of coercive power can reduce referent power since the former involves punishment, making us less likely to identify with the power user. Reward power can increase referent power, while legitimate power through its association with high status may have a similar enhancing effect on referent power. The general point to be emphasised is that while different types of power can be theoretically identified, in practice they are hard to separate. The use of power in real life is likely therefore to involve more than one form.

NORMATIVE AND INFORMATIONAL SOCIAL INFLUENCE

Before discussing the different ways in which influence can be exerted on others, it is useful to ask why individuals are susceptible to it and what psychological benefits this might bring them. While many different factors have been suggested to account for this tendency to conform, the most important relate to two basic needs, already encountered: firstly, to be liked and, secondly, to have personal views supported by others. This latter need, the desire to be correct or right, can be satisfied through two different sources of information, namely our own experiences and information provided by others. In our lives we learn quickly to depend upon both sources of information to give us a more balanced view of the environment. Informational social influence therefore relies upon the individual's trust in the correctness of judgements made by people.

The impact of social influence is best illustrated in a series of classic experiments carried out by Asch (1955). In these studies Asch wanted to determine whether individuals would rely on their own judgements or be swayed by the judgements of those around them. This was a test of the effect of informational social influence: would individuals rely on information gathered through their senses or on the information provided by others? To create a meaningful discrepancy between these two sources of information, Asch devised a simple comparison task requiring the individual to select one of three lines of differing length as equal in length to a standard line. The task was constructed so that it was obvious that one of the three lines was the correct choice for each of the twelve sets of comparisons made in the study. Unknown to his subjects, Asch included seven accomplices in each group-testing session along with each new subject. These confederates were asked to select an obviously wrong line in the comparisons, and the group was organised so that all but one of these individuals called out their choices to the experimenter before the naive subject. To Asch's surprise he found that in one third of trials his naive subjects gave incorrect responses. In other words subjects were prepared to put their trust in the information of others, even when this conflicted with the information gained through their own eyes. Subsequent discussions with subjects revealed that many subjects in the experiment knew that the choices made were in error, but did not wish to appear different from other members of the group. Recent investigation of this effect by Jennings and George (1984) suggests that while some subjects respond to informational social influence by experiencing genuine changes in their perceptions, the vast majority do not and simply go along to be accepted by other members of the group.

Given the impact that information provided by others can have on people, it is worthwhile to outline briefly the psychological and communicative value that this information provides. Firstly, it serves as a basis for self-evaluation in providing us with a comparator against which we can examine and modify our views and abilities. The process of social comparison has been found to operate extensively both in very young children (Mosatche and Bragonier, 1981) and in school and college settings (Marsh and Parker, 1984). Indeed, it can be found in most aspects of society.

A second and related value that information from others provides has to do with feedback. Festinger (1954), in his theory of social comparison, suggests that we select out specific others on the basis of their similarity to us to gain more relevant feedback about ourselves. This feedback can be used in several different ways to aid the individual. It can function to protect at times when an accurate or realistic self-appraisal may be damaging. This can be done by comparing ourselves to others who are of lower ability. Sachs (1982) has revealed how the individual is more receptive to positive rather than accurate information when they are feeling down. Hakmiller (1966) reports a similar effect among students who have performed badly in exams. Such individuals tend to choose a classmate who scores more poorly than themselves to gain a more favourable comparison. Information from others can thus boost people's self-images through seeking comparisons that show them up more favourably. Wilson and Benner (1971) suggest that individuals with high and low levels of self-esteem may use different strategies in selecting potential comparators. Those with high esteem are more likely to seek out people who are successful, since they will gain most information and self-worth from such comparisons. Those with low esteem seek out individuals lower in ability to avoid any negative effects that would derive from upward comparisons.

The final use to which information from others can be put is to achieve self-improvement through the selection of superior comparators (Nosanchuk and Erickson, 1985). This strategy appears to be most common in competitive situations, although it has both advantages and disadvantages for the individual. By comparing ourselves to superior others we can, according to Cialdini *et al.* (1976), 'borrow status' from them. However, choosing an individual who is too far above oneself in ability can pose problems in terms of self-esteem. This appears to be one reason why people who have mental disorders have particular problems in this regard (see Parker and Kleiner, 1968).

If individuals rely too heavily on their own judgements, their general views about the world and the way other people view them may be very different from reality. The psychological importance of perceiving oneself accurately is an essential prerequisite for meaningful communication. If individuals do not pay attention to information provided by others to both validate and correct their views about the world, they will experience difficulty in both attaining a stable view of themselves and in interacting meaningfully with those around them. (Issues of self-enhancement versus self-verification were addressed in Chapter Two.)

The second source of influence identified in the Asch study depends on the need to be liked by others. This form is termed normative social influence and involves the use of referent others to tell us what we should and should not do in different social settings. Deutsch and Gerard (1955), for example, were able to increase group members' conformity through promising rewards to those groups that made fewest errors on experimental tasks. The increased interdependency of group members following the promise of reward led to a significant improvement in group conformity compared with a control condition. Felson and Reed (1986) utilised normative influence to explain the shared expectations that group members experienced in evaluating themselves. This shows that evaluations in groups are constrained by shared group norms that largely determine individual behaviour.

Riesman (1950), in an early study of the 'reference-others' chosen by Americans, distinguishes between 'inner-directed' and 'other-directed' choices. For some (inner-directed) individuals the family serves as a point of reference from which they learn the appropriate rules and behaviours to deal with life. These rules and values are subsequently internalised giving the individual a sense of what is right and wrong; an internal yardstick against which new events can be judged. With the increasing demands of society and the subsequent need for increased communication, Riesman argues that American society has become dominated by other-directed reference choices. Reflecting the greater complexity of society, other-directed individuals rely on external peers and friends to determine morality and behaviour. This enables a more flexible and changing yardstick to be developed through which the actions and behaviours of more diverse others can be judged and understood. Reference-others thus provide individuals with values and norms and, equally importantly, with a way of defining themselves through social comparisons. (See Goffman (1959) for an alternative conceptualization of the way that referent-others operate in terms of self-presentation.)

TYPES OF SOCIAL INFLUENCE

In this section the different types of social influence that can be used by individuals will be examined along with the advantages and disadvantages of each. The implications of these strategies in applied settings will be discussed along with ways in which they can be resisted. Before outlining the different types of influence that have been studied, however, it is worth quickly examining the evidence which suggests that women and men may both react differently to, and also employ different influence strategies. This is an important question, since any attempt to describe the utility of contrasting approaches would have to consider such differences (Crutchfield, 1955). Fortunately, recent research suggests that not only do men and women not differ in their susceptibility to such strategies (Rule et al., 1985; Bisanz and Rule, 1989), but furthermore use them in similar ways (see Eagly and Johnson, 1990).

One area where gender differences have been reported is in studies of male and female speech and in conversational interruptions. Lakoff (1975), in an examination of the content of male and female speech, found that the former tended to be direct, assertive and adult while the latter was immature, overly polite and passive. Her findings were based on differences between the sexes in the use of qualifiers such as 'probably' or 'sort of' and 'tag questions' which soften the impact of statements. While much of this work was based on small samples and subjective evaluations, experimental research suggests that such differences exist (Crosby and Nyquist, 1977). These differences are important since Zimmerman and West (1975) relate conversational interruptions (the ability to change the topic of conversation) to social power. In a study of adult conversations they found that while males and females showed similar rates of interruption when interacting with members of their own sex, males interrupted significantly more in interactions between the sexes. Similarly, Ridgeway et al. (1985) report the use of significantly more nonverbal signals of social power (e.g. longer eye contact and decreased time in turn-taking during conversations) by males than females in mixed-sex pairings. (See Berger, 1985 for a more detailed discussion of this issue.) These gender differences are of more benefit in highlighting the subtle forms through which social power can be expressed since they may be caused by sex role stereotyping.

Authority influence

The most direct technique that can be employed to change the behaviour of others is to demand that they comply with your instructions. This is the least subtle of all the techniques of social influence and is associated with the use of legitimate power. Obeying a police officer's or doctor's instructions can be explained in terms of their legitimate authority, but disturbing evidence suggests that we can be just as susceptible to those lacking in such power.

Milgram (1965, 1974), in a series of now famous experiments, demonstrated the extent to which people would blindly obey instructions from others. In his experiments subjects were told that they would be helping in an experiment into the effects of punishment on learning. Their experimental role was to deliver shocks to another person when they made mistakes during a simple learning task. In reality, the learner was a confederate of the experimenter's who made large numbers of mistakes that had to be punished by moving to a higher shock level. The shock levels ranged from 15 to 450 volts via thirty different switches on the equipment. Unknown to the experimental subjects, the learner was not actually receiving any current, but pretending to be responding as one would expect at each level of intensity.

Subjects soon found themselves facing a dilemma. Should they continue to give shocks to the subject at ever-increasing levels, convinced that they were clearly causing suffering to the other individual, or disobey the experimenter? When subjects complained about the effects on the learner, the experimenter at first responded with 'Please go on' and at later stages with 'It is essential that you continue' and 'You have no choice; you must go on'. Faced with this situation, Milgram found that 65 per cent of his subjects went right through to the maximum 450 volt setting. At first, it was thought that such startling results could only occur in a laboratory, as opposed to real life settings, but a series of experiments soon displayed the robustness of this effect (Kilham and Mann, 1974; Milgram, 1974).

While there are clearly ethical problems raised by such research, it nevertheless suggests several techniques that can be employed to influence others. The first of these is to employ influence in small steps rather than to demand that people comply with extreme requests. In the Milgram experiment it is extremely unlikely that individuals would have obeyed the authority figure if they had been asked to deliver 450 volts straight away. Once an individual starts to obey the small instructions given by another they are more likely to continue with later larger ones. One of the most critical aspects of authority influence, therefore, is to employ a strategy that is gradual in nature gaining acceptance through a series of steps.

A second strategy that can be successfully employed is to highlight authority through titles, badges, uniforms or suits that remind people that they are dealing with someone of importance. Wilson (1968), in a study of Australian college students' ratings of an unknown visiting academic, varied the title (student, demonstrator, lecturer, senior lecturer, professor) with which the visitor was introduced to different classes. Following these introductions the classes were asked to estimate the visitor's height. It was found that his perceived height increased by two and a half inches when introduced as a professor as opposed to a student. The clear relationship between perceived height and status conferred by means of a simple title demonstrates the power of signals of authority. Many other studies have shown similar effects for uniforms and business suits (Bushman, 1984, 1988). An important consideration raised by this study, and one that has been noted by people who make commercials for television, is that the title by itself is enough to convince us. We tend to believe actors who play the parts of scientists or doctors on television even though we may be aware that they are acting.

The effects of authority even reach into areas that one might presume would be resistant to such influence. Hofling *et al.* (1966) were concerned that nursing staff might be following instructions from doctors without using their training to determine whether these instructions were correct. To test this, they made phone calls to nurses on wards in which they identified themselves as a doctor and asked the nurse to give a drug to a specific patient. This drug was prescribed over the phone, at a dose that nurses would know was dangerous, by an individual the nurse had never met before. Despite these breaches of both hospital procedure and dosage, 95 per cent of the nurses would have given the patient the drug if they had not been intercepted.

The influence of authority, while considerable, can be effectively countered by several strategies. Firstly, if individuals can see someone else standing up to an authority figure, they are less likely to obey (Powers and Geen, 1972). Secondly, if people are reminded that they, and not others, are responsible for the consequences of their actions, they are much less likely to obey authority figures. Finally, as people become more familiar with the operation of authority, they appear to be able to resist instructions both by questioning the authority's motives and expertise and by being aware of the type of influence that is being exerted upon them (see Sherman, 1980).

Reciprocation strategies

An unspoken rule of life, and one that is shown in Chapter Nine to play a significant part within relationships, is reciprocation of rewards. When someone gives you something, you are placed under an obligation to pay them back. Clearly, this rule applies in all human societies and the success of cooperative living depends upon it (see Gouldner, 1960; Leakey and Lewin, 1978). In its most simplistic form this strategy involves the offer of a seemingly free gift. This can be anything from a free sample to doing a small favour for another. Once delivered this initial gift makes the individual more likely to reciprocate. Many sales representatives use this technique both to introduce a new customer to their product and to engender an obligation to buy larger quantities of the product on a subsequent visit.

A more subtle variation of the reciprocation rule involves making use of the finding that having a small request granted is likely to lead to compliance with a much larger later request. Two competing explanations have been offered to explain the success of this strategy. Rittle (1981) believes that individuals who assent to small requests come to view helping in a much less threatening and more positive way. When the boss appears and you are aware that he is going to get you to do something, you may feel under threat and prepare to resist. However, when the request is much smaller than anticipated, the situation becomes less threatening. With defences lowered, one is less prepared for any subsequent larger request. An alternative explanation for the success of the multiple request strategy is that agreeing to a small request leads to changes in the way we view ourselves. Having complied with the small request, we come to see ourselves as being helpful. Having done so, we then find it difficult to refuse a further demand, since this would be inconsistent with our new self-image. While both explanations have received experimental support, the need-for-consistency explanation is attracting more interest (see Eisenberg et al., 1987).

The other compliance strategy that is based on multiple requests is the aptly called 'door-in-the-face' technique. This works in exactly the opposite way to the 'foot-in-the-door' strategy mentioned above. Rather than making a small request first, the individual makes a large one that is followed by a much smaller demand. Cialdini et al. (1975) confronted students with a large request (to serve as unpaid volunteer counsellors for two hours a week for two years). When this was refused, they asked for a much smaller favour: taking delinquents to the zoo on a two hour trip. They found that 50 per cent of students approached using this strategy agreed to this latter request, compared to only 17 per cent of students in a control group who received the smaller request alone. As with the foot-in-the-door strategy two explanations have been offered for the success of this approach. One relates compliance to the need for reciprocal concessions. By backing down to a lower request when an initial attempt is refused, we concede ground. Faced with a second request, the recipient may feel obligated to make a similar concession in return to balance this out. Pendleton and Batson (1979) offer an alternative explanation that focuses on self-presentation. Refusing a unrealistically large request, they argue, is justifiable and does not harm our self-image. If we then go on to refuse a smaller request as well, we will find this more difficult to justify since it makes us look unreasonable. Under this view we prefer to take a small material loss rather than a drop in self-image. While both the foot-in-the-door and the door-in-the-face strategies are successful, it appears that the former may be more so in a much wider range of contexts. (See Cann et al., 1975; Patch, 1986.)

Both the foot-in-the-door and the door-in-the-face strategies rely on the need to reciprocate or balance out the rewards that flow between individuals. It is also clear that people can make subtle use of this principle to control the behaviour of others. This is one of the most difficult methods to counter. Cialdini (1988) suggests that simply rejecting favours or gifts when offered, although successful, is too abrasive a technique to be used in such circumstances. It also denies the reciprocation principle that plays such a central role in interactions. Instead, Cialdini suggests we should accept such gifts or concessions in good faith but be prepared to redefine them as tricks if necessary. Once such redefinition of the reason for the original gift occurs, the need to reciprocate is removed.

Ingratiation strategies

A further set of techniques that rely upon enhancing the rewarding aspects of the individual are ingratiation strategies. Chapter Six summarises one well-documented strategy based upon promoting interpersonal attraction through pointing out the similarities between interactors. The more similarities that can be highlighted the more that person will be liked, making the other in turn more likely to follow his or her suggestions (see Byrne, 1971). Alternative techniques can be usefully subdivided into those that try to enhance other people's perceptions of the ingratiating individual and those which try to enhance their perceptions of themselves.

Self-enhancement strategies include such simple but effective techniques as improving one's dress and grooming; presenting information that suggests one is competent, sincere and intelligent; or associating oneself with persons or occasions that are viewed positively by the other. While these strategies are straightforward, they require the employment of considerable social skill to achieve a balanced performance. Baron (1986) highlights graphically the pitfalls that can befall individuals who try to portray too glowing a picture of themselves in interview settings. The ability to use such techniques subtly, interlaced with appropriate self-disclosure and self-deprecation skills to counterbalance impressions that the individual may not be open and honest, is essential. Self-deprecation techniques provide the other person with negative information about the speaker, making the latter appear more human and trustworthy.

The most common strategy, known as other-enhancement, makes use of the verbal and nonverbal cues outlined in Chapters Three and Four. This involves the use of eye contact and other positive nonverbal cues such as smiles and nods to express an interest in the other person. The improvement in communication that occurs as a result is backed up by the use of praise to boost the self-esteem of the other person. This technique is partially adopted in counselling to encourage the development of smoother interactions and to build trust, but perhaps is found in its fullest form (with flattery included) in management settings (see Linden and Mitchell, 1988).

Incidental and bi-directional influence

In understanding the impact of power upon the individual, it is necessary to acknowledge the role of unintentional influence as well as that which is intentional. In Chapter Two, the role of observational learning was outlined stressing the important part that models (both real and mediated) can play in influencing the behaviour of others (Sims and Manz, 1981; Dickson et al., 1989). Clearly, people will adopt modelled behaviour without being asked to do so both through identifying with the model and because they perceive that either reward or expectancy of reward will follow from behaving in this way.

In addition, it is important to note that influence does not operate in a vacuum; it occurs through interactions between individuals. The bi-directional nature of influence emerged largely as a result of work by developmental psychologists into interactions between parents and young children. At first it was thought that influence could only flow in one direction, with parents influencing children but not the other way around. Research quickly indicated, however, that even young children influence the behaviour of their parents (see Bell, 1971; Stone *et al.*, 1973). The acknowledgement of bi-directional and unintentional influence in the operation of power underlines both the importance of viewing power within an interactionist framework and the need for those who set out to influence others to possess well-developed social skills to employ influence strategies.

CONCLUSION

In this chapter the concepts of power and social influence were examined, highlighting the central role that rewards play both in conferring power on people and in the types of influence they exert. Power, following Huston (1983), was defined as the ability to achieve ends through (intentional) influence. The different bases of power – legitimate, reward, coercive, expert, referent and information – were examined in turn, and the advantages and disadvantages of each were outlined. While distinctions can be made between these in theoretical terms, in practice they are found to have considerable interdependence. The reasons why individuals are susceptible to social influence were examined in terms of the psychological and communicative value that normative and informational influence provides. These allow us to compare ourselves to others to ensure our views of the world are correct and to protect or improve ourselves by making either downward or upward comparisons. In addition, normative social influence provides us with referent others to tell us what we should and should not do in different social settings and distribute rewards accordingly.

Sex differences in social influence were addressed to illustrate the subtle ways in which the process can be expressed through eye contact, communication interruptions, and turn-taking. It was argued that while such differences exist, they reflect sex role stereotyping rather than underlying differences between the sexes.

Three different types of social influence strategies were examined, based on authority, reciprocation and ingratiation. Each of these operates through the use of reward and was found to be highly effective if used subtly. Ways of resisting each of these strategies were presented, enabling individuals to recognise and counter their effects.

Finally, the importance of viewing power and social influence in an interactionist sense was highlighted through the role of bi-directional and unintentional influence. These effects, combined with the need for subtlety in the use of influence techniques, suggest that the use of power and social influence is likely to be highly dependent upon the development of appropriate social skills if such strategies are to be successfully employed.

Chapter 9

Rewarding relationships

INTRODUCTION

The role of interpersonal rewards in determining the ways in which relationships develop, how they are strengthened and built up, and how they can weaken and end are discussed in this chapter. Levinger's (1983) five-stage model, which suggests that relationships can be classified into acquaintance, build-up, consolidation, deterioration and ending phases, each with its own unique characteristics, is adopted as a useful framework. The use of rewards within relationships is examined at both a theoretical and a practical level. Drawing upon reinforcement, exchange and equity theories, the role of rewarding behaviour is outlined while the specific skills and strategies which are required to either build up, maintain or repair damaged relationships are discussed. The way in which individuals need to vary the use of these strategies and skills at different stages is highlighted by drawing upon both theoretical studies and an examination of the practical problems faced by partners. The potential benefits of adopting a skill-based approach to understanding relationships are discussed along with the practical value that this approach offers those who work in this area in a professional capacity.

THEORIES OF RELATIONSHIPS

In order to understand why people engage in relationships, it seems sensible to ask the question why such associations are necessary in the first place and what benefits they offer. This will be looked at from two perspectives: firstly, the value of relationships will be addressed through an examination of the theoretical explanations that have been offered to account for them and, secondly, the practical and psychological benefits that relationships offer will be highlighted in terms of the physical and emotional support they provide.

By adopting an evolutionary perspective, sociobiological theories attempt to explain familial liaisons in terms of the protection of shared genes. The argument here is that humans like animals have a vested interest in ensuring that their genes will survive and spread through the population. Since the genetic make-up of family members is similar, it is argued that we have developed over time strategies which will serve to protect our family gene pools and help them to survive into future generations. While it appears reasonable to suggest that genetic factors play a part in determining social bonds, the evidence is much stronger for their effects on animals than for humans.

Nevertheless, recent animal evidence suggests that need for affiliation (the need to engage in friendly interactions) may have a biological basis (DeWaal, 1989), and Wright (1984) proposes a similar intrinsic motivation in humans to establish meaningful relationships. Although it is generally accepted that humans have a need to affiliate with others, it is equally clear that there are strong individual differences in this respect. Following the pioneering efforts of Murray (1938), recent work on need for affiliation has found that those who are high on this trait are more self-confident and spend more time talking to others, therefore making more friends (Crouse and Mehrabian, 1977; Byrne and Greendlinger, 1989). The way in which need for affiliation works within differing settings is further clarified by Hill (1987). He suggests that four different motives underpin it: social comparison (whereby the individual affiliates in order to reduce uncertainty and threat); positive stimulation (the need for contact with others); emotional support (the need to gain support from others in times of stress); and attention (improving self-perception and self-esteem by gaining attention from others). This line of research is quite promising since it allows the researcher to predict under which circumstances individuals will affiliate with others. Those who are high on emotional support, for example, will be more likely to affiliate when they are faced with a problem, whereas those who are high on attention will be most likely to affiliate when they feel they can gain attention and praise from others. While need for affiliation may predispose individuals towards contact with others, they require the necessary social skills to turn such contacts into something more enduring.

A persuasive account of relationships is offered by those theorists who have followed a reinforcement- or reward-based perspective. As has been highlighted in Chapter Six, people who are rewarding in any of a number of different ways are generally rated as being more attractive than those who do not offer these rewards (Foa and Foa, 1975). In fact, it appears that simply being associated with a rewarding event is enough to increase an individual's attractiveness, irrespective of the role that the person plays in this event. Perhaps the most straightforward account of the role of reward in attraction is offered by Clore and Byrne's (1974) reinforcement–affect model outlined in Chapter Six and, according to which, we like anyone who makes us feel good and dislike anyone who makes us feel bad. The model also predicts, it will be recalled, that we will also react positively or negatively to individuals on the basis of their *association* with these events in our environment. In this sense, individuals are judged not on the basis of their own actions, but through the medium of the emotionally arousing context in which they find themselves. The well-known attraction strategy of taking someone out on a date to be wined and dined operates, at least on one level, by association. Researchers, however, have pointed to the limitations in following a simple reinforcement-centred description of relationships in which benefits to each must be donated by the other. Within an enduring union, it is common for one member to gain satisfaction from the rewards that the other receives in addition to their own. It has been suggested that focusing on rewards for their own sake within relationships appears to deny the natural concern expressed by members for equity in their distribution (Kelley and Thibaut, 1978).

Social exchange theory (Thibaut and Kelley, 1959) proposes an extension of reinforcement theory whereby individuals seek to maximise the rewards that they obtain while at the same time attempting to minimise the costs. Under this view of relationships partners are able to weigh up the potential gains and losses to themselves of entering into a liaison. This involves comparing the benefits of each new relationship with those obtained from other past experiences and from new potential ones. An essential feature of exchange theories is the notion of reciprocity of rewards, with couples expecting rewards to be returned to them in direct proportion to those that they give out. Much of the research into social exchange theory has been hampered by the laboratory-based settings within which studies have been carried out, the prisoners' dilemma game being a well-known example. This experimental procedure faces two individuals with conflicting choices between cooperation and competition. Each player is unaware of the moves of the other. They are told that if they both confess to a crime, they will receive a stiff sentence (eight years) but not the maximum possible (ten years). If one player confesses and turns in the other, that player will receive a sentence of only three months while the other will receive a full ten-year sentence. If neither prisoner confesses, they will both receive a one-year sentence. These games are felt by some researchers to be similar to real life tendencies towards cooperation and competition (but see Dawes, 1980).

The individualistic nature of the moves made by players in such games has, however, been criticised by others, including Argyle (1988b), for not adequately reflecting the interactional nature of real and enduring associations. It is becoming increasingly clear that any simplistic version of social exchange theory that does not pay attention to the interdependent nature of actions within relationships is likely to be unsuccessful. This criticism of early versions is best illustrated by the fact that it is only when liaisons are in their early stages, and when they are starting to deteriorate, that the individuals involved tend to think in terms of exchange of rewards (Murstein et al., 1977). Kelley and Thibaut (1978), in a refinement of the theory, reflect these considerations by inclusion of empathic concern for the other partner. This recognises the ongoing nature of relationships, with rewards being viewed not simply from an individual perspective but from a realisation of the couple's interdependence.

The notion of fairness in the allocation of rewards within relationships present in both early and later versions of social exchange theory is a central tenet of *equity theory* (Hatfield et al., 1979). This proposes that members expect the rewards they receive to reflect the effort that they put in. If relationships are ultimately perceived as inequitable, they are likely to be ended.

One of the major problems facing researchers into relationships is the multidisciplinary nature of this topic. It is becoming more acceptable to view relationships as events which require both a social psychological and a wider sociological focus in order to appreciate their complexity. The need to take into account societal factors is well illustrated by the work of Argyle *et al.* (1985) on relationship rules. They found that different cultures impose varying but widely accepted rule structures on a range of social liaisons, reflecting the power of wider social forces in determining the basic stipulations involved.

The physical and psychological benefits of fellowship are well documented. One function of friends is to provide the individual with emotional stability by reaffirming that things are being seen in similar ways to others (Duck, 1991). Friendships also provide us with valuable emotional support in times of stress. They can have benefits as well in terms of self-esteem. This can occur simply through the awareness that other individuals value you enough to choose to spend time with you, or by allowing you to accept responsibility for different aspects of their lives. Weiss (1974) points to a more general positive consequence of being in relationships – that of perceiving oneself as a member of a group. This is an important aspect which appears to apply to everyone. Even those individuals who do not like relationships claim that they do so by choice rather than through circumstance, highlighting well this social need to feel accepted. Duck (1991) also stresses the need to communicate with others about ourselves as an important feature of friendships. These communications may in many cases be about seemingly trivial things and last only for a few minutes, yet they are apparently rated as being highly significant by the participants (Duck *et al.*, 1991).

While conclusive evidence about the effects of lack of relationships on mental and physical health is hard to gather, longitudinal studies such as those by Peterson *et al.* (1988) suggest that pessimism in early adulthood is associated with greater risk of poor health in later life. There is a growing literature on the importance of stable social bonds for the maintenance of mental health (Lynch, 1977; Gerstein and Tesser, 1987).

STAGES IN RELATIONSHIPS

This section examines the evolution of relationships, using Levinger's (1983) five-stage model, together with the particular skills and strategies that are required to deal successfully with each.

Acquaintance

The first stage in relationships, following Levinger, is that of acquaintance. A number of factors have been found to be important in determining whether initial contact will be made with another person. Perhaps the most widely researched of these is physical attractiveness which was outlined in detail in Chapter Six. It has been found that both male and female subjects are strongly influenced by physical attractiveness (Folkes, 1982; Feingold, 1990). Initially, it was assumed that females were not affected to the same extent as males by this variable. However, many of these early studies employed a self-report methodology which simply highlighted differences in reporting between the sexes rather than genuine gender variations. As we have seen, attractive individuals are rated as being more interesting, sociable, dominant, socially skilled, and successful than their unattractive counterparts (Feingold, 1990). This bias or halo effect, working in favour of attractive individuals, is found across all age groups (Johnston and Pittenger, 1984) but for the most part is not backed up by objective evidence. It is worth noting, however, that attractive individuals have been found to have better social skills and to be more popular than their less attractive counterparts (O'Grady, 1989; Feingold, 1990). There is little doubt that many initial contacts are made on the basis of attractiveness, although people generally appear to prefer individuals who are similar in this respect to themselves ('the matching hypothesis', Berscheid et al., 1971).

Another factor which determines whether people will form relationships is propinquity which determines the frequency with which they interact. To get acquainted with an individual it is necessary to interact with them regularly. The power of the environment in determining contact between individuals has been well documented in social psychological research (Nahemow and Lawton, 1975; Ebbesen et al., 1976). Through such accidental contacts an unknown individual becomes familiar and less threatening, making communication more likely. Segal (1974) found that students in university who were assigned seats alphabetically were much more likely to become friendly with those next to them. In college settings friendship choices are affected significantly more by propinquity than any other single factor. This is a remarkable testament to its impact since other factors such as similarity of background or social class might be expected to be more influential. Repeated contact with an individual generally leads to a more positive evaluation of them. This appears only to hold, however, if the individual concerned is viewed initially in neutral or positive terms. Repeated exposure to someone who is rated as unpleasant leads to reduced liking (Swap, 1977).

Similarity is another factor which, it will be recalled, influences initial contacts. On the basis of both reinforcement and balance theories of attraction we should be attracted to those who are similar to ourselves. In reward terms having people agree with us is pleasurable, so we will tend to like those individuals who share our attitudes or views. When someone produces views which are similar to our own, it provides us with confirmatory evidence that our views are correct. This validation of views or attitudes through social comparison also makes the individual feel good and makes it more likely that they will like the other person (Goethals, 1986).

It is clear that people differ not only in their need to affiliate with others, but also in the social skills required to cope with such interactions. Relationships do not simply happen; they have to be worked at if they are to function properly. The view that relationships can be treated this way has until recently been frowned upon since it implies an artificiality in our interactions. Research suggests, however, that individuals learn the skills that need to be employed in forming bonds with others in their adult life through earlier family-based interactions. Ickes and Turner (1983) report that first-born children are not as socially skilled as subsequent children in a family. In addition, children who come from families where they have had the opportunity to interact with siblings of the other sex tend to display a greater ease in later cross-sex interactions.

Hazan and Shaver (1987) have been able to demonstrate that the types of attachments we form with our parents closely mirror the attachments we later develop in adult life. They have identified three types of attachment style, each of which appears to have consequences for later relationship development. Those who form secure attachments, where their parents were readily available and responsive to their needs, tend to form secure and stable relationships. Children who have had fussy or anxious parents, who are available only some of the time, tend to become anxious adults who are insecure in their relationships. Finally, those who had parents who were unresponsive or rejecting tend to avoid adult relationships altogether, preferring to immerse themselves in work or other activities.

Acquaintance skills

In this initial stage of forming a partnership, a number of important social skills can be identified which are essential if that partnership is to function properly. These skills include: being able to recognise and select those social situations where interactions will have the best chance to develop; being able to demonstrate a positive evaluation of the other person through appropriate verbal and nonverbal cues; ensuring equity in the provision of rewards; and being able to assess the relationship needs of another individual. Each of these skills will be examined in terms of the differing demands that various stages of relationships place upon the individuals concerned.

There is little doubt that, for many, making and establishing relationships is a new and anxiety-provoking experience. Langston and Cantor (1989), in a longitudinal study of students, set out to determine why some are socially very successful while others are not. On the basis of their findings they proposed a three-process model. They claim that the individual firstly makes a 'task appraisal' which, if negative, results in their viewing social encounters as threatening and anxiety-provoking. A 'strategy' for dealing with social interactions then has to be devised. If individuals appraise such interactions negatively, they are more likely to develop constrained and overly conservative strategies to deal with them. The final result of appraising the task negatively and the adoption of a constrained strategy for dealing with others is a 'performance outcome' which is unsuccessful. According to this analysis people who view interactions negatively fail because the strategies they adopt do not allow them to open up to others. Thorne (1987) found that socially constrained individuals ask questions about others they meet, but appear to lack the confidence to disclose information about themselves. Successful individuals by contrast have greater confidence in their task appraisals and adopt a more open strategy which is more likely to establish friendships.

One of the first set of skills that is required at this early stage of forming an association is to be able to recognize social situations which will be conducive to its further development. Duck and Miell (1986) report that those who are developing close contacts initially spend most of their time in public as opposed to private places. In most cultures the individual is aided in this venture by a set of culturally defined locations where relationships can be played out. In addition, culture-specific rules define how individuals are expected to act towards one another during different stages of a relationship.

One of the most powerful factors in developing a meaningful fellowship with another person is the ability to demonstrate that you evaluate them highly. In one sense, this can be accomplished simply by being physically present since you are in fact implicitly informing the other person that you have chosen to be with them. Perhaps more importantly, however, it is necessary for the individual to be able to demonstrate through either verbal or nonverbal rewards this positive evaluation. Research has shown that if this evaluative information can be conveyed and is reciprocated a close association is very likely to follow (Condon and Crano, 1988). The effects of such interpersonal evaluations are translated very quickly into behaviour. Curtis and Miller (1986) in an ingenious experiment asked subjects to fill in a survey. They were subsequently divided into two groups who were informed that their survey results had led a stranger to either like or dislike them. When they later interacted with this individual, subjects who expected to be liked made more eye contact, spoke in a warmer tone, and were more self-disclosing than those who had been led to believe the stranger disliked them.

One of the most striking features of initial relationships is the way in which rewards are expected to be reciprocated. In the early stages of relationships this exchange of rewards is 'watched' quite closely by those involved since it serves to cement the union. Rewards can take the form of physical gifts or, as previously outlined, the use of verbal and nonverbal reinforcements such as nods and smiles to indicate enjoyment and attention. The exchange of rewards in many ways serves as a signal both to those within the developing relationship and to those outside it that a friendship exists (Chown, 1981). While this concern with equity is quite normal in the initial stages of relationships, immediate and demonstrable reciprocity becomes less important, as we have seen, as they evolve.

An important type of reward that people offer in the early part of a relationship is self-disclosure, whereby they give the other individual a piece of information about themselves which they are expected to respect (Berg and McQuinn, 1989). In effect, one individual is rewarding the other by trusting that other with personal information which could be used to the discloser's disadvantage.

The skill of being able to identify the relationship needs of another person is highlighted well by Duck (1991). This involves skills such as listening and the provision of appropriate verbal and nonverbal feedback to indicate attention and to assess the similarity between ourselves and the partner. The ability to judge whether another individual is likely to be compatible with you requires an assessment of their background, education and interests. Research demonstrates that individuals who attempt to form relationships which do not take account of these factors are likely to be unsuccessful (Rodin, 1982).

Build-up

The process through which social bonds develop from initial acquaintance to the establishment of a more stable arrangement is difficult to chart accurately. This is because relationships can develop in at least two ways. They may occur through a gradual build-up over time of the contacts between individuals, leading to a more gradual movement from acquaintance to build-up phases. Alternatively, there can be a marked transition point at which the relationship moves clearly from one stage to the next (see Huston and Levinger, 1978). Despite these differences it is possible to distinguish a number of features which mark out the move from initial acquaintance to the establishment of a less transient union.

As a relationship develops, the two individuals increase the amount of contact that they have with one another. This usually involves increasing contact across an ever-widening circle of activities. Whereas in the initial acquaintance stage the other individual might be contacted by special arrangement only or through propinquity, as the relationship deepens there is an expectation that they will be together more often. Tolhuizen (1989), in a study of dating couples, found that one of the most common strategies adopted by them was to increase the amount of time they spent together. In tandem with this increase in contact there is normally an increase in the intimacy of conversation. The more superficial interaction that marks out the acquaintance stage has to be replaced with a communication style that reflects this increased intimacy. The need for information about the other person becomes more important since each individual has to decide whether the relationship has promise for them. Not surprisingly, this stage is also associated with an increase in self-disclosure which focuses on a careful examination of the information that is being imparted along with an assessment of the risks that this implies if such disclosures are not reciprocated. Miell (1987) reports that close friends tend to disclose more information about their own personality than do acquaintances.

Along with this increased contact and disclosure there is a necessary development in the commitment that members are expected to display towards the relationship. In exchange theory terms this commitment is expressed through putting in personal time and effort which cannot be retracted. At this stage the individual may assess the rewards and costs of both staying within the present relationship and of replacing it with another. The relationship is therefore at a crucial stage since decisions have to be made about the desirability of advancing it or its continuation at a lower level of intimacy. Since these decisions cannot be taken in isolation, it is necessary for each member to be aware of both their own hopes and expectations for the relationship and those of the other person. Movement to a more stable arrangement thus requires that the individuals bring into play, albeit in a different way, the skills they already utilise with acquaintances.

Build-up skills

As relationships continue, the need to determine the attitudes and beliefs of the other partner becomes important. This need to gain more detailed information is well documented in longitudinal studies (e. g. Van Lear and Trujillo, 1986). To do this we require skills necessary to make accurate assessments of the personality of others and to help them in turn to make similar judgements about us. Gaining this information depends upon a growth in commitment which allows the appropriate use of self-disclosure skills. These skills can be classified into direct and indirect disclosure techniques. Direct disclosure refers to the deliberate provision of personal information about the self. Indirect disclosure, by contrast, refers to the way in which personality characteristics of the individual can be conveyed through either intentional or unintentional cues. (In Chapter Four the rewarding aspects of smiles, nods and eye contact were outlined.) These same cues can provide information about the personality of the individual. In interactions we expect these behaviours to occur in a particular integrated manner. When for example someone stares at us for too long, we immediately attribute this to that person being rude, aggressive or drunk!

The management of the intimacy level of disclosures is a skill which has been identified (Derlega *et al.*, 1985). This has been shown to be dependent on knowing when and where such disclosures are most appropriate and how to pace them (Chelune, 1979). If disclosures are made at either an inappropriate time or at too fast a pace, they are likely to confuse the recipient and lead to resentment. Participants who force the pace of interactions by disclosing too much about themselves are in effect forcing the other to reciprocate, something they may be unwilling to do. Duck (1991) suggests that individuals who disclose too quickly may also suffer by losing credibility since self-disclosure is supposed to be reserved for certain selected others. If someone discloses too much about themselves, can they really be trusted to keep the other's disclosures secret? Inadequate self-disclosure skills will almost certainly lead to negative impressions about the individual concerned. Fortunately, people can be taught (in trusting environments) the degree of disclosure that is required in differing stages of relationships.

With acquaintances, equity between rewards given and those received is expected. When relationships develop further, the nature of this exchange changes. La Gaipa (1977) suggests that the value and type of rewards alter as individuals form more intimate relationships. Rather than an exchange of physical gifts which signal intimacy, more abstract exchanges of information are found. There is much less emphasis on strict temporal reciprocation of rewards, with partners being more willing to extend the time span over which equity may take place. Indeed, the very notion of keeping close track of rewards within relationships is likely to mitigate against the development of a meaningful liaison.

In line with this more relaxed view of rewards, Morton and Douglas (1981) suggest that individuals within developing relationships focus to a greater extent on an assessment of attitudes and beliefs, rather than on the more factual information exchanges that are characteristic of the acquaintance stage. This is also reflected in greater flexibility in rules governing bodily contact and intimacy. Honeycutt *et al.* (1989) suggest that as relationships evolve, the past history of the association becomes an important aspect for participants. This sense of a shared past in which differences in accounts between partners are removed over time appears to give a stability that they might not otherwise obtain. Baxter (1987) highlights the special significance that interpersonal events of particular significance take on as future anchor points in relationships.

Consolidation

Here individuals seek ways in which to maintain interest and variety in being together. There is a continued growth in commitment to the relationship with public pledges such as marriage, or private pledges and shared social networks adding a new societal reinforcement (Hinde, 1979). The major features of this stage are the need to provide continuing evidence of positive evaluation; the need to avoid jealousy; a perception that both individuals are being equally rewarded; and the need to ensure a high level of mutual satisfaction with the relationship.

The most important single factor within the consolidation stage is the phenomenon of commitment. Numerous researchers in the social sciences are in almost unanimous agreement that commitment is the key anchoring variable in accounting for stability within relationships (see Becker, 1960; Kelley, 1983). Kelley (1983) offers a most persuasive account of how commitment can vary, utilising Levinger's (1976) analysis of the different positive and negative forces acting on individuals sharing a common social bond. He argues that they examine the rewards (pros) and the costs (cons) associated with the liaison. Rewards include love for the other person; the positively viewed activities and status that accrue through the relationship; the costs that would be involved in terms of lost investment in ending it; and the negotiation and settlements this would necessarily involve. On the 'con' side are included all those factors which serve to draw the individual out of the relationship: the comparative attractiveness of alternatives; the physical or psychological costs in terms of effort or anxiety associated with one's partner; and the need to experiment due to lack of interest or variety. As the balance between rewards and costs within an association is likely to vary over time, it is unlikely that members constantly monitor it. Kelley instead proposes that a longer time span is involved, with commitment to the relationship depending upon rewards outweighing costs in an enduring manner. Rusbult (1980) conceptualises commitment similarly, seeing it as being positively related to 'outcomes' (rewards minus costs) and negatively related to the attractiveness of possible alternative relationships. Many investigators assume, according to Kelley, that commitment can be viewed as a stable function of reward–cost differences over time which ignores the variability which is found in practice (see Kelley, 1983). In practice, commitment should be defined in terms of both reward–cost differences and their variability.

Consolidation strategies

Based on a theoretical examination of commitment in terms of rewards and costs, it is possible to highlight a number of skills or strategies which will serve to strengthen partnerships. Firstly, it is necessary to ensure that an overall fairness or equity exists, along the lines already mentioned, in terms of what members put into and get out of their union. Thereafter, individuals' perceptions of the rewards within relationships can be improved by emphasising the positive aspects of interactions and by highlighting the negative costs of bringing them to an end. Walster *et al.* (1978), in keeping with this perspective, have identified a general style which appears to be effective in maintaining relationships. This style is based on the notion of perceived fairness, reflecting the idea that people are not necessarily striving to *maximise* relational rewards. In established liaisons there is a concern for the rewards that the other person gets as well. This is not to say that partners can always accurately assess the rewards and costs that accrue from relationships (Hatfield and Traupmann, 1981). They do appear to be concerned, however, in so far as they can assess it, that there should be an equitable balance. This more balanced view of distribution is also shown in the way in which people are prepared to tolerate non-reciprocation in terms of either rewards or disclosures.

It is also important to distinguish between psychological and physical rewards and costs since these have been shown to lead to differing ways of dealing with perceived inequity. Hatfield and Traupmann (1981) suggest that people can decide to respond to perceived inequity either by doing something about it in a physical sense, or by altering their attitude towards the other person.

Commitment to relationships can be improved by focusing attention on the past history of positive interactions that have occurred within them. Since satisfaction with a liaison has been identified as a factor which contributes to the growth of commitment, reminding individuals of the positive nature of past interactions will serve to strengthen their current sense of togetherness (Hinde, 1979). In line with this, Rosenblatt (1977) points to the shared nature of patterns of living that become associated with relationships, something that is not found with mere acquaintances.

A second strategy for enhancing commitment is to focus on the amount of investment that individuals have put into a relationship in terms of time, self-disclosure and effort. Most people who put effort into an activity come to feel that it must be worthwhile (Aronson, 1961), and that they will eventually be rewarded for their efforts (Lerner *et al.*, 1976). Jemmott *et al.* (1989) point out that the availability of alternative partners is an important factor to be considered here, since individuals are more likely to view the present association more positively when alternative partners are not readily available. In general, however, the evidence suggests that highlighting the investments that people have made in the past in both initiating and maintaining relationships can be a powerful way of strengthening them (Rusbult, 1980).

Accentuating the social costs of ending partnerships is another strategy which can be employed to rekindle commitment. This involves working through the problems that would have to be faced if partners were to go their separate ways. This has been found to be most effective in circumstances where a stable social network of valued individuals has been established whose opinions matter to those in the relationship. Where such social networks are lacking, strategies which focus on the costs of ending relationships may be counterproductive since they highlight negative as opposed to positive aspects of the union. For this reason any strategy which is based on highlighting positive aspects of being together rather than dwelling on the negative consequences associated with it is likely to be more successful.

Deterioration and ending

It is a sad fact of life that relationships, like any other type of once valued activity which ceases to be sufficently rewarding, can start to deteriorate and may eventually be abandoned. Unfortunately, due to their nature, this is likely to involve considerable emotional upheaval and conflict for those involved. It is impossible to commit oneself for any period of time to a liaison which has involved exchanges of rewards and shared experiences and not feel a sense of loss and bitterness at its demise. For a relationship to start to deteriorate, it requires at least one partner to view it in a more negative manner. The way in which members respond to such crises seems to depend on both their age and their level of self-esteem. Baxter (1984) suggests that differing types of disengagement strategies are adopted by older and younger couples. Older individuals tend to prefer drifting apart rather than the more confrontational style that is commonly found among younger couples. Rusbult and Zembrodt (1983) suggest that responses to relationship problems can be either passive or active. Partners either wait for improvement to occur or for things to get worse (passive), or decide to leave each other or work to improve things (active). Later research by Rusbult et al. (1990) suggests that self-esteem appears to be linked to the choice of strategy that individuals will employ. For those high in self-esteem active responses are most common while those lower in self-esteem seem to prefer passive strategies. These findings are important, since they suggest that individuals who have low self-esteem are most likely to choose passive strategies which have been found to result in greater distress (Rusbult et al., 1986).

Duck (1982) suggests that break-up can be best described in five phases: breakdown, intrapsychic, dyadic, social and 'grave dressing'. The breakdown phase is one in which a realisation that a problem or problems exist within the relationship is noted by one or both partners. At this stage they are unlikely to confide this to their partner or other people. This can lead them either to ascribe it to particular circumstances which may improve with time or to move to the next phase, the intrapsychic. This phase, according to Duck, is where the individual starts to inform others in appropriate settings about experienced grievances within the relationship. The partner is seldom informed about the problem but instead social support is sought to reassure the aggrieved individual that he/she is right to complain. In the dyadic phase the partner is finally confronted with the problem and this can lead either to conflict or to a joint acknowledgement of it.

The social phase refers to the point in the breakdown where third parties become involved in the dispute and tends to encourage those who know the partners to take sides. The final phase, the aptly named 'grave dressing', occurs when the relationship is acknowledged by both parties to be over, and is in essence a period of necessary readjustment. McCall (1982) presents a good account of the elaborate structure that surrounds this phase in terms of both convincing oneself that the relationship is over and providing a convincing account of it for others.

Break-up strategies

A number of different strategies have been suggested to try to mend deteriorating relationships. Before outlining these it is important to note that a satisfactory solution to break-up problems is unlikely to work unless three factors can be identified in the relationship. These are: firstly, a high level of satisfaction generally with the relationship; secondly, the acknowledgement by both parties of the time and effort that has gone into building it; and thirdly, the absence of new compensatory attachments (Rusbult, 1980; Simpson, 1987). The second general point worth noting from research is the impact of what Rusbult *et al.* (1990) call passive or active strategies in dealing with relationship problems. Those who adopt a wait-and-see perspective are most unlikely to seek out the more active strategies which might help their failing union.

Following Duck's (1982) model of break-up, it is clear that it is during the intrapsychic phase that members are most likely to gain from external intervention since this is where they first make their problem known to others. Most interventions at this phase by counsellors centre on trying to get the individual to think about the relationship in a more balanced way. Since the troubled individual is likely to focus on the specific problem and to blame the partner, techniques which focus attention on both positive and negative aspects of the partner are helpful along with encouragement to examine the individual's own role in the problem and its solution.

Within the dyadic phase Duck suggests that couples should be helped to communicate more carefully to avoid falling into what Gottman (1979) refers to as a 'cross-complaining cycle' where accusations are merely traded. It is important to ascertain whether the parties simply view problems in terms of personal fault, which allows little scope for progress, or whether they can be encouraged to agree that they can both do things which would improve the situation. If a couple have been in a relationship for some time, it is unlikely that they did not at some point in the past have a more positive attitude towards shared activities. Given this, Holmes and Boon (1990) suggest that repairing relationships depends upon the individuals discovering whether these past positive aspects are still available or, failing that, whether they can be rebuilt. Castaneda *et al.* (1986) point out that in cases where shared activities appear to have been neglected, household chores can become even more boring and routine. While many of the less attractive duties associated with relationships cannot be avoided, they can be examined with a view to sharing them more equitably.

During the social phase, the individuals are actively soliciting support from those around them. Given the nature of social networks it is likely that old social grievances will be brought to the fore to support either party. It is here, for example, that you find that your mother-in-law really couldn't stand you after all! Strategies at this juncture can either attempt to support the individual by offering alternative and comparative viewpoints which enable the person to understand more clearly what is happening or, on the other hand, help to construct a 'grave dressing' which they can live with. This should concentrate on building up the individual's self-confidence by ensuring that they have satisfactory reasons why their relationship did not work so that they can undertake more productive associations in the future.

CONCLUSION

It is clear that individuals enter relationships in order to fulfil a number of basic social needs. Among these are the need to be positively valued by others, the need to communicate about views of the world in order to reassure oneself of their validity, and the need to provide emotional support in times of stress. While these factors are in themselves rewarding, some can be successfully attained through mere acquaintanceship with others. As relationships deepen, there is an increase in the amount of self-disclosure and above all in commitment to the other person. Rewards in established relationships tend to flow more from a shared as opposed to an individualistic perspective with increased levels of intimacy and information sharing replacing the more reciprocal nature of reward exchanges found in initial liaisons. Rewards in established relationships stem from a shared sense of fairness or equity over a much longer timespan. The positive nature of past activities and new more intimate communicative strategies are used to enable partners to develop a sense of shared past and a unique interactive style which is based on common perceptions and experiences. One could go so far as to conclude that the very nature of rewards has to be revised in the light of this shared perspective, since the reinforcement history of a relationship is likely to play as significant a part as current rewards to those involved. In short, relationships illustrate the complexity of human interaction and the need to develop models such as that proposed in Chapter One which take account of both present and contextual factors in communication.

Finally, from the point of view of those interested in interventions to help relationships, a number of important conclusions are warranted. Firstly, it has to be acknowledged that different strategies will have to be employed to help individuals according to the stage and phase of relationship they have attained. These strategies all involve an enhancement of the rewarding features of relationships through emphasising either the positive aspects of prior interactions or the negative aspects associated with ending the association. Perhaps the best advantage of adopting a stage-based approach to understanding human relationships is that it offers those interested in resolving problems and maintaining satisfying associations a more systematic way of handling human interactions.

Chapter 10

Overview and concluding comments

INTRODUCTION

The thesis advanced in the preceding pages emphasises the distribution of social rewards in the operation and regulation of interpersonal conduct. Engaging with another can be a tremendously fulfilling experience or, on the other hand, the source of much pain and frustration depending upon the extent to which it enables both parties to further their goals and meet the needs which underlie them. This is true not only of everyday liaisons but also of professional associations. Compared with some instances of the former, the latter are often more transient, less intimate, and much easier to annul. Nevertheless, the importance of social rewards still stands. While much of what has been said is of relevance to everyday relationships, the focus of application in this book has been with those working in what has been labelled by Ellis and Whittington (1981) as the 'Interpersonal Professions'. We can think of groupings such as teachers, doctors, nurses, counsellors, managers and social workers, to name but a few, where the major part of the working day is spent interacting with others and where the outcome of the service provided is effected by this means. Here the professional (or paraprofessional) represents a potential source of reward for the client, patient or pupil. This can come about in different ways. Outcomes resulting from contacts with teachers, doctors and counsellors can take a tangible form. These outcomes are obviously important, and professionals are assessed in terms of them. But, in addition, the manner in which pupils, patients, clients, etc., are engaged as fellow social beings should not be dismissed. In a fascinating account of his professional maturation as a physician, Henry Eisenberg discloses his growing realisation that outcomes are not enough:

> Fortunately, the recognition that there's more to being a doctor than just being a good technician and getting good results came before it was too late for me to do anything but turn the thought over endlessly in my mind while rocking on a retirement porch somewhere.... I had wrapped myself up in *materia medica* like a mummy and, like a mummy, I found it difficult to bend.... As a doctor, it made my relationships with patients perfunctory and unrewarding.
>
> (Eisenberg *et al.*, 1986, pp. 158–159)

MacLeod Clark (1985) points out that a sizeable and seemingly increasing proportion of the complaints which come before the NHS Ombudsman each year stem from poor communication with patients. Relating to those to whom a service is proffered can, therefore, be more or less rewarding on its own account. These two sources, process and outcome, should not, of course, be thought of as operating totally independently. When, for instance, a positive outcome relies upon patient compliance with some course of action prescribed by the practitioner, greater levels of patient satisfaction with the relationship enjoyed are facilitative (Ley, 1988). In this book, though, we have focused not so much on material, external rewards derivable from professional involvement, but with the positivity of the engagement process manifested in verbal and nonverbal communication.

The importance of the interpersonal dimension of professional practice is becoming ever more widely acknowledged. This is evidenced, for instance, by the upsurge of books and training courses in this area. These, in turn, have no doubt been spurred by recent stipulations on the part of professional bodies with responsibilities for monitoring and improving standards of education and training in their various domains of influence, to the effect that trainees should develop interpersonal, as well as cognitive and practical, skills (Dickson *et al.*, 1989). Again those researchers who have been intent on analysing what exactly it is that effective practitioners actually do when involved in such activities as teaching (Turney *et al.*, 1983), interviewing and counselling (Ivey and Authier, 1978), or speech therapy (Saunders and Caves, 1986) have isolated a component of practice that has to do with responding positively so as to reward and reinforce appropriately. It might therefore be assumed that teachers, managers, coaches and interviewers would be particularly adept in their use of these techniques. As has been revealed, one of the consistent findings to emerge from the literature suggests that this assumption is unsustainable. Hence the primary aim of this book has been to make some small contribution in this direction by heightening awareness of self as rewarding agent, the effects of such positive reactions on others, and some of the determining variables that seem to be implicated.

A central premise of our thinking is that interpersonal communication can be construed as skilled activity. Early attempts defined social skill in terms of the ability of the individual to interact with other people so as to evoke positive rather than negative consequences (Libet and Lewinsohn, 1973). But *providing* rewards can also be regarded as skilled interaction to the extent that it represents a contextually appropriate and behaviourally facilitative means of relating effectively and efficiently to other people so as to accomplish warrantable objectives (Dickson, 1988). As depicted in the model outlined in Chapter One, interactors pursue goals within a person/situation framework. When interacting, they make perceptions of the situation, themselves, the other, and how they are being received by him or her. In so doing they interpret and attach meaning to what is happening thereby making some sort of sense of it. Furthermore, this information is utilised in the ongoing operation of making decisions and selecting strategies considered most likely to accomplish the goal being sought. These are then translated into action. Because of the dynamically interdependent nature of the process, interactors are at one and the same time senders and receivers of information; each affects and is affected by the other in a system of reciprocal influence. In seeking to satisfy personal ends, therefore, each also provides the other with data of relevance to that other's goal quests. This feedback, if perceived, can in turn be considered and subsequently acted upon. Each of these elements, namely goals, perception, mediating processes, responses and feedback, together with personal and situational factors, is implicated in the exchange of rewards. Furthermore, social interchange can in turn and to varying degrees impact upon both personal characteristics and situational factors in a system of reciprocal determinism.

In responding to the other, interactors make possible the provision of social rewards. This may be in what is said, through praise, reflective statements, self-disclosures, etc.; how it is said, bearing in mind the importance of the nonverbal accompaniments of speech; and in the other nonvocal features of nonverbal communication, including smiles, posture, head-nods, eye contact, and gestures. We have seen how the operation of such feedback may be interpreted in accordance with several contrasting theoretical positions. Firstly, it may be regarded as a source of reinforcement, increasing the probability of the preceding behaviour recurring in future under comparable circumstances. In the view of some extreme behaviourists this is accomplished in a largely automatic, reflexive fashion without the need for any sort of conscious awareness or cognitive mediation. The weight of current thinking seems to be, though, that this is probably not typical of much of human activity. Alternative attempts to account for reinforcing effects involving information processing were outlined in Chapter Two.

Secondly, as suggested by Fitts and Posner (1973), feedback enables insights to be gleaned into the extent to which the performer has achieved the set goal or is on course to do so. This interpretation necessitates an intervening stage of information processing and decision-making. The role of attribution processes which determine the meaning attached to experienced events and, therefore, their likely rewarding potential was explored in Chapter Seven. Accordingly, not all instances of praise will necessarily be construed positively. Deci and Porac (1978), it will be recalled, postulated that reactions of this type can be thought to furnish information leading to quite different judgements and consequent responses. On the one hand, they can reflect on the efficiency and effectiveness with which tasks are being achieved and act as a basis for further effort or corrective action. Alternatively, they may herald an attempt by the other to control and subjugate. If the latter construction is placed on such episodes, it is highly unlikely that the sorts of positive reaction typically associated with the receipt of genuine rewards will be forthcoming.

While reviewing some of the research focusing upon the influential effects of reinforcers, we have been at pains to stress that no aspect of interpersonal behaviour should be thought to have absolute qualities in this respect. The relativity and subjectivity which pertains is encapsulated, for instance, in the thinking underlying the concept of Reinforcement value (Rotter, 1982). Whether or not some action is experienced positively will depend upon a plethora of concomitant variables, to be turned to shortly, surrounding the provider, the recipient and the circumstances of the episode.

Thirdly, feedback can be held to contribute an essentially motivational input effecting continued effort. However, a number of differing accounts of the underlying mechanisms was again encountered. For many the concept of goal is implicated. While particular goals pursued in any interactive encounter can be enormously varied, yet it seems that the satisfaction of several underlying needs and motives are fundamentally paramount. These include the need to feel in control of events which impinge and to be able to predict happenings; the need to belong socially and to gain the respect and approval of those who matter; and the need to exercise mastery and manifest competence in one's dealings with the world and others. Outcomes which meet these requirements or hold out the promise of doing so are likely to be positively received and acted upon. Vroom (1964) has also stressed the value bestowed upon outcomes which are more externally derived. Bandura (1989), in particular, has accentuated the motivational consequences of information signalling movement towards projected end states; it is not only the achievement of those states which counts. In addition to more commonly thought of incentive value which is externally derived and stems from the projected attainment of tangible outcomes, the satisfaction of personal standards governing goal-directed behaviour should not be overlooked as an energising source of skilled performance.

As emphasised in Chapter One, while it is relatively easy to conceptually prise these different feedback mechanisms apart, in practice they most likely overlap and merge to varying extents (Salmoni *et al.*, 1984). But feedback is a much broader notion than reward, and not all instances of it can be thought of in this way. Although feedback may be positive or negative, reward has a mainly positive connotation. Some elements of feedback will serve to reward, but not all.

It is possible, in dealing with the topics of rewards and rewarding, to do so at a number of different conceptual levels. Shifts of emphasis across these will be evident in the foregoing chapters. At the micro end of things we can focus on fine-grained verbal and nonverbal behaviours and chart their reinforcing impact on quite limited and specific outcome effects. At an intermediate level of analysis we can think of broader dimensions of interpersonal activity such as warmth and empathy which are expressed much more inclusively. (Indeed, humanistic psychologists would typically take exception to the reductionist stance adopted in Chapter Five, arguing that these attitudes represent underlying values towards others and cannot be adequately defined as composites of molecular behaviours.) Moving further towards the macro extreme we encounter the full-blown humanistic stances represented in the second chapter by the work of Carl Rogers and Eric Berne. Here, in so far as concepts such as positive regard and stroking can be equated with the provision of interpersonal rewards, the process is construed much more holistically in its operation. It is people in their totality who are rewarding, not isolated aspects of what they do with and for each other!

Turning attention to the sorts of outcome associated with rewarding episodes, we again find that these can be identified on a micro–macro dimension. At the micro level, the effects of various social reinforcers on increasing the instances of quite precisely circumscribed behaviours within some transient and frequently research-engendered encounter were considered. This contrasts with the role of rewards of a much less distinct coinage that operate to sustain established relationships in the ways sketched in the preceding chapter.

In addition to their direct effects on what the other does, the distribution of rewards may also serve to empower the rewarder in relation to the rewarded, thus facilitating the operation of social influence. Attitudes can also be modified. The act of making rewards available often enhances the attraction of the provider in the eyes of the recipient. One way of accounting for this is in terms of the Byrne–Clore model presented in Chapter Six. Moreover, attractive people, it seems, are more likely to be reacted to positively by those with whom they come in contact. But it is not only attitudes towards the recipient that are implicated; attitudes towards self can also be shaped in this way. Depending upon how it is cast, being exposed to rewarding others can lead to the emergence of a favourable self-concept and heightened self-esteem. On the other hand, and under particular sets of circumstances, being praised may actually create an undermining of one's confidence in one's ability, as was pointed out in Chapter Seven.

So far we have been considering the effects of positive reactions of others which are directly experienced in the course of interpersonal contact. However, we also decide upon courses of action as a result of witnessing others benefit from acting in that manner. Vicarious reinforcement must not be overlooked. Allied to this is the role of social rewards in furthering the modelling process. Although, according to Bandura (1977), rewards are not essential for learning of this type to take place, they assist by making it more likely that particular behavioural displays will be attended to, that the resulting information will be retained, and that there will be sufficient incentive for the individual to actually implement such learning in behavioural terms.

Many of the conclusions reached in this book have been hedged around with caveats, qualifications and provisos. The words of Lieberman (1990) quoted in the introductory chapter, to the effect that the principle of using rewards isn't quite as simple as it sounds, come echoing back. Perhaps this is one reason why professionals fail to use such practices with the aplomb that might be imagined. The remainder of this concluding chapter will be given over to attempting to tease out and summarise some of the central findings to emerge together with the significant variables that seem to apply. The fact that we have not restricted our coverage to one particular paradigmatic approach to the study of the phenomenon complicates this task. These summary statements will be grouped under factors to do with the nature of the reward, the rewarder, the rewarded and, finally, the circumstances of rewarding. Some of the practical guidelines and recommendations will draw upon the work of O'Leary and O'Leary (1977), Brophy (1981), Karoly and Harris (1986), and Schwartz (1989).

FACTORS RELATING TO REWARDS

1 The value attached to any social reward will differ from person to person. The thinking behind this proposition is encapsulated in the Social Learning theory concept of Reinforcement value. Likewise in the parlance of Transactional Analysis, we must acknowledge the importance of 'Different strokes for different folks'. Early experience of being treated well or poorly by significant others leads to the creation of fixed views of self, the world, other people, and how best to gain recognition from them. It may even be the case that what was intended as a genuine compliment or word of praise will be distorted to render it more in keeping with the sorts of strokes to which that individual has become accustomed.

2 We cannot think of specific behaviours being rewarding in any absolute or categorical sense. This is an extension of the previous point. Although we have specified, in Chapters Three and Four, certain verbal and nonverbal behaviours which suggest positivity as normally used in social contact and which seem to have reinforcing potential across a range of situations, yet it should not be thought that these behaviours must invariably operate in this manner. While attention from others is commonly welcomed, Sajwaj and Dillon (1977) remind us that when such attention has been consistently associated with aversive experiences, it may come to have punishing connotations and be actively avoided. Furthermore, according to Premack (1965), virtually any social behaviour can come to serve as a reinforcer if made contingent upon the performance of some other less likely action.

We have also seen how, within the context of well-established relationships, the nature of rewards shared by partners changes from that which typically applied in the initial stages of the formation of the association to become less readily recognisable and more unique to that particular liaison as it develops.

3 Rewards do not have to be directly experienced to be effective in regulating what people think, feel and do. They can function vicariously through being observed by others.

4 While external, material inducements may reduce the degree of intrinsic interest that the performer has in a task, this seems to be not necessarily so in the case of verbal rewards. Indeed, when these are seen as relevant to the performance of the task and supportive of it, levels of intrinsic motivation enjoyed may even be increased (Sakurai, 1990).

5 Rewards from others must be seen to be genuine and authentic, rather than manipulative, to be effective.

6 Social reinforcers, when used to strengthen specific targeted responses, should be meaningfully varied to minimise loss of potency. This loss can come about if over-reliance is placed on a single expression. For example, if every attempt is responded to with 'Good', this word quickly loses its effect through failing to provide any differential feedback or underlying sense of appreciation.

7 Rewards seem to work best to motivate and direct when the recipient appreciates

why they are being offered. If the intention is to enhance learning and performance at a certain task, then the rewarder should:

- specify the particulars of the accomplishment being praised;
- decide upon criteria for praising and preferably agree these with the recipient in advance, so reducing the chances of what is happening being constructed as the mere exercise of reward power;
- draw attainment criteria from that individual's previous levels of performance rather than those of peers;
- focus the recipient's attention on the task and his or her accomplishment at it rather than on the reward and the rewarder;
- ensure that the attribution of the cause of the positive reaction encompasses effort invested in the task and does not undermine self-beliefs in ability (Brophy, 1981).

8 Findings on the magnitude of the reward are inconsistent. However, much of this work has been on material inducements. Attempting to quantify those that are more interpersonal in nature poses problems as mentioned in Chapter Two. Nevertheless, if thought of in terms of degree of intensity, Hargie *et al.* (1987) stress that social reinforcement should be in keeping with the extent of the accomplishment as appreciated by the performer. 'Over-praise' may result in misinterpretation and faulty attribution. It can lead to the recipient seriously questioning their own ability, or the agent's judgement and motives (Brophy, 1981).

Excess may be counterproductive for a different reason. As mentioned in Chapter Eight, cognitive dissonance can operate to make greater changes to underlying attitudes in the direction of behaviour brought about by an inducement, when that inducement is small rather than large. It is much more difficult to reconcile doing something which is at odds with one's beliefs and attitudes for a trivial recompense. Furthermore small, frequent rewards, implicitly provided, may be more effective when the intention is to exert control and influence through the exercise of power.

Recipients' judgements of what is fair and equitable are also implicated. Workers have been found to express less satisfaction with rewards received when those recompenses amounted not only to less, but also more than was expected (Lawler, 1983). Similarly, as mentioned in Chapter Six, when rewards are donated on a charitable basis thereby placing the recipient under an obligation to the provider, the level of attraction of the provider is less than would be expected were reciprocation possible.

FACTORS RELATING TO REWARDERS

1 It has already been established that the same social reward will probably be valued differently by different recipients. That value will be additionally modified depending upon the source. In other words, certain characteristics of the

person providing the reward will render it more or less significant. These particular characteristics vary, however, with a plethora of factors pertaining to recipients, making a straightforward and categorical listing difficult. Nevertheless, the following rewarder features seem to be important:

- Credibility/respect. It appears from a number of research studies that positive reactions to accomplishments are more impactful when provided by individuals regarded as having expertise in that area and therefore credible and worthy of respect.
- Prestige. Again prestigious rewarders will be more likely to be successful. However, as noted by Krasner (1962, p. 70) in relation to therapists, 'the reinforcing value of therapist "prestige" does not exist for all potential patient groups. A group such as delinquents may consider a therapist to be a "square", thus decreasing the likelihood of reinforcement from such a source being effective.' Prestige may rest upon different exploits and reputations for contrasting sections of the community!
- Status. It would seem from some of the empirical evidence reviewed earlier that, at least for young people, higher status individuals are more acceptable sources of reward than peers. Stock (1978), for example, revealed that praise by the experimenter had a greater impact on quality and quantity of work carried out than that by a fellow student. Nevertheless, it may be that this effect is considerably tempered when the peer has acknowledged and relevant expertise.
- Age. When it comes to modifying aspects of self-concept, it would appear that, while parents are most influential in the earlier years, peers begin to take on a greater role with the onset of adolescence. How these young people dress, groom and present themselves becomes influenced by fellow adolescents with whom they associate.
- Similarity. Within the constraints identified in Chapter Six, and mindful of the points just made to do with expertise, status, etc., it seems that similarity in salient characteristics such as socioeconomic status and ethnic background (McGrade, 1966) may enhance the attraction of the source and promote a reinforcing outcome (Sapolsky, 1960).

2 The manner in which the accomplishments of another are reacted to, whether or not they are praised for example, will depend upon the standards of competence applied by the assessor. These standards and criteria, as already mentioned, should be ideally shared with and preferably jointly determined by the performer. The process of shaping behaviour from initial crude attempts at some task to the progressive refinement of performance is reliant upon the systematic inflation of standards required to be reached in order for rewards to be forthcoming. The part played by attributional processes was also mentioned in Chapter Seven.

3 The agent's past history of offering rewards to a particular individual should not be overlooked. Other things being equal, it is likely that recipients will have

greater expectations of receiving positive responses from sources supplying them in the past. Having said that, a word of praise or compliment from someone who has seldom reinforced us in this way before can be even more telling, assuming of course that we regard this other as credible, there is no suspected ulterior motive, and so on. According to the Gain/Loss theory advanced by Aronson (1969), the gain in esteem resulting from this scenario has a more potent effect than does constant praise. This may come about because, in contrast to what had gone before, the positivity of this reaction seems all the greater. Perhaps the heightened effect is a result of reduced anxiety. Alternatively, the unexpected praise can be interpreted as due to recipients believing that they are now demonstrating their competence and this being appreciated by the rewarder. Some even recommend the use of praise together with criticism for inappropriate behaviour (Acker and O'Leary, 1987).

Again, if an agent habitually rewards not only us but also everyone else on the merest pretext, any specific instance will probably have little impact. Rewards for particular tasks can be devalued if the agent dispenses them too liberally.

FACTORS RELATING TO RECIPIENTS

1 While the point is not accepted unanimously, it appears that the reinforcing effect of rewards in modifying specific practices is more pronounced when the recipient is aware of the nature of the contingency. The contiguous association with the receiver, or indeed some third party who just happens to be present, of pleasurable experiences resulting from rewards being received, as was mentioned in Chapter Five in relation to interpersonal attraction, has a considerable affective component and is generally held to be based on somewhat different underlying principles of conditioning (Bower and Hilgard, 1981).

2 The meaning attached to rewards and recipients' reactions to them are shaped by the attributions which are brought into play. Rewards that are believed to be genuinely provided, stem from the degree of proficiency with which a difficult task was conducted, and proffer information on its accomplishment rather than representing an attempt at control, will tend to enhance performance and promote positive self-perceptions. But as we have seen in Chapter Seven, under circumstances where recipients have little knowledge of their ability at the task, assume that the rewarding agent has such insights, are informed that the task is relatively easy, and notice that others who appear to be equally successful are not reacted to in this manner, the result may be to attribute the rewards to their own low ability at this type of endeavour.

3 The impact of social rewards such as praise is influenced by personality characteristics of those to whom they are made available. It seems that people who are high in need for approval (Crowne and Marlowe, 1964), self-monitoring (Snyder, 1987), extroversion (Gupta and Shukla, 1989), and low in self-esteem

(Smith and Smoll, 1990) are more prone to the conditioning effects of this type of contingency.

Apart from general levels of self-esteem, individuals' beliefs in their ability to successfully carry out a particular project, and their feelings of self-efficacy, will have a bearing upon outcomes pursued and hence possible rewards attainable.

Locus of control is a further significant personality factor. Those who are essentially internally oriented have a firm regard for their ability to operate on the environment in order to make things happen as they want them. They can earn rewards through their effort. Externally oriented counterparts have a less optimistic view of their impact upon the world. Rewards that are received are often put down to luck, chance or some external happening.

4   In addition to personality, several other personal factors have been implicated with greater likelihood of succumbing to reinforcement. Socioeconomic status is one such variable around which much debate has centred. While earlier claims that verbal rewards, including praise, work best with middle-class pupils now seem untenable, it may still be the case that this variable is influential but in a much more complex fashion involving interactions with other factors like ethnic background and gender (Miller and Eller, 1985).

5   Attractive recipients are generally more likely to be responded to positively by others. Hore (1971) produced rather disturbing evidence that the more physically attractive female student received higher grades on teaching practice. Likewise, brighter pupils receive a disproportionate amount of the teacher's attention, it has been claimed. Interestingly, unsolicited teacher help may be attributed to low ability on the part of the pupil by an uninformed outsider.

6   Males and females appear to differ in several respects in relation to social rewards and their effects. There is some limited evidence that boys may be more receptive to peer praise than girls when taking part in a problem-solving activity (Henry et al., 1979). Females were found to react more positively to a surreptitious touch on the hand compared with male counterparts (Fisher et al., 1975), and to respond to an interviewer's reflective statements by disclosing more personal detail and at greater depth, in a piece of research by Feigenbaum (1977).

7   With regard to the effects of rewards on self-concept, the extent of modification appears to correlate with age. Susceptibility to the self-defining reactions of others has been thought to peak in early adolescence, according to Elkind (1967). A firmly established self-concept and high self-esteem are further factors which militate against casual change.

8   Recipients are typically not passively exposed to the reactions of others but rather are actively implicated in the process. For the most part it seems that those reactions sought will be essentially positive and in the best interests of promoting self-enhancement (Tesser, 1988), although others have cautioned that self-verification or preserving a consistent, even if negative self-image is also important (Swann et al., 1990).

Different strategies for securing desired reactions from social partners, particularly those with whom we do not have an enduring relationship, include self-presentation and ingratiation. Another approach involves comparing our achievements with those of others. If we do not manage to secure our goal, the next best thing is to reassure ourselves by establishing that others also failed. Of course, the chances of this discovery will very much depend upon whom we choose to compare ourselves with. As mentioned in Chapter Eight, those with low self-esteem tend to seek out others of low ability.

CIRCUMSTANTIAL FACTORS OF REWARDING

1 In relation to frequency of reward, it has already been noted that profligacy can serve to devalue the reward on offer. Nevertheless, in the initial stages of establishing some novel habit or way of doing something, it is advisable to reinforce quite frequently. These levels can be gradually reduced as the response becomes established (Lieberman, 1990).

   Intermittent reinforcement has been discovered to produce much higher rates of behaviour with greater resistance to extinction than continuous rewards. But the different patterns of responding to alternative schedules so typical of animal experimentation are less characteristic of conditioning with people. Lowe (1979) believes that this is due to the way in which people interpret the relationship between response and reward in making sense of what is taking place.

2 In order for the different social behaviours mentioned in the past pages to operate as effective reinforcers, it is imperative that their application be made contingent upon the response targeted. This is a consistent finding. But it does not mean that the non-contingent use of interpersonal rewards will prove futile. It may serve to put the other at ease, as Saigh (1981) speculates, or define the situation in a particular manner (Bennett and Jarvis, 1991). Moreover, it may create impressions of the agent as a warm, friendly individual (Siegman, 1987). It is highly unlikely, however, to selectively reinforce.

3 The reinforcing process is further enhanced when rewards are provided quite soon after the response in question. As far as offering feedback is concerned, it makes sense for this information on performance to be provided with little delay. From a motivational point of view the prospect of an immediately available inducement is more compelling than having to wait some time for it to become available (Schwartz, 1989). Nevertheless, delays can occur without seriously jeopardising the outcome if the recipient is aware that the reward is forthcoming and retains the connection between it and the activity to which it relates (Lieberman, 1990).

4 Rewards will have a differential impact on account of the nature of the activity to which they relate. When the task necessitates considerable concentration in the acquisition of some demanding skill, lavish praise may be detrimental due perhaps to the distraction of being made self-conscious (Baumeister *et al.*,

1990). Furthermore, as we have seen in Chapter Seven, success after having tried hard is likely to be attributed to either ability or effort as a consequence of the task being presented as 'task-involving' or 'ego-involving' (Jagacinski and Nicholls, 1987).

5 The overall situation within which rewards are acquired will help determine their desirability. While teacher praise in the classroom may be acceptable, similar behaviour in the playground could be off-putting to that pupil. But the environment operates at another level to modify the likelihood of rewards. Wheldall and Lam (1987) reported that teachers tended to make greater use of positive responses to pupils seated in rows rather than in groups.

6 The relationship between interactors and the stage which it has reached is another circumstantial factor that helps shape the types of reward on offer in furthering that union.

ETHICAL CONSIDERATIONS

Before leaving the topic of social rewards in professional practice, a few additional words need to be said on the ethical nature of the enterprise. This dimension has been acknowledged at several points in the book. An in-depth consideration doing justice to the philosophical profundity of the debate around these concerns will not be contemplated here. The interested reader is referred to several of the excellent publications which are available (e.g. O'Leary *et al.*, 1972; Purtilo and Cassel, 1981; Beauchamp and Childress, 1983; Barnard, 1986; Fairbairn and Fairbairn, 1987; and Goodlad *et al.*, 1990). The essential issue, as it applies here, is this: given that rewards of different sorts can be used to bring about changes in what people do, how they feel, and the attitudes which they hold, *should* they be so used? The answer to this question will probably hinge on several considerations that take into account the intentions of the agent, the expertise of the agent, the extent of the recipient's awareness and understanding of what is proposed, the likelihood of the intervention causing physical or psychological distress, whether or nor the recipient has given free and full consent to such an intervention, the degree of respect which he has been accorded, and the effects of this rewarding action in meeting his needs and interests. As a very crude rule of thumb, and at the risk of trivialising the complexity of the matter, ethical requirements tend to be more successfully satisfied when an intervention does not cause distress; is conducted with the informed consent of the recipient who is aware that it is taking place; does not expose the recipient to harm, hurt or distress; and the intention on the part of the agent in initiating the intervention is to further the recipient's best interests, and the outcome has indeed this desired effect.

While rewards can be used manipulatively to further the interests of the source and, some would hold, may do so with little awareness on the part of the unsus-pecting person to whom they are directed that such influence is being wrought, they do not have to be used in this manner. Indeed many of the above ethical stipulations are in keeping with pragmatic guidelines already mentioned. A common approach to the initiation of professional involvement in a range of contexts involves establishing, at the outset, agreed objectives and a mutually acceptable agenda. This may be formalised in some sort of written contract in certain settings. For example, Lang and van der Molen (1990) discuss contracting procedures as part of the commencement of a counselling involvement. This is very much in keeping with the current move in the health and caring professions towards promoting patient/client empowerment (Parsons, 1991). It also makes possible a situation typified by two people working together towards a common goal such that the positivity of their reactions one to the other is derived from this mutual quest. It is in such a climate of openness and agreement that the sorts of social reward explored in this book tend to be maximally facilitative.

References

Abramson, L.Y., Seligman, M.E.P. and Teasdale, J.D. (1978) Learned helplessness in humans: Critique and reformulation. *Journal of Abnormal Psychology*, 87, 49–74.

Acker, M. and O'Leary, S. (1987) Effects of reprimands and praise on appropriate behaviour in the classroom. *Journal of Abnormal Child Psychology*, 15, 549–557.

Adams, G.R. (1977) Physical attractiveness, personality and social reactions to peer pressure. *Journal of Psychology*, 96, 287–296.

Albee, G. (1969) Emerging concepts of mental illness and models of treatment: The psychological point of view. *American Journal of Psychiatry*, 125, 870–876.

Alicke, M.D., Smith, R.H. and Klotz, M.L. (1986) Judgements of physical attractiveness: The role of faces and bodies. *Personality and Social Psychology Bulletin*, 12, 381–389.

Allen, K. and Stokes, T. (1987) Use of escape and reward in the management of young children during dental treatment. *Journal of Applied Behaviour Analysis*, 20, 381–389.

Allison, J. (1989) The nature of reinforcement. In S. Klein and R. Mowrer (eds) *Contemporary Learning Theory: Instrumental Conditioning Theory, and the Impact of Biological Constraints on Learning*. Lawrence Erlbaum Assocs, Hillsdale, N.J.

Allison, M. and Ayllon, T. (1980) Behavioural coaching in the development of skills in football, gymnastics and tennis. *Journal of Behaviour Analysis*, 13, 297–314.

Altmann, H.A. (1973) Effects of empathy, warmth and genuineness in the initial counselling interview. *Counselor Education and Supervision*, 12, 225–228.

Anderson, C. and Jennings, D. (1980) When experiences of failure promote expectations of success: The impact of attributing failure to ineffective strategies. *Journal of Personality*, 45, 393–407.

Anderson, D., Crowell, C., Doman, M. and Howard, G. (1988) Performance posting, goal setting and activity contingent praise as applied to a university hockey team. *Journal of Applied Psychology*, 73, 87–95.

Arenson, S. (1978) Age and dress of experimenter in verbal conditioning. *Psychological Reports*, 43, 823–827.

Argyle, M. (1975) *Bodily Communication*. Methuen, London.

Argyle, M. (1983) *The Psychology of Interpersonal Behaviour*. Penguin, Harmondsworth.

Argyle, M. (1988a) *Bodily Communication* (2nd edn). Methuen, London.

Argyle, M. (1988b) Social relationships. In M. Hewstone *et al.* (eds) *Introduction to Social Psychology*. Blackwell, Oxford.

Argyle, M., Alkema, F. and Gilmour, R. (1972) The communication of friendly and hostile attitudes by verbal and non-verbal signals. *European Journal of Social Psychology*, 1, 385–402.

Argyle, M. and Cook, M. (1976) *Gaze and Mutual Gaze*. Cambridge University Press, Cambridge.

Argyle, M., Henderson, M. and Furnham, A. (1985) The rules of social relationships. *British Journal of Social Psychology*, 24, 125–139.

Aronfreed, J. (1970) The socialization of altruistic and sympathetic behaviour: Some theoretical and experimental analyses. In J. Macaulay and L. Berkowitz (eds) *Altruism and Helping Behaviour*. Academic Press, New York.

Aronson, E. (1961) The effect of effort on the attractiveness of rewarded and unrewarded stimuli. *Journal of Abnormal and Social Psychology*, 63, 375–380.

Aronson, E. (1969) The theory of cognitive dissonance: A current perspective. In L. Berkowitz (ed.) *Advances in Experimental Social Psychology*, Vol. 4. Academic Press, New York.

Aronson, E. (1984) *The Social Animal*. W.H. Freeman, New York.

Asch, S.E. (1951) Effects of group pressure upon the modification and distortion of judgment. In H. Guetzkow (ed.) *Groups, Leadership and Men*. Carnegie, Pittsburgh.

Asch, S.E. (1955) Opinions and social pressure. *Scientific American*, 193, 31–35.

Aspy, D. (1975) Empathy: Let's get the hell on with it. *The Counselling Psychologist*, 5, 10–14.

Aspy, D.N. and Hadlock, W. (1966) The effect of empathy, warmth and genuineness on elementary students' reading achievement. Unpublished thesis. University of Florida.

At Emery Air Freight: Positive reinforcement boosts performance (1973) *Organizational Dynamics*, 1, 41–50.

Atkinson, J. and Raynor, J. (1974) *Motivation and Achievement*. Winston, Washington, D.C.

Authier, J. (1986) Showing warmth and empathy. In O. Hargie (ed.) *A Handbook of Communication Skills*. Croom Helm, London.

Ayllon, T. and Azrin, N. (1968) *The Token Economy: A Motivational System for Therapy and Rehabilitation*. Prentice-Hall, Englewood Cliffs, N.J.

Backman, C. (1988) The self: A dialectical approach. In L. Berkowitz (ed.) *Advances in Experimental Social Psychology*, Vol. 21. Academic Press, New York.

Baldock, J. and Prior, D. (1981) Social workers talking to clients: A study of verbal behaviour. *British Journal of Social Work*, 11, 19–38.

Baldwin, J. and Baldwin, J. (1981) *Behaviour Principles in Everyday Life*. Prentice-Hall, Englewood Cliffs, N.J.

Bandura, A. (1977) *Social Learning Theory*. Prentice-Hall, Englewood Cliffs, N.J.

Bandura, A. (1986) *Social Foundations of Thought and Action: A Social Cognitive Theory*. Prentice-Hall, Englewood Cliffs, N.J.

Bandura, A. (1989) Self-regulation of motivation and action through internal standards and goal systems. In L. Pervin (ed.) *Goal Concepts in Personality and Social Psychology*. Lawrence Erlbaum Assocs, Hillsdale, N.J.

Bandura, A., Lipsher, D. and Miller, P. (1960) Psychotherapists' approach avoidance reactions to patients' expressions of hostility. *Journal of Consulting Psychology*, 24, 1–8.

Barker, G. and Graham, S. (1987) Developmental study of praise and blame as attributional cues. *Journal of Educational Psychology*, 79, 62–66.

Barnabei, F., Cormier, W.H. and Nye, L.S. (1974) Determining the effects of three counselling verbal responses on client verbal behaviour. *Journal of Counseling Psychology*, 21, 355–359.

Barnard, D. (1986) Communication skills and moral principles in health care: Aspects of their relationship and implications for professional education. *Patient Education and Counseling*, 8, 349–358.

Barnes, D. and Rosenthal, R. (1985) Interpersonal effects of experimenter attractiveness, attire and gender. *Journal of Personality and Social Psychology*, 48, 435–436.

Barnlund, D. (1976) The mystification of meaning: Doctor–patient encounters. *Journal of Medical Education*, 51, 716–725.

Baron, R.A. (1986) Self-presentation in job interviews: When there can be too much of a good thing. *Journal of Applied Social Psychology*, 16, 16–28.

Baron, R. (1988) Negative effects of destructive criticism: Impact on conflict, self-efficacy, and task performance. *Journal of Applied Psychology*, 73, 199–207.

Baron, R., Cowan, G., Ganz, R. and McDonald, M. (1974) Interaction of locus of control and type of reinforcement feedback: Considerations of external validity. *Journal of Personality and Social Psychology*, 30, 285–292.

Barrios, B., Corbitt, L., Estes, J. and Topping, J. (1976) Effect of social stigma on interpersonal distance. *Psychological Record*, 26, 343–348.

Baumeister, R., Hutton, D. and Cairns, K. (1990) Negative effects of praise on skilled performance. *Basic and Applied Social Psychology*, 11, 131–148.

Baxter, J. and Rozelle, R. (1975) Nonverbal expression as a function of crowding during a simulated police–citizen encounter. *Journal of Personality and Social Psychology*, 32, 40–54.

Baxter, J.C., Becker, J. and Hooks, W. (1963) Defensive style in the families of schizophrenics and controls. *Journal of Abnormal and Social Psychology*, 66, 512–518.

Baxter, L.A. (1984) Trajectories of relationship disengagement. *Journal of Social and Personal Relationships*, 1, 29–48.

Baxter, L.A. (1987) Symbols of relationship identity in relationship cultures. *Journal of Social and Personal Relationships*, 4, 261–279.

Baxter, L.A. and Wilmot, W. (1986) Interaction characteristics of disengaging, stable and growing relationships. In R. Gilmour and S.W. Duck (eds) *The Emerging Field of Personal Relationships* Lawrence Erlbaum, Hillsdale, N.J.

Bayes, M. (1972) Behavioural cues of interpersonal warmth. *Journal of Counseling and Clinical Psychology*, 39, 333–339.

Beauchamp, T. and Childress, J. (1983) *Principles of Biomedical Ethics*. Oxford University Press, New York.

Becker, H.S. (1960) Notes on the concept of commitment. *American Journal of Sociology*, 66, 32–40.

Beharry, E.A. (1976) The effect of interviewing style upon self-disclosure in a dyadic interaction. *Dissertation Abstracts International*, 36, 4677B.

Bell, R.Q. (1971) Stimulus control of parent or caretaker behavior by offspring. *Developmental Psychology*, 4, 63–72.

Bem, D. (1972) Self-perception theory. In L. Berkowitz (ed.) *Advances in Experimental Social Psychology*, Vol. 6. Academic Press, New York.

Bennett, M. and Jarvis, J. (1991) The communicative function of minimal responses in everyday conversation. *The Journal of Social Psychology*, 131, 519–523.

Benson, P.L., Karabenick, S.A. and Lerner, R.M. (1976) Pretty please: The effects of physical attractiveness, race and sex on receiving help. *Journal of Experimental Social Psychology*, 12, 409–415.

Berg, J.H. and McQuinn, R.D. (1989) Loneliness and aspects of social support networks. *Journal of Social and Personal Relationships*, 6, 359–372.

Berger, C. (1985) Social power and interpersonal communication. In M. Knapp and G. Miller (eds) *Handbook of Interpersonal Communication*. Sage, Beverly Hills, Calif.

Berger, C. (1989) Goals, plans and discourse comprehension. In J. Bradac (ed.) *Message Effects in Communication Science*. Sage, Newbury Park, Cal.

Berkowitz, L. (ed.) (1988) *Advances in Experimental Social Psychology*, Vol. 21. Academic Press, New York.

Berne, E. (1964) *Games People Play*. Grove Press, New York.

Bernstein, B. (1961) Social class and linguistic development: A theory of social learning. In A.J. Holsey, J. Flond and A. Anderson (eds) *Economy, Education and Society*. Free Press, Glencoe, Ill.

Berscheid, E. (1981) An overview of the psychological effects of physical attractiveness. In

G.W. Lucker, K.A. Ribbens and J.A. McNamara Jr (eds) *Psychological Aspects of Facial Form*. CHGD, Michigan.

Berscheid, E. (1983) Emotion. In H. Kelley, E. Berscheid, A. Christensen. *et al.* (eds) *Close Relationships*. W.H. Freeman, New York.

Berscheid, E. (1985) Interpersonal attraction. In G. Lindzey and E. Aronson (eds) *Handbook of Social Psychology*, Vol. 2 (3rd edn). Random House, New York.

Berscheid, E., Dion, K., Walster, E. and Walster, G.W. (1971) Physical attractiveness and dating choice: A test of the matching hypothesis. *Journal of Experimental Social Psychology*, 7, 173–189.

Berscheid, E. and Walster, E.H. (1972) Beauty and the best. *Psychology Today*, 5, 424.

Betz, B.J. (1963) Bases of therapeutic leadership in psychotherapy with the schizophrenic patient. *American Journal of Psychotherapy*, 17, 196–212.

Bierstedt, R. (1950) An analysis of social power. *American Sociological Review*, 6, 7–30.

Bingham, W., Moore, B. and Gustad, J. (1959) *How to Interview*. Harper and Brothers, New York.

Birdwhistell, R.L. (1970) *Kinesics and Context*. University of Pennsylvania Press, Philadelphia.

Bisanz, G.L. and Rule, B.G. (1989) Gender and the persuasion schema: A search for cognitive invariants. *Personality and Social Psychology Bulletin*, 15, 4–18.

Boddy, J., Carvier, A. and Rowley, K. (1986) Effects of positive and negative verbal reinforcement on performance as a function of extroversion-introversion: Some tests of Gray's Theory. *Personality and Individual Differences*, 7, 81–88.

Bolles, R. (1975) *The Theory of Motivation*. Harper and Row, New York.

Bonem, M. and Crossman, E. (1988) Elucidating the effects of reinforcement magnitude. *Psychological Bulletin*, 104, 348–362.

Borden, M. (1972) *Purposive Explanation in Psychology*. Harvard University Press, Cambridge, Mass.

Borkowski, J., Weyhing, R. and Carr M. (1988) Effects of attributional retraining on strategy-based reading comprehension in learning disabled children. *Journal of Educational Psychology*, 80, 46–53.

Bourget, L.G.C. (1977) Delight and information specificity on elements of positive interpersonal feedback. *Dissertation Abstracts International*, 38, 1946B–1947B.

Bower, G. and Hilgard, E. (1981) *Theories of Learning*. Prentice-Hall, Englewood Cliffs, N.J.

Bower, G., McLean, J. and Meachan, J. (1966) Value of knowing when reinforcement is due. *Journal of Comparative and Physiological Psychology*, 62, 184–192.

Brammer, L. (1973) *The Helping Relationship*. Prentice-Hall, Englewood Cliffs, N.J.

Breakwell, G. (1990) *Interviewing*. Routledge, London.

Brehm, S. and Brehm, J. (1981) *Psychological Reactance: A Theory of Freedom and Control*. Academic Press, New York.

Breland, K. and Breland, M. (1961) The misbehaviour of organisms. *American Psychologist*, 16, 681–684.

Brenner, M. (1985) Survey interviewing. In M. Brenner, J. Brown and D. Canter (eds) *The Research Interview: Uses and Approaches*. Academic Press, London.

Brewer, W. (1974) There is no convincing evidence for operant and classical conditioning in humans. In W. Weimer and D. Palermo (eds) *Cognition and Symbolic Processes*. Lawrence Erlbaum, Hillsdale, N.J.

Brickman, P., Rabinowitz, V.C., Karuza, J., Coates, D., Cohn, E. and Kidder, L. (1982) Models of helping and coping. *American Psychologist*, 37, 368–384.

Brooks, W. and Heath, R. (1985) *Speech Communication*. W.C. Brown, Dubuque, Iowa.

Brophy, J. (1981) Teacher praise: A functional analysis. *Review of Educational Research*, 51, 5–32.

Brown, B., Frankel, B. and Fennell, M. (1989) Hugs and shrugs; parental and peer influence on continuity of involvements in sport by female adolescents. *Sex Roles*, 20, 397–409.

Brown, K., Willis, B. and Reid, D. (1981) Differential effects of supervisor verbal feedback and feedback plus approval on institutional staff performance. *Journal of Organizational Behaviour Management*, 3, 57–68.

Brundage, L., Derlega, V. and Cash, T. (1977) The effects of physical attractiveness and need for approval on self-disclosure. *Personality and Social Psychology Bulletin*, 3, 63–66.

Bruner, J. and Taguiri, R. (1954) The perception of people. In G. Lindzey (ed.) *Handbook of Social Psychology*. Addison-Wesley, Reading, Mass.

Brunner, L.J. (1979) Smiles can be back-channels. *Journal of Personality and Social Psychology*, 37, 728–734.

Bryan, J. and Freed, F. (1982) Corporal punishment: Normative data and sociological and psychological correlates in a community college population. *Journal of Youth and Adolescence*, 11, 77–87.

Buck, R. (1988) *Human Motivation and Emotion*. Wiley, New York.

Bugental, D., Kaswan, J., Love, L. and Fox, M. (1970) Child versus adult perception of evaluative messages in verbal, vocal and visual channels. *Developmental Psychology*, 2, 267–375.

Bull, P. (1978) The psychological significance of posture. Unpublished Ph.D. thesis, University of Exeter.

Bull, P. (1983) *Body Movement and Interpersonal Communication*. Wiley and Sons, Chichester.

Buller, M. and Buller, D. (1987) Physicians' communication style and patient satisfaction. *Journal of Health and Social Behaviour*, 28, 375–388.

Burgoon, J. (1985) Nonverbal signals. In M. Knapp and G. Miller (eds) *Handbook of Interpersonal Communication*. Sage, Beverly Hills, Cal.

Burgoon, J. and Aho, L. (1982) Field experiments on the effects of violations of conversational distance. *Communication Monographs*, 49, 71–88.

Burgoon, J. and Jones, S. (1976) Toward a theory of personal space expectation and their violations. *Human Communication Research*, 2, 131–146.

Burgoon, M. and Koper, R.J. (1984) Non-verbal and relational communication associated with reticence. *Human Communication Research*, 10, 601–627.

Busch, P. and Wilson, D.T. (1976) An experimental analysis of a salesman's expert and referent bases of social power in the buyer–seller dyad. *Journal of Marketing Research*, 13, 3–11.

Bushman, B.J. (1984) Perceived symbols of authority and their influence on compliance. *Journal of Applied Social Psychology*, 14, 501–508.

Bushman, B.J. (1988) The effects of apparel on compliance: A field experiment with a female authority figure. *Personality and Social Psychology Bulletin*, 14, 459–467.

Buss, A. (1983) Social rewards and personality. *Journal of Personality and Social Psychology*, 44, 553–563.

Butler-Sloss, E. (1988) *Report of the Inquiry into Child Abuse in Cleveland, 1987*. HMSO, London.

Byrne, D. (1961) Interpersonal attraction and attitude similarity. *Journal of Abnormal and Social Psychology*, 62, 713–715.

Byrne, D. (1971) *The Attraction Paradigm*. New York: Academic Press, New York.

Byrne, D. and Clore, G. (1967) Effectance arousal and attraction. *Journal of Personality and Social Psychology Monograph*, 6, Whole no. 638.

Byrne, D. and Greendlinger, V. (1989) Need for affiliation as a predictor of classroom friendships. Unpublished manuscript, State University of New York.

Byrne, D. and Nelson, D. (1965) Attraction as a linear function of proportion of positive reinforcements. *Journal of Personality and Social Psychology*, 1, 659–663.

Cairns, L. (1986) Reinforcement. In O. Hargie (ed.) *A Handbook of Communication Skills*. Croom Helm, London.

Cann, A., Sherman, S.J. and Elkes, R. (1975) Effects of initial request size and timing of a second request on compliance: The foot-in-the-door and the door-in-the-face. *Journal of Personality and Social Psychology*, 32, 774–782.

Cannell, C. and Kahn, R. (1968) Interviewing. In G. Lindzey and E. Aronson (eds) *The Handbook of Social Psychology*, Vol. 2. Addison-Wesley, Reading, Mass.

Cannell, C., Oksenberg, L. and Converse, J. (1977) Striving for response accuracy: Experiments in new interviewing techniques. *Journal of Marketing Research*, 14, 306–321.

Cappella, J.N. (1981) Mutual influence in expressive behaviour: adult–adult and infant–adult dyadic interaction. *Psychological Bulletin*, 89, 101–132.

Capella, J.N. (1984) The relevance of the microstructure of interaction to relationship change. *Journal of Social and Personal Relationships*, 1, 239–264.

Carkhuff, R. and Berenson, B. (1967) *Beyond Counselling and Therapy*. Holt, Rinehart and Winston, New York.

Carter, J.A. (1978) Impressions of counselors as a function of counselor physical attractiveness. *Journal of Counseling Psychology*, 25, 28–34.

Carver, C. and Scheier, M. (1988) *Perspectives on Personality*. Allyn and Bacon, Boston.

Cary, M.S. (1978) Does civil inattention exist in pedestrian passing? *Journal of Personality and Social Psychology*, 36, 1185–1193.

Cash, T.F., Begley, P.J. McConn, D.A. and Weise, B.C. (1975) When counselors are heard but not seen: Initial impact of physical attractiveness. *Journal of Counseling Psychology*, 22, 273–279.

Cash, T.F. and Kehr, J. (1978) Influence of non-professional counselors' physical attractiveness and sex on perceptions of counselor behavior. *Journal of Counseling Psychology*, 25, 336–342.

Cash, T.F. and Salzbach, R.F. (1978) The beauty of counseling: Effects of counselor physical attractiveness and self-disclosure on perceptions of counselor behavior. *Journal of Counseling Psychology*, 25, 283–291.

Castaneda, G., Hendrick, S. and Fanary, R. (1986) Housework allocation, role conflicts and coping strategies in dual-career couples. Paper presented at Southwest Psychological Association, Fort Worth, Tex.

Catano, V. (1976) Effectiveness of verbal praise as a function of expertise of its source. *Perceptual and Motor Skills*, 42, 1283–1286.

Cavior, N. and Dokecki, P.R. (1971) Physical attractiveness, perceived attitude similarity and academic achievement as contributors to interpersonal attraction among adolescents. *Developmental Psychology*, 9, 44–54.

Chambliss, C. and Murray, E.J. (1979) Cognitive procedures for smoking reduction: Symptom attribution versus efficacy attribution. *Cognitive Therapy and Research*, 3, 91–95.

Charny, E.J. (1966) Psychosomatic manifestations of rapport in psychotherapy. *Psychosomatic Medicine*, 28, 305–315.

Cheek, J. and Hogan, R. (1983) Self-concepts, self-presentations and moral judgements. In J. Suls and A. Greenwald (eds) *Psychological Perspectives on the Self*, Vol. 2. Lawrence Erlbaum Assocs, Hillsdale, N.J.

Chelune, C.J. (1979) Measuring openness in interpersonal communication. In G.J. Chelune (ed.) *Self Disclosure*. Jossey Bass, London.

Chown, S.M. (1981) Friendship in old age. In S.W. Duck and R. Gilmour (eds) *Personal Relationships 2: Developing Personal Relationships*. Academic Press, London.

Cialdini, R.B. (1985) *Influence: Science and Practice*. Scott Foresman, Glenview, Ill.

Cialdini, R.B. (1988) *Influence: Science and Practice* (2nd edn). Scott Foresman, Glenview, Ill.

Cialdini, R.B., Borden, R.J., Thorne, A., Walker, M.R. and Freeman, S. (1976) Basking in reflected glory. *Journal of Personality and Social Psychology*, 34, 366–375.

Cialdini, R.B., Vincent, J.E., Lewis, S.K., Catalan, J., Wheeler, D. and Darby, B. L. (1975) Reciprocal concessions procedure for inducing compliance: The door-in-the-face technique. *Journal of Personality and Social Psychology*, 31, 206–215.

Cipani, E. (1990) The communicative function hypothesis: An operant behaviour perspective. *Journal of Behaviour Therapy and Experimental Psychiatry*, 21, 239–274.

Clairborn, C.D. (1979) Effects of counselor interpretation, restatement and nonverbal behaviour on perceptions of the counselor and the counselor's ability to influence. *Dissertation Abstracts International*, 39, 505B.

Clay, M.M. (1969) Reading errors and self correction behaviour. *British Journal of Educational Psychology*, 39, 47–56.

Clifford, M. (1975) Physical attractiveness and academic performance. *Child Study Journal*, 5, 201–209.

Clifford, M. and Walster, E. (1973) The effect of physical attractiveness on teacher expectations. *Sociology of Education*, 46, 248–257.

Clore, G.L. (1977) Reinforcement and affect in attraction. In S.W. Duck (ed.) *Theory and Practice in Interpersonal Attraction*. Academic Press, London.

Clore, G.L. and Byrne, D. (1974) A reinforcement–affect model of attraction. In T.L. Huston (ed.) *Foundations of Interpersonal Attraction*. Academic Press, New York. Also in T.L. Huston (ed.) *Perspectives on Interpersonal Attraction*. Academic Press. New York and London.

Clore, G., Wiggins, N. and Itkins, S. (1975) Judging attraction from nonverbal behaviour: The gain phenomenon. *Journal of Counseling and Clinical Psychology*, 43, 491–497.

Condon, J.W. and Crano, W.D. (1988) Inferred evaluation and the relationship between attitude similarity and interpersonal attraction. *Journal of Personality and Social Psychology*, 54, 789–797.

Conger, R. and Killeen, P. (1974) Use of concurrent operants in small group research: A demonstration. *Pacific Sociological Review*, 17, 399–416.

Cook, H. (1985) Generality and generalization of social reinforcer efficacy subsequent to satisfaction. *The Journal of Psychology*, 119, 527–33.

Cook, M. (1970) Experiments on orientation and proxemics. *Human Relations*, 23, 61–76.

Cooley, C. (1902) *Human Nature and the Social Order*. Charles Scribner's Sons, New York.

Cooper, H. (1977) Controlling personal rewards – professional teachers' differential use of feedback and the effects of feedback on the students' motivation to perform. *Journal of Educational Psychology*, 69, 419–427.

Cormier, W.H. and Cormier, L.S. (1979) *Interviewing Strategies for Helpers: A Guide to Assessment, Treatment and Evaluation*. Brooks/Cole, California.

Cramer, R., Lutz, D., Bartell, P., Dragna, M., and Helzer, K. (1989) Motivating and reinforcing functions of the male sex role: Social analogues of partial reinforcement, delay of reinforcement, and intermittent shock. *Sex Roles*, 20, 551–773.

Crosby, F. and Nyquist, L. (1977) The female register: An empirical study of Lakoff's hypotheses. *Language in Society*, 6, 313–322.

Crouse, B.B. and Mehrabian, A. (1977) Affiliation of opposite-sexed strangers. *Journal of Research in Personality*, 11, 38–47.

Crowell, C., Anderson, C., Abel, D. and Sergio, J. (1988) Task clarification, performance feedback and social praise: Procedures for improving the customer service of bank tellers. *Journal of Applied Behaviour Analysis*, 21, 65–71.

Crowne, D. and Marlowe, D. (1964) *The Approval Motive*. Wiley, New York.

Crutchfield, R.S. (1955) Conformity and character. *American Psychologist*, 10, 191–198.

Cummings, N.A. (1979) Turning bread into stones: Our modern anti-miracle. *American Psychologist*, 34, 1119–1129.

Curran, J. (1979) Social skills: Methodological issues and future directions. In A. Bellack and M. Hersen (eds) *Research and Practice in Social Skills Training*. Plenum, New York.

Curtis, R.C. and Miller, K. (1986) Believing another likes or dislikes you: Behavior making the beliefs come true. *Journal of Personality and Social Psychology*, 51, 284–290.

D'Augelli, A.R. (1974) Nonverbal behavior of helpers in initial helping interactions. *Journal of Counseling Psychology*, 21, 360–363.

Davey, G. (1981) Behaviour modification in organizations. In G. Davey (ed.) *Applications of Conditioning Theory*. Methuen, London.

Davey, G. (1988) Trends in human operant theory. In G. Davey and C. Cullen (eds) *Human Operant Conditioning and Behaviour Modification*. Wiley, Chichester.

Davey, G. (1989) *Ecological Learning Theory*. Routledge, London.

Davies, M. (1985) *The Essential Social Worker: A Guide to Positive Practice*. Gower, Aldershot.

Dawes, R.M. (1980) Social dilemmas. In M. Rosenzweig and L. Porter (eds) *Annual Review of Psychology*, 31, 169–193.

Day, B.R. (1961) A comparison of personality needs of courtship couples and same-sex friends. *Sociology and Social Research*, 45, 435–440.

Day, W. (1980) The historical antecedents of contemporary behaviourism. In R. Rieber and K. Salzinger (eds) *Psychology: Theoretical-Historical Perspectives*. Academic Press, New York.

de Charms, R. (1976) *Enhancing Motivation: Change in the Classroom*. Irvington, New York.

Deci, E.L, Nezlek, J. and Sheinman, L. (1981) Characteristics of the rewarder and intrinsic motivation of the rewardee. *Journal of Personality and Social Psychology*, 40, 1–10.

Deci, E. and Porac, J. (1978) Cognitive evaluation theory and the study of human motivation. In M. Lepper and D. Greene (eds) *The Hidden Costs of Rewards: New Perspectives on the Psychology of Human Motivation*. Lawrence Erlbaum Assocs, Hillsdale, N.J.

Deci, E. and Ryan, R. (1980) The empirical exploration of intrinsic motivational processes. In L. Berkowitz (ed.) *Advances in Experimental Psychology*, Vol. 13. Academic Press, New York.

Deitz, S.R., Littman, M. and Bentley, B.J. (1984) Attribution of responsibility for rape: The influence of observer empathy, victim resistance and victim attractiveness. *Sex Roles*, 10, 261–280.

DeNike, L. and Spielberger, C. (1963) Induced mediating states in verbal conditioning. *Journal of Verbal Learning and Verbal Behaviour*, 1, 339–345.

DePaulo, B., Kenny, D., Hoover, C., Webb, W. and Oliver, P. (1987) Accuracy of person perception: Do people know what kinds of impressions they convey? *Journal of Personality and Social Psychology*, 52, 303–315.

Derlega, V. and Berg, J. (eds) (1987) *Self-disclosure: Theory, Research and Therapy*. Plenum Press, New York.

Derlega, V.J., Winstead, B.A., Wong, P.T.P. and Hunter, S. (1985) Gender effects in an initial encounter: A case where men exceed women in disclosure. *Journal of Social and Personal Relationships*, 2, 25–44.

Deutsch, M. and Gerard, H.B. (1955) A study of normative and informational influence upon individual judgement. *Journal of Abnormal and Social Psychology*, 61, 181–189.

DeWaal, F. (1989) *Peacemaking among Primates*. Harvard University Press, Cambridge, Mass.

Dickinson, A. (1989) The detrimental effects of extrinsic reinforcement on 'intrinsic motivation'. *The Behaviour Analyst*, 12, 1–15.

Dickson, A. (1985) *Assertiveness and You – A Woman In Your Own Right*. Quartet Books, London.

Dickson, D. (1981) Microcounselling: An evaluative study of a programme. Unpublished Ph.D. thesis, Ulster Polytechnic.

Dickson, D. (1986) Reflecting. In O. Hargie (ed.) *A Handbook of Communication Skills*. Croom Helm, London.

Dickson, D. (1988) *Improving the communication skill of health professionals: A structured approach to training*. Paper presented at the London Conference of the British Psychological Society, City University, London, 19 and 20 December.

Dickson, D. (1989) Interpersonal communication in the health professions: A focus on training. *Counselling Psychology Quarterly*, 2, 345–367.

Dickson, D., Hargie, O. and Morrow, N.C. (1989) *Communication Skills Training for Health Professionals*. Chapman and Hall, London.

Dickson, D. and Mullan T. (1990) An empirical investigation of the effects of a microcounselling programme with social work students: The acquisition and transfer of component skills. *Counselling Psychology Quarterly*, 3, 267–283.

Dies, R.R. and Greenberg, B. (1976) Effects of physical contact in an encounter group context. *Journal of Consulting and Clinical Psychology*, 44, 400–405.

Dillard, J. (1990) The nature and substance of goals in tactical communication. In M. Cody and M. McLaughlin (eds) *The Psychology of Tactical Communication*. Multilingual Matters, Clevedon.

Dillon, J. (1990) *The Practice of Questioning*. Routledge, London.

DiMatteo, M. and DiNicola, D. (1982) *Achieving Patient Compliance: The Psychology of the Medical Practitioner's Role*. Pergamon, New York.

Dinkmeyer, D. (1971) Contributions to teleoanalytic theory and techniques of school counseling. In C. Beck (ed.) *Philosophical Guidelines for Counseling*. W. S. Brown, Dubuque, Iowa.

Dion, K. (1972) Physical attractiveness and evaluation of children's transgressions. *Journal of Personality and Social Psychology*, 24, 207–213.

Dion, K. and Berscheid, E. (1974) Physical attractiveness and peer perception among children. *Sociometry*, 37, 1–12.

Dion, K., Berscheid, E. and Walster, E. (1972) What is beautiful is good. *Journal of Personality and Social Psychology*, 24, 285–290.

Dodds, R. (1983) Love and joy in the gymnasium. In G. Martin and D. Hrycaiko (eds) *Behaviour Modification and Coaching: Principles, Procedures and Research*. C.C. Thomas, Springfield, Ill.

Domjan, M. and Burkhard, B. (1986) *The Principles of Learning and Behaviour*. Brooks Cole, Monterey, Cal.

Donohue, G. and Tryon, W. (1985) A functional analysis of social reinforcement in vicarious verbal conditioning. *Pavlovian Journal*, 20, 140–148.

Drucker, P. (1954) *The Practice of Management*. Harper, New York.

Duck, S. (1977) *The Study of Acquaintance*. Gower Press, Farnborough.

Duck, S. (1982) A topography of relationship disengagement and dissolution. In S.W. Duck (ed.) *Personal Relationships 4: Dissolving Personal Relationships*. Academic Press, London.

Duck, S. (1986) *Human Relations: An Introduction to Social Psychology*. Sage, London.

Duck, S. (1988) *Relating to Others*. Open University Press, Milton Keynes.

Duck, S.W. (1991) *Friends for Life* (2nd edn). Harvester, New York.

Duck, S.W. and Miell, D.E. (1986) Charting the development of personal relationships. In R. Gilmour and S. W. Duck (eds) *The Emerging Field of Personal Relationships*. Lawrence Erlbaum, Hillsdale, N.J.

Duck, S.W., Rutt, D.J., Hurst, M. and Strejc, H. (1991) Some evident truths about communication in everyday relationships: All communication is not created equal. *Human Communication Research* (in press).

Dudley, W. and Blanchard, E. (1976) Comparison of experienced and inexperienced interviewers on objectively scored interview behaviour. *Journal of Clinical Psychology*, 32, 690–697.

Dulany, D. (1968) Awareness, rules and propositional control: A confrontation with S-R behaviour theory. In T. Dixon and D. Horton (eds) *Verbal Behaviour and General Behaviour Theory*. Prentice-Hall, Englewood Cliffs, N.J.

Duncan, S. (1972) Some signals and rules for taking speaking turns in conversations. *Journal of Personality and Social Psychology*, 23, 283–292.

Duncan, S. and Fiske, D.W. (1977) *Face-to-face Interaction: Research, Methods and Theory*. Lawrence Erlbaum, Hillsdale, N.J.

Dunham, P. (1977) The nature of reinforcing stimuli. In W. Honig and J. Staddon (eds) *Handbook of Operant Behaviour*. Prentice-Hall, Englewood Cliffs, N.J.

Dweck, C. (1975) The role of expectations and attributions in the alleviation of learned helplessness. *Journal of Personality and Social Psychology*, 31, 674–685.

Eagly, A.H. and Johnson, B.T. (1990) Gender and leadership style: A meta analysis. *Psychological Bulletin*, 108, 2, 233–256.

Ebbesen, E.B., Kjos, G.L. and Konecni, V.J. (1976) Spatial ecology: Its effects on the choice of friends and enemies. *Journal of Experimental Social Psychology*, 12, 505–518.

Egan, G. (1982) *The Skilled Helper*. Brooks/Cole, Monterey, Cal.

Egan, G. (1986) *The Skilled Helper* (3rd ed). Brooks/Cole, Monterey, Cal.

Egan, G. (1990) *The Skilled Helper* (4th ed). Brooks/Cole, Monterey, Cal.

Ehrlich, R.P., D'Augelli, A.R. and Danish, S.J. (1979) Comparative effectiveness of six counselor verbal responses. *Journal of Counseling Psychology*, 26, 290–298.

Eicher, J.B. and Kelley, E.A. (1972) High school as a meeting place. *Michigan Journal of Secondary Education*, 13, 12–16.

Eisenberg, G., Eisenberg, A. and Eisenberg, H. (1986) *Night Calls*. Berkley, New York.

Eisenberg, N., Cialdini, R.B., McCreath, H. and Shell, R. (1987) Consistency based compliance: When and why do children become vulnerable? *Journal of Personality and Social Psychology*, 52, 1174–1181.

Ekman, P. (1982) *Emotion in the Human Face*. Cambridge University Press, Cambridge.

Ekman, P. and Oster, H. (1979) Facial expressions of emotion. *Annual Review of Psychology*, 30, 527–555.

Elder, J. (1978) *Transactional Analysis in Health Care*. Addison-Wesley, Menlo Park, Cal.

Elkind, D. (1967) Egocentrism in adolescence. *Child Development*, 38, 1025–1034.

Ellis, A. and Beattie, G. (1986) *The Psychology of Language and Communication*. Weidenfeld and Nicolson, London.

Ellis, R. and Whittington, D. (1981) *A Guide to Social Skill Training*. Croom Helm, London.

Emmons, R. (1989) The personal striving approach to personality. In L. Pervin (ed.) *Goal Concepts in Personality and Social Psychology*. Lawrence Erlbaum, Hillsdale, N.J.

Epling, W. and Pierce, W. (1988) Applied behaviour analysis: new directions from the laboratory. In G. Davey and C. Cullen (eds) *Human Operant Conditioning and Behaviour Modification*. Wiley, Chichester.

Erwin, P.G. and Calev, A. (1984) The influence of Christian name stereotypes on the marking of children's essays. *British Journal of Educational Psychology*, 54, 223–227.

Estes, W. (1971) Reward in human learning: Theoretical issues and strategic choice points. In R. Glaser (ed.) *The Nature of Reinforcement*. Academic Press, New York.

Fairbairn, S. and Fairbairn, G. (eds) (1987) *Psychology, Ethics and Change*. Routledge and Kegan Paul, London.

Fantino, E. (1977) Conditioned reinforcement: Choice and information. In W. Honig and J. Staddon (eds) *Handbook of Operant Behaviour*. Prentice-Hall, Englewood Cliffs, N.J.

Fantuzzo, J., Rohrbeck, C., Hightower, A. and Work, W. (1991) Teachers' use and children's preferences of rewards in elementary school. *Psychology in the Schools*, 28, 175–181.

Faraone, S. and Hurtig, R. (1985) An examination of social skill, verbal productivity, and Gottman's model of interaction using observational methods and sequential analyses. *Behavioural Assessment*, 7, 349–366.

Feather, N. (1982) *Expectations and Actions*. Lawrence Erlbaum Assocs, Hillsdale, N.J.

Feigenbaum, W.M. (1977) Reciprocity in self-disclosure within the psychological interview. *Psychological Reports*, 40, 15–26.

Feingold, A. (1990) Gender differences in effects of physical attractiveness on romantic attraction: A comparison across five research paradigms. *Journal of Personality and Social Psychology*, 59, 981–993.

Feldman, S.D. (1971) The presentation of shortness in everyday life – height and heightism in American society: Towards a sociology of stature. Paper presented at the meetings of the American Sociological Association.

Felson, R. (1985) Reflected appraisal and the development of self. *Social Psychology Quarterly*, 48, 71–78.

Felson, R. (1989) Parents and the reflected appraisal process: A longitudinal analysis. *Journal of Personality and Social Psychology*, 56, 965–971.

Felson, R. B. and Reed, M.D. (1986) Reference group and self-appraisals of academic ability and performance. *Social Psychology Quarterly*, 49, 103–109.

Ferster, C. and Skinner, B.F. (1957) *Schedules of Reinforcement*. Appleton-Century-Crofts, New York.

Festinger, L. (1954) A theory of social comparison processes. *Human Relations*, 7, 117–140.

Festinger, L., and Carlsmith, J.M. (1959) Cognitive consequences of forced compliance. *Journal of Abnormal and Social Psychology*, 58, 203–210.

Fisher, J., Rytting, M. and Helsin, R. (1975) Hands touching hands: Affective and evaluative effects of interpersonal touch. *Sociometry*, 39, 416–421.

Fisher, S. and Groce, S. (1990) Accounting practices in medical interviews. *Language in Society*, 19, 225–250.

Fitts, P. and Posner, M. (1973) *Human Performance*. Prentice-Hall, London.

Flaherty, D. (1982) Incentive contrast: A review of behavioural changes following shifts in reward. *Animal Learning and Behaviour*, 10, 409–440.

Flanders, N. and Simon, A. (1969) Teacher effectiveness. In R. Ebel (ed.) *Encyclopaedia of Educational Research*. Macmillan, New York.

Fletcher, G. (1984) Psychology and common sense. *American Psychologist*, 39, 203–213.

Foa, U.G. and Foa, E.B. (1975) *Resource Theory of Social Exchange*. General Learning Press, Morrison, N.J.

Folkes, V.S. (1982) Forming relationships and the matching hypothesis. *Journal of Personality and Social Psychology*, 8, 631–636.

Foot, H.C., Chapman, A.J. and Smith, J.R. (1977) Friendship and social responsiveness in boys and girls. *Journal of Personality and Social Psychology*, 35, 401–411.

Forbes, R.J. and Jackson, P.R. (1980) Nonverbal behaviour and the outcome of selection interviews. *Journal of Occupational Psychology*, 53, 65–72.

Forgas, J. (1985) *Interpersonal Behaviour*. Pergamon, Oxford.

Franzoi, S.L. and Herzog, M.E. (1987) Judging physical attractiveness: What body aspects do we use? *Personality and Social Psychology Bulletin*, 13, 34–44.

Frazee, H.E. (1953) Children who later become schizophrenic. *Smith College Studies Social Work*, 23, 125–149.

Frederiksen, L. and Johnson, R. (1981) Organizational behaviour management. In M. Hersen, R. Eisler and P. Miller (eds) *Progress in Behaviour Modification*, Vol. 12. Academic Press, New York.

Freedman, J. (1978) *Happy People*. Harcourt Brace Jovanovich, New York.

French, J.R.P. and Raven, B. (1959) The bases of social power. In D. Cartwright (ed.) *Studies in Social Power*. University of Michigan Press, Ann Arbor.

Fretz, B.R., Corn, R., Tuemmler, J. and Bellet, W. (1979) Counselor nonverbal behaviours and client evaluations. *Journal of Counseling Psychology*, 26, 304–311.

Geller, D., Goodstein, L., Silver, M. and Sternberg, W. (1974) On being ignored: The effects of the violation of implicit rules of social interaction. *Sociometry*, 37, 541–556.

Gergen, K. (1969) *The Psychology of Behaviour Exchange*. Addison-Wesley, Reading, Mass.

Gerstein, L. H. and Tesser, A. (1987) Antecedents and responses associated with loneliness. *Journal of Social and Personal Relationships*, 4, 329–363.

Giacolone, R. and Rosenfeld, P. (1987) Impression management concerns and reinforcement interventions. *Group and Organization Studies*, 12, 445–453.

Giles, H. and Chavasse, W. (1975) Communication length as a function of dress style and social status. *Perceptual and Motor Skills*, 40, 961–962.

Glaser, R. (ed.) (1971) *The Nature of Reinforcement*. Academic Press, New York.

Glass, D. and Singer, J. (1972) *Urban Stress*. Academic Press, New York.

Goethals, G.R. (1986) Fabricating and ignoring social reality: Self-serving estimates on consensus. In J. Olsen, P. Herman and M. P. Zanna (eds) *Relative Deprivation and Social Comparison*. Lawrence Erlbaum, Hillsdale, N.J.

Goffman, E. (1959) *The Presentation of Self in Everyday Life*. Doubleday, New York.

Goffman, E. (1972) *Relations in Public: Micro-studies of the Public Order*. Penguin, Harmondsworth.

Goldman, M. (1980) Effect of eye-contact and distance on the verbal reinforcement of attitude. *Journal of Social Psychology*, 111, 73–78.

Goldman, W. and Ewis, P. (1977) Beautiful is Good: Evidence that the physically attractive are more socially skillful. *Journal of Experimental Social Psychology*, 13, 125–130.

Gompertz, K. (1960) The relation of empathy to effective communication. *Journalist Quarterly*, 37, 533–546.

Goodlad, J., Soder, R. and Sirotnik, K. (eds) (1990) *The Moral Dimensions of Teaching*. Jossey Bass, San Francisco.

Goodstein, L.D. (1965) Behaviour theoretical views of counseling. In B. Stefflre (ed.) *Theories of Counseling*. McGraw-Hill, New York.

Goss, C.S. (1984) Therapeutic influence as a function of therapist attire and the seating arrangement in an initial interview. *Journal of Clinical Psychology*, 40, 52–57.

Gottman, J.M. (1979) *Marital Interaction: Experimental Investigations*. Academic Press, New York.

Gouldner, A.W. (1960) The norm of reciprocity: A preliminary statement. *American Sociological Review*, 25, 161–178.

Graham, S. (1984) Communicating sympathy and anger to black and white students: The cognitive (attributional) consequences of affective cues. *Journal of Personality and Social Psychology*, 47, 40–54.

Graham, S. (1991) A review of attribution theory in achievement contexts. *Educational Psychology Review*, 3, 5–39.

Graham, S. and Barker, G. (1990) The downside of help: An attributional-developmental analysis of helping behavior as a low ability cue. *Journal of Educational Psychology*, 82, 7–14.

Graves, J.W. and Robinson, J.D. (1976) Proxemic behaviour as a function of inconsistent verbal and nonverbal messages. *Journal of Counseling Psychology*, 23, 333–338.

Graziano, W., Brothen, T. and Berscheid, E. (1978) Height and attraction: Do men and women see eye-to-eye? *Journal of Personality*, 46, 128–145.

Green, R. (1977) Negative reinforcement as an unrewarding concept – a plea for consistency. *Bulletin of the Psychological Society*, 30, 219–222.

Greenberg, L. and Clarke, K. (1979) Differential effects of the two-chair experiment and empathic reflections at a conflict marker. *Journal of Counseling Psychology*, 26, 1–8.

Greene, L.R. (1977) Effects of verbal evaluative feedback and interpersonal distance on behavioural compliance. *Journal of Counseling Psychology*, 24, 10–14.

Greenspoon, J. (1955) The reinforcing effect of two spoken sounds on the frequency of two responses. *American Journal of Psychology*, 68, 409–416.

Griffiths, R. (1973) The future development of MT technique – some possibilities. APLET International Conference on Educational Technology, April.

Griffitt, W. (1970) Environmental effects of interpersonal affective behaviour: Ambient effective temperature and attraction. *Journal of Personality and Social Psychology*, 15, 240–244.

Grush, J., Clore, G.L., and Costin, F. (1975) Dissimilarity and attraction: When difference makes a difference. *Journal of Personality and Social Psychology*, 32, 783–789.

Gudykunst, W. (1991) *Bridging Differences: Effective Intergroup Communication*. Sage, London.

Gupta, S. and Shukla, A. (1989) Verbal operant conditioning as a function of extroversion and reinforcement. *British Journal of Psychology*, 80, 39–44.

Gupton, T. and LeBow, M. (1971) Behavior management in a large industrial firm. *Behavioral Therapy*, 2, 78–82.

Gussman, K. and Harder, D. (1990) Offspring personality and perceptions of parental use of reward and punishment. *Psychological Reports*, 67, 923–930.

Haase, R.F. and Tepper, D. (1972) Non-verbal components of empathic communication. *Journal of Counseling Psychology*. 19, 417–424.

Hakmiller, K.L. (1966) Threat as a determinant of downward comparison. *Journal of Experimental Social Psychology*, 1, 32–39.

Hall, E.T. (1966) *The Hidden Dimension*. Doubleday, Garden City, N.Y.

Hall, J., Roter, D. and Katz, N. (1988) Meta-analysis of correlates of provider behaviour in medical encounters. *Medical Care*, 26, 657–673.

Hamachek, D. (1987) *Encounters with the Self*. CBS College Publishing, New York.

Hargie, O. (1980) An evaluation of a microteaching programme. Unpublished doctoral dissertation. Ulster Polytechnic, N. Ireland.

Hargie, O. (1986) Self-disclosure. In O. Hargie (ed.) *A Handbook of Communication Skills*. Croom Helm, London.

Hargie, O. and Maidment, P. (1979) *Microteaching in Perspective*. Blackstaff Press, Dundonald, N. Ireland.

Hargie, O. and Marshall, P. (1986) Interpersonal communication: A theoretical framework. In O. Hargie (ed.) *A Handbook of Communication Skills*. Croom Helm, London.

Hargie, O., Saunders, C. and Dickson, D. (1987) *Social Skills in Interpersonal Communication*. Croom Helm, London.

Harrigan, J.A. and Rosenthal, R. (1986) Nonverbal aspects of empathy and rapport in physician–patient interaction. In P.D. Blanck, R. Buck and R. Rosenthal (eds) *Nonverbal Communication in the Clinical Context*. Pennsylvania State University Press, Pennsylvania.

Harris, A. and Harris, T. (1986) *Staying OK*. Pan Books, London.

Hart, B. and Risley, T.R. (1980) In vivo language intervention: Unanticipated general effects. *Journal of Applied Behavior Analysis*, 13, 407–432.

Harter, S. (1990) Causes, correlates and the functional role of global self-worth: A life-span perspective. In R. Sternberg and J. Kolligian (eds) *Competence Considered*. Yale University Press, New Haven, Conn.

Haslett, B. and Ogilvie, J. (1988) Feedback processes in small groups. In R. Cathcart and L. Samovar (eds) *Small Group Communication*. W. C. Brown, Dubuque, Iowa.

Hatcher, C., Brooks, B. and Associates (1977) *Innovations in Counseling Psychology.* Jossey-Bass, San Francisco.

Hatfield, E. and Traupmann, J. (1981) Intimate relationships: A perspective from equity theory. In S. W. Duck and R. Gilmour (eds) *Personal Relationships 1: Studying Personal Relationships.* Academic Press, London.

Hatfield, E., Utne, M.K. and Traupmann, J. (1979) Equity theory and intimate relationships. In R.L. Burgess and T.L. Huston (eds) *Exchange Theory in Developing Relationships.* Academic Press, New York.

Hawkes, G.R. and Egbert, R.L. (1954) Personal values and the empathetic response: Their inter-relationships. *Journal of Educational Psychology*, 45, 469–476.

Hazan, C. and Shaver, P. (1987) Romantic love conceptualized as an attachment process. *Journal of Personality and Social Psychology*, 52, 511–524.

Heider, F. (1958) *The Psychology of Interpersonal Relations.* Wiley, New York.

Heller, M. and White, M. (1975) Rates of teacher approval and disapproval to higher and lower ability classes. *Journal of Educational Psychology*, 67, 796–800.

Henry, S., Medway. F. and Scarbo, H. (1979) Sex and locus of control as determinants of children's responses to peer versus adult praise. *Journal of Educational Psychology*, 71, 604–612.

Hensley, W.E. (1981) The effects of attire, location, and sex on aiding behavior: A similarity explanation. *Journal of Nonverbal Behavior*, 6, 3–11.

Herbert, M. (1989) *Discipline: A Positive Guide to Parents.* Basil Blackwell, Oxford.

Herman, C., Zanna, O. and Higgins, R. (eds) (1986) *The Ontario Symposium: Social Influence, 5.* Lawrence Erlbaum Assocs, Hillsdale, N.J.

Hermansson, G.L., Webster, A. C. and McFarland, K. (1988) Counselor deliberate postural lean and communication of facilitative conditions. *Journal of Counseling Psychology*, 35, 149–153.

Heron, J. (1990) *Helping the Client: A Creative Practical Guide.* Sage, London.

Hermstein, R. (1970) On the law of effect. *Journal of the Experimental Analysis of Behaviour*, 7, 185–188.

Heshka, S. and Nelson, Y. (1972) Interpersonal speaking distance as a function of age, sex and relationship. *Sociometry*, 35, 491–498.

Heslin, R. (1974) Steps toward a taxonomy of touching. Paper presented at the convention of the MidWestern Psychological Association, Chicago, May.

Heslin, R. and Alper, T. (1983) A bonding gesture. In J. Wiemann and R. Harrison (eds) *Non-Verbal Interaction: Sage Annual Review of Communication Research*, Vol. 11. Sage Publications, London.

Hewes, D. and Planalp, S. (1987) The individual's place in communication science. In C. Berger and S. Chaffee (eds) *Handbook of Communication Science.* Sage, London.

Highlen, P.S. and Baccus, G.K. (1977) Effects of reflection of feeling and probe on client self-referenced affect. *Journal of Counseling Psychology*, 24, 440–443.

Hildum, D. and Brown, R. (1956) Verbal reinforcement and interviewer bias. *Journal of Abnormal Psychology*, 53, 108–111.

Hill, C.E. (1987) Affiliation motivation: People who need people but in different ways. *Journal of Personality and Social Psychology*, 52, 1008–1018.

Hill, C.E. and Gormally, J. (1977) Effects of reflection, restatement, probe and non-verbal behaviours on client affect. *Journal of Counseling Psychology*, 24, 92–97.

Hill, C.E. and Stephany, A. (1990) Relation of nonverbal behaviour to client reactions. *Journal of Counseling Psychology*, 37, 22–26.

Hinde, R.A. (1979) *Towards Understanding Relationships.* Academic Press, London.

Hofling, C.K., Brotzman, E., Dalrymple, S., Graves, N. and Pierce, C.M. (1966) An experimental study of nurse–physician relationships. *Journal of Nervous and Mental Disease*, 143, 171–180.

Holahan, C.J. (1972) Seating patterns and patient behaviour in an experimental dayroom. *Journal of Abnormal Psychology*, 80, 115–124.

Holahan, C.J. (1977) Consultation in environmental psychology: A case study of a new counseling role. *Journal of Counseling Psychology*, 24, 151–254.

Holmes, J.G. and Boon, S.D. (1990) Developments in the field of close relationships: Creating foundations for intervention strategies. *Personality and Social Psychology Bulletin*, 16, 23–41.

Honeycutt, J.M., Cantrill, J.G. and Greene, R.W. (1989) Memory structures for relational escalation: A cognitive test of the sequencing of relational actions and stages. *Human Communication Research*, 16, 62–90.

Hore, T. (1971) Assessment of teaching practice: An 'Attractive' hypothesis. *British Journal of Educational Psychology*, 41, 302–305.

Hull, C. (1943) *Principles of Behaviour*. Appleton-Century-Crofts, New York.

Hulse, S., Egeth, H. and Deese, J. (1980) *The Psychology of Learning*. McGraw-Hill, New York.

Huston, T.L. (1983) Power. In H. Kelley *et al.* (eds) *Close Relationships*. Freeman and Company, New York.

Huston, T.L. and Levinger, G. (1978) Interpersonal attraction and relationships. *Annual Review of Psychology*, 29, 115–156.

Hutchins, P., Williams, R. and McLaughlin, T. (1989) Using group contingent free time to increase punctuality and preparedness of high school special education students. *Child and Family Therapy*, 11, 59–70.

Ickes, W. and Turner, M. (1983) On the social advantages of having an older, opposite-sex sibling: Birth order effects in mixed-sex dyads. *Journal of Personality and Social Psychology*, 45, 210–222.

Ivey, A. (1971) *Microcounselling: Innovations in Interviewing Training*. C.C. Thomas, Springfield, Ill.

Ivey, A. and Authier, J. (1978) *Microcounselling: Innovations in Interviewing, Counselling, Psychotherapy and Psychoeducation*. C.C. Thomas, Springfield, Ill.

Ivey, A.E. and Gluckstern, N.B. (1974) *Basic Attending Skills*. Microtraining Associates, North Amherst, Mass.

Jacobs, M. (1990) A controlled explosion? – a decade of counselling training. *British Journal of Guidance and Counselling*, 18, 113–126.

Jagacinski, C. and Nicholls, J. (1987) Competence and affect in task involvement and ego involvement: The impact of social comparison information. *Journal of Educational Psychology*, 79, 107–114.

James, W. (1890) *The Principles of Psychology*. Holt, New York.

Janis, I. (1983) The role of social support in adherence to stressful decisions. *American Psychologist*, 38, 143–160.

Jemmott, J.B., Ashby, K.L. and Lindenfeld, K. (1989) Romantic commitment and the perceived availability of opposite sex persons: On loving the one you're with. *Journal of Applied Social Psychology*, 19, 1198–1211.

Jennings, L.B. and George, S.G. (1984) Group induced distortion of visually perceived linear extent: The Asch effect revisited. *The Psychological Record*, 34, 133–148

Johnston, D.F. and Pittenger, J.B. (1984) Attribution, the attractiveness stereotype, and the elderly. *Developmental Psychology*, 20, 1168–1172.

Jones, E. (1990) *Interpersonal Perception*. Freeman and Company, New York.

Jones, E.E. and Wortman, C. (1973) *Ingratiation: An Attributational Approach*. General Learning Press, Morristown, N.J.

Jones, W., Hobbs, S. and Hockenbury, D. (1982) Loneliness and social skill deficits. *Journal of Personality and Social Psychology*, 42, 682–689.

Kaats, G.R. and Davis, K.E. (1970) The dynamics of sexual behaviour of college students. *Journal of Marriage and the Family*, 32, 390–399.

Kanfer, F. (1968) Verbal conditioning: A review of its current status. In T. Dixon and D. Horton (eds) *Verbal Behaviour and General Behaviour Therapy*. Prentice-Hall, Englewood Cliffs, N.J.

Kanfer, F. and Goldstein, A. (1986) *Helping People Change: A Textbook of Methods*. Pergamon, New York.

Karoly, P. and Harris, A. (1986) Operant methods. In F. Kanfer and A. Goldstein (eds) *Helping People Change: A Textbook of Methods*. Pergamon, New York.

Kaufman, A., Baron, A. and Kopp, R. (1966) Some effects of instructions on human operant behaviour. *Psychonomic Monograph Supplements*, 1, 243–250.

Kazdin, A. (1988) The token economy: A decade later. In G. Davey and C. Cullen (eds) *Human Operant Conditioning and Behaviour Modification*. Wiley, Chichester.

Keenan, A. (1976) Effects of non-verbal behaviour of interviewer on candidates' performance. *Journal of Occupational Psychology*, 49, 171–176.

Kelley, H.H. (1967) Attribution theory in social psychology. In D. Levine (ed.) *Nebraska Symposium on Motivation*, Vol. 15. University of Nebraska Press, Lincoln.

Kelley, H.H. (1983) Love and commitment. In H.H. Kelley *et al*. (eds) *Close Relationships*. Freeman, New York.

Kelley, H.H. and Thibaut, J.W. (1978) *Interpersonal Relations: A Theory of Interdependence*. Wiley, New York.

Kelly, E.W. and True, J.H. (1980) Eye contact and communication of facilitation conditions. *Perceptual and Motor Skills*, 51, 815–820.

Kelly, G. (1955) *The Psychology of Personal Constructs*. Norton, New York.

Kelman, H.C. (1974) Attitudes are alive and well and gainfully employed in the sphere of action. *American Psychologist*, 29, 310–335.

Kendon, A. (1981) Geography and gesture. *Semiotica*, 37, 129–163.

Kendon, A. (1983) Gesture and speech: How they interact. In J. Wiemann, and R. Harrison (eds) *Nonverbal Interaction. Sage Annual Reviews of Communication Research*, Vol. II. Sage Publications, London.

Kennedy, T., Timmons, E. and Noblin, C. (1971) Nonverbal maintenance of conditioned verbal behaviour following interpretations, reflections and social reinforcers. *Journal of Personality and Social Psychology*, 20, 112–117.

Kennedy, W. and Willcutt, H. (1964) Praise and blame as incentives. *Psychological Bulletin*, 62, 323–332.

Kennelly, K. and Mount, S. (1985) Perceived contingency of reinforcement, helplessness, focus of control and academic performance. *Psychology in the Schools*, 22, 465–469.

Kilham, W. and Mann, L. (1974) Level of destructive obedience as a function of transmitter and expectant roles in the Milgram obedience paradigm. *Journal of Personality and Social Psychology*, 29, 696–702.

Kimble, G. (1961) *Hilgard and Marquis Conditioning and Learning*. Appleton-Century-Crofts, New York.

Kimble, G. and Schlesinger, K. (eds) (1985) *Topics in the History of Psychology*. Lawrence Erlbaum Assocs, Hillsdale, N.J.

Kleck, R.E. (1969) Physical stigma and nonverbal cues emitted in face-to-face interaction. *Human Relations*, 22, 51–60.

Kleinke, C.L. (1975) Effects of false feedback about response lengths on subjects' perception of an interview. *Journal of Social Psychology*, 95, 99–104.

Kleinke, C.L. (1977) Effects of dress on compliance to requests in a field setting. *Journal of Social Psychology*, 101, 223–224.

Kleinke, C.L. (1986) *Meeting and Understanding People*. W.H. Freeman and Company, New York.

Kleinke, C.L. and Tully, T.B. (1979) Influence of talking level on perceptions of counselors. *Journal of Counseling Psychology*, 26, 23–29.

Klinger, E., Barta, S. and Maxeiner, M. (1981) Current concerns: Assessing therapeutically relevant motivation. In P. Kendall and S. Hollon (eds) *Assessment Strategies for Cognitive Behavioural Interventions*. Academic Press, New York.

Knapp, M.L. (1972) *Nonverbal Communication in Human Interaction*. Holt, Rinehart and Winston, New York.

Knapp, M.L. (1978) *Nonverbal Communication in Human Interaction* (2nd edn). Holt, Rinehart and Winston, New York.

Knapp, M.L., Hart, R., Friedrich, G. and Schulman, G. (1973) The rhetoric of good-bye: Verbal and nonverbal correlates of leave-taking. *Speech Monographs*, 40, 182–198.

Kolb, D.A. (1965) Achievement motivation training for under achieving high school boys. *Journal of Personality and Social Psychology*, 2, 783–792.

Komaki, J. (1982) Managerial effectiveness: Potential contributions of the behavioural approach. *Journal of Organizational Behaviour Management*, 3, 71–83.

Komaki, J. and Barnett, F. (1977) A behavioural approach to coaching football: Improving the play execution of the offensive backfield on a youth football team. *Journal of Applied Behaviour Analysis*, 10, 657–664.

Komaki, J., Blood, M. and Holder, D. (1980) Fostering friendliness in a fast food franchise. *Journal of Organizational Behaviour Management*, 2, 151–165.

Kopelman, R. (1983) Improving productivity through objective feedback: A review of the evidence. *National Productivity Review*, 83, 43–55.

Kopera, A.A., Maier, R.A. and Johnson, J.E. (1971) Perception and physical attractiveness: The influence of group interaction and group co-action on ratings of the attractiveness of photographs of women. *Proceedings of the 79th Annual Convention of the American Psychological Association*, 6, 317–318.

Korda, M. (1976) *Power in the Office*. Weidenfeld and Nicolson, London.

Koulack, D. and Tuthill, J.A. (1972) Height perception: A function of social distance. *Canadian Journal of Behavioural Science*, 4, 50–53.

Krasner, L. (1962) The therapist as a social reinforcement machine. In H. Strupp and L. Luborsky (eds) *Research in Psychotherapy*, Vol. 2. American Psychological Association, Washington, D.C.

Krebs, D. and Adinolf, A.A. (1975) Physical attractiveness, social relations and personality style. *Journal of Personality and Social Psychology*, 31, 245–253.

Kreps, G. (1988) The pervasive role of information in health and health care: Implications for health communication policy. In J. Anderson (ed.) *Communication Yearbook, II*. Sage, Beverly Hills, Cal.

Kruglanski, A. (1978) Endogenous attribution and intrinsic motivation. In M. Lepper and D. Greene (eds) *The Hidden Costs of Reward: New Perspectives on the Psychology of Human Motivation*. Academic Press, New York.

Kulka, R.A. and Kessler, J.B. (1978) Is justice really blind? – the influence of litigant physical attractiveness on juridical judgement. *Journal of Applied Social Psychology*, 8, 366–381.

Kunin, C. and Rodin, M. (1982) The interactive effects of counselor gender, physical attractiveness and status on client self-disclosure. *Journal of Clinical Psychology*, 38, 84–90.

Kurth, S.B. (1970) Friendship and friendly relations. In G.J. McCall, M. McCall, N. Denzin, G. Shuttles and S. Kurth (eds) *Social Relationships*. Aldine, Chicago.

Kurtz, P.D., Marshall, E.K. and Banspach, S.W. (1985) Interpersonal skill-training research: a 12 year review and analysis. *Counselor Education and Supervision*, 24, 249–263.

La France, M. (1979) Non-verbal synchrony and rapport: Analysis by the cross-lag panel technique. *Source Psychology Quarterly*, 42, 66–70.

La Gaipa, J.J. (1977) Interpersonal attraction and social exchange. In S.W. Duck (ed.) *Theory and Practice in Interpersonal Attraction*. Academic Press, London.

La Gaipa, J.J. (1982) Rules and rituals in disengaging from relationships. In S.W. Duck (ed.) *Personal Relationships 4: Dissolving Personal Relationships*. Academic Press, London.

Laird, J.D. (1974) Self attribution of emotion: The effects of expressive behaviour in the quality of emotional experience. *Journal of Personality and Social Psychology*, 29, 475–486.

Lakoff, R. (1975) *Language and Woman's Place*. Harper and Row, New York.

Lambert, M.J., Bergin, A.E. and Collins, J.L. (1978) Therapist-induced deterioration in psychotherapy. In A. S. Gurman and A. M. Razin (eds) *Effective Psychotherapy: A Handbook of Research*. Pergamon Press, Oxford.

Landy, D. and Aronson, E. (1960) The influence of the character of the criminal and his victim on the decision of simulated juries. *Journal of Experimental Social Psychology*, 5, 141–152.

Lang, G. and van der Molen, H. with Trower, P. and Look, R. (1990) *Personal Conversations: Roles and Skills for Counsellors*. Routledge, London.

Langer, E.J. and Rodin, J. (1976) The effects of choice and enhanced personal responsibility for the aged: A field experiment in an institutional setting. *Journal of Personality and Social Psychology*, 34, 191–198.

Langston, C.A. and Cantor, N. (1989) Social anxiety and social constraint: When making friends is hard. *Journal of Personality and Social Psychology*, 56, 649–661.

Larsen, K. and Smith, C. (1981) Assessment of nonverbal communication in the patient–physician interview. *Journal of Family Practice*, 12, 481–488.

Laver, J. and Hutcheson, S. (eds) (1972) *Communication in Face-to-Face Interaction*. Penguin, Harmondsworth.

Lawler, E. (1983) Reward systems in organizations. In J. Lorsch (ed.) *Handbook of Organizational Behaviour*. Prentice-Hall, Englewood Cliffs, N.J.

Lea, M. and Duck, S.W. (1982) A model for the role of similarity of values in friendship development. *British Journal of Social Psychology*, 21, 301–310.

Leahey, T. (1987) *A History of Psychology: Main Currents in Psychological Thought*. Prentice-Hall, Englewood Cliffs, N.J.

Leakey, R. and Lewin, R. (1978) *People of the Lake*. Doubleday, New York.

Lees, L. and Dygdon, J. (1988) The initiation and maintenance of exercise behaviour: A learning theory conceptualization. *Clinical Psychology Review*, 8, 345–353.

Lepper, M. and Greene, D. (1978) Overjustification research and beyond: Toward a means-ends analysis of intrinsic and extrinsic motivation. In M. Lepper and D. Greene (eds) *The Hidden Costs of Reward: New Perspectives on the Psychology of Human Motivation*. Wiley, New York.

Lepper, M.R. and Greene, D. (1978) *The Hidden Costs of Reward*. Lawrence Erlbaum, Hillsdale, N.J.

Lerner, M.J., Miller, D.T. and Holmes, J.G. (1976) Deserving and the emergence of forms of justice. *Advances in Experimental Social Psychology*, 9, 133–162.

Lerner, R.M. and Karabenick, S.A. (1974) Physical attractiveness, body attitudes and self-concept in late adolescents. *Journal of Youth and Adolescence*, 3, 307–316.

Lerner, R.M., Karabenick, S.A. and Stuart, J.L. (1973) Relations among physical attractiveness, body attitudes, and self-concept of male and female college students. *Journal of Psychology*, 85, 119–129.

Levinger, G. (1976) A social psychological perspective on marital dissolution. *Journal of Social Issues*, 32, 21–47.

Levinger, G. (1983) Development and change. In H.H. Kelley *et al.* (eds) *Close Relationships*. Freeman, New York.

Levinger, G. and Breedlove, J. (1966) Interpersonal attraction and agreement: A study of marriage partners. *Journal of Personality and Social Psychology*, 3, 367–72.

Lewin, K. (1938) *The Conceptual Representation and Measurement of Psychological Forces*. Duke University Press, Durham, N.C.

Lewis, K.N. and Walsh, W.B. (1978) Physical attractiveness: Its impact on the perception of a female counselor. *Journal of Counseling Psychology*, 25, 210–216.

Ley, P. (1988) *Communication with Patients: Improving Communication, Satisfaction and Compliance*. Croom Helm, London.

Liberman, B.L. (1978) The role of mastery in psychotherapy: Maintenance of improvement and prescriptive change. In J.D. Frank *et al.* (eds) *The Effective Ingredients of Successful Psychotherapy*. Brunner/Mazel, New York.

Libet, J. and Lewinsohn, P. (1973) Concept of social skill with special reference to the behaviour of depressed persons. *Journal of Consulting and Clinical Psychology*, 40, 304–312.

Lidtz, T., Cornelison, A., Fleck, S. and Terry, D. (1957) The intra-familial environment of schizophrenic patients. *American Journal of Psychiatry*, 114, 241–248.

Lieberman, D. (1990) *Learning: Behaviour and Cognition*. Wadsworth, Belmont, Cal.

Liggett, J. (1974) *The Human Face*. Stein and Day, New York.

Linden, R.C. and Mitchell, T.R. (1988) Ingratiatory behaviors in organizational settings. *Academy of Management Review*, 13, 572–587.

Locke, E. and Latham, G. (1984) *Goal Setting: A Motivational Technique that Works*. Prentice-Hall, Englewood Cliffs, N.J.

Logan, F. (1971) Incentive theory, reinforcement and education. In R. Glaser (ed.) *The Nature of Reinforcement*. Academic Press, New York.

Lombardo, J., Weiss, R. and Stich, M. (1973) Effectance reduction through speaking in reply and its relation to attraction. *Journal of Personality and Social Psychology*, 28, 325–332.

Lorr, M. and McNair, D.M. (1966) Methods relating to evaluation of therapeutic outcome. In L. A. Gottschalk and A. H. Auerbach (eds) *Methods of Research in Psychotherapy*. Appleton-Century-Crofts, New York.

Lott, A. and Lott, B. (1968) A learning theory approach to interpersonal attitude. In A. Greenwald, T. Brock and T. McOstrom (eds) *Psychological Foundations of Attitudes*. Academic Press, New York.

Lott, B. and Lott, A. (1985) Learning theory in contemporary social psychology. In G. Lindzey and E. Aronson (eds) *The Handbook of Social Psychology*, Vol. 1. Random House, New York.

Lovitt, T. and Hansen, C. (1976) The use of contingent skipping and drilling to improve oral reading and comprehension. *Journal of Learning Disabilities*, 9, 481–487.

Lowe, C. (1979) Determinants of human operant behaviour. In M. Zeiler and P. Harzem (eds) *Advances in Analysis of Behaviour*, Vol. 1. Wiley, Chichester.

Luthans, F. and Kreitner, R. (1975) *Organizational Behaviour Modification*. Scott Foresman, Glenview, Ill.

Lynch, J.J. (1977) *The Broken Heart: The Medical Consequences of Loneliness*. Basic Books, New York.

Lysakowski, R. and Walberg, H. (1981) Classroom reinforcement and learning: A quantitative synthesis. *Journal of Educational Research*, 75, 69–77.

McBee, G. and Justice, B. (1977) The effects of interviewer bias on mental illness questionnaire responses. *The Journal of Psychology*, 95, 67–75.

McCall, G. (1982) Becoming unrelated: The management of bond dissolution. In S. W. Duck (ed.) *Personal Relationships 4: Dissolving Personal Relationships*. Academic Press, London.

McDowell, J. (1988) Matching theory in natural human environments. *The Behavior Analyst*, 11, 95–109.

McGrade, B. (1966) Effectiveness of verbal reinforcers in relation to age and social class. *Journal of Personality and Social Psychology*, 4, 555–560.

McHenry, R. (1981) The selection interview. In M. Argyle (ed.) *Social Skills and Work.* Methuen, London.

McKenzie, T. and Rushall, B. (1974) Effects of self-recording on attendance and performance in a competitive swimming training environment. *Journal of Applied Behaviour Analysis*, 7, 191–206.

McLaughlin, M. (1984) *Conversation: How Talk is Organised.* Sage, Beverly Hills, Cal.

McLaughlin, T. and Williams, R. (1988) The Token Economy. In J. Witt, S. Elliott and F. Gresham (eds) *Handbook of Behavior Therapy in Education*. Plenum, New York.

MacLeod Clark, J. (1985) The development of research in interpersonal skills in nursing. In C. Kagan (ed.) *Interpersonal Skills in Nursing: Research and Applications*. Croom Helm, London.

McNaughton, S.S. and Glynn, T. (1981) Delayed versus immediate attention to oral reading errors. *Educational Psychology*, 1, 57–65.

McNaughton, S.S., Glynn, T. and Robinson, V. (1987) Pause, prompt and praise: Effective tutoring for remedial reading. *Positive Products*, Birmingham.

Mahon, B. R. and Altman, H. (1977) Skill training: Cautions and recommendations. *Counselor Education and Supervision*, 17, 42–50.

Maier, S. (1989) Learned helplessness: Event covariation and cognitive changes. In S. Klein and R. Mowrer (eds) *Contemporary Learning Theory: Instrumental Conditioning Theory and the Impact of Biological Constraints on Learning*. Lawrence Erlbaum Assocs, Hillsdale, N.J.

Major, B. and Heslin, R. (1982) Perceptions of cross-sex and same-sex nonreciprocal touch: It is better to give than to receive. *Journal of Nonverbal Behaviour*, 6, 148–161.

Makin, P., Cooker, C. and Cox, C. (1989) *Managing People at Work*. British Psychological Society, Leicester.

Marisi, D. and Helmy, K. (1984) Intratask integration as a function of age and verbal praise. *Perceptual and Motor Skills*, 58, 936–939.

Markus, H. and Cross, S. (1990) The interpersonal self. In L. Pervin (ed.) *Handbook of Personality: Theory and Research*. Guilford Press, New York.

Marquis, K. (1970) Effects of social reinforcement on health reporting in the household interview. *Sociometry*, 33, 203–215.

Marsh, H.W. and Parker, J. W. (1984) Determinants of student self-concept: Is it better to be a relatively large fish in a small pond even if you don't learn to swim well? *Journal of Personality and Social Psychology*, 47, 213–231.

Martens, B., Halperin, S., Rummel, J. and Kilpatrick, D. (1990) Matching theory applied to contingent teacher attention. *Behavioural Assessment*, 12, 139–157.

Martin, G. and Hrycaiko, D. (eds) (1983) *Behaviour Modification and Coaching: Principles, Procedures and Research*, C. C. Thomas, Springfield, Ill.

Martin, G., Le Page, R. and Koop, S. (1983) Applications of behaviour modification for coaching age-group competitive swimmers. In G. Martin and D. Hrycaiko (eds) *Behaviour Modification and Coaching: Principles, Procedures and Research*. C.C. Thomas, Springfield, Ill.

Maslach, C. (1978) The client role in staff burn-out. *Journal of Social Issues*, 34, 111–124.

Maslow, A.H. and Mintz, N.L. (1956) Effects of esthetic surroundings: 1. Initial effects of three esthetic conditions upon perceiving 'energy' and 'well-being' in faces. *Journal of Psychology*, 61, 153–157.

Mason, H. and Pratt, T. (1980) Communication skills and patient care. *American Journal of Pharmacy Education*, 43, 189–196.

Matarazzo, R. (1978) Research on the teaching and learning of psychotherapeutic skills. In

S. L. Garfield and A. E. Bergin (eds) *Handbook of Psychotherapy and Behaviour Change: An Empirical Analysis*. Wiley, New York.

Matarazzo, J.D. and Wiens, A.N. (1972) *The Interview: Research on its Anatomy and Structure*. Aldine-Atherton, Chicago.

Mathes, E.W. and Kahn, A. (1975) Physical attractiveness, happiness, neuroticism and self-esteem. *Journal of Psychology*, 90, 27–30.

Mayfield, E. (1972) Value of peer nominations in predicting life insurance. *Journal of Applied Psychology*, 46, 6–13.

Mead, G. (1934) *Mind, Self and Society*. University of Chicago Press, Chicago.

Mehrabian, A. (1969) Inference of attitudes from the posture, orientation and distance of a communicator. *Journal of Consulting and Clinical Psychology*, 33, 330–336.

Mehrabian, A. (1972) *Nonverbal Communication*. Aldine-Atherton, Chicago.

Mehrabian, A. and Friar, J.T. (1969) Encoding of attitude by a seated communicator via posture and position cues. *Journal of Consulting and Clinical Psychology*, 33, 330–336.

Melloh, R.A. (1964) Accurate empathy and counselor effectiveness. Unpublished doctoral dissertation, University of Florida.

Merbaum, M. (1963) The conditioning of affective self-references by three classes of generalized reinforcer. *Journal of Personality*, 31, 179–191.

Meyer, W.U., Bachmann, M., Biermann, U., Hempelmann, M., Ploger, F. and Spiller, H. (1979) The informational value of evaluative behaviour: Influence of praise and blame on perceptions of ability. *Journal of Educational Psychology*, 71, 259–268.

Meyer, W.U., Mittag, W. and Engler, U. (1986) Some effects of praise and blame on perceived ability and affect. *Social cognition*, 4, 293–308.

Michelson, L., Sugai, D., Wood, R. and Kazdin, A. (1983) *Social Skills Assessment and Training with Children*. Plenum, New York.

Miell, D.E. (1987) Remembering relationship development: Constructing a context for interaction. In R. Burnett, P. McGee and D. Clarke (eds) *Accounting for Relationships*. Methuen, London.

Mikulineer, M. (1986) Attributional processes in the learned helplessness paradigm: Behavioral effects of global attributions. *Journal of Personality and Social Psychology*, 51, 1248–1256.

Milgram, S. (1965) Some conditions of obedience and disobedience to authority. *Human Relations*, 18, 57–76.

Milgram, S. (1974) *Obedience to Authority: An Experimental View*. Harper and Row, New York.

Millar, A.G. (1970) Role of physical attractiveness in impression formation. *Psychonomic Science*, 19, 241–243.

Millar, R., Crute, V. and Hargie, O. (1992) *Professional Interviewing*. Routledge, London.

Miller, J. and Eller, B. (1985) An examination of the effect of tangible and social reinforcers on intelligence test performance of middle school students. *Social Behaviour and Personality*, 13, 147–157.

Miller, N. (1951) Learnable drives and rewards. In S. Stevens (ed.) *Handbook of Experimental Psychology*. Wiley, New York.

Miller, N. (1963) Some reflections on the law of effect produce a new alternative to drive reduction. In M. Jones (ed.) *Nebraska Symposium on Motivation*. University of Nebraska, Lincoln.

Miller, N. and Dollard, J. (1941) *Social Learning and Imitation*. Yale University Press, New Haven, Conn.

Miller, R., Brickman, P. and Bolen, D. (1975) Attribution versus persuasion as a means of modifying behavior. *Journal of Personality and Social Psychology*, 31, 430–441.

Mills, M.C. (1983) Adolescents' self-disclosure in individual and group theme-centred modelling, reflecting and probing interviews. *Psychological Reports*, 53, 691–701.

Mischel, W. (1973) Toward a cognitive social learning reconceptualization of personality. *Psychological Review*, 80, 252–283.

Mischel, W. (1990) Personality dispositions revisited and revised: A view after three decades. In L. Pervin (ed.) *Handbook of Personality Theory and Research*. Guilford Press, New York.

Mitchell, K.M., Bozarch, J.D. and Krauft, C.C. (1977) A re-appraisal of the therapeutic effectiveness of accurate empathy, non-possessive warmth and genuineness. In A. S. Gurman and A. M. Razin (eds) *Effective Psychotherapy: A Handbook of Research*. Pergamon Press, Oxford.

Mizes, J. (1985) The use of contingent reinforcement in the treatment of a conversion disorder: A multiple baseline study. *Journal of Behaviour Therapy and Experimental Psychiatry*, 16, 341–345.

Montagu, M.F.A. (1971) *Touching: The Human Significance of the Skin*. Columbia University Press, New York.

Montegar, C., Reid, D., Madsen, C. and Erwell, M. (1977) Increasing institutional staff-to-resident interaction through inservice training and supervisor approval. *Behavior Therapy*, 8, 533–540.

Moore, J.S., Graziano, W. and Millar, M.G. (1987) Physical attractiveness, sex role orientation and the evaluation of adults and children. *Personality and Social Psychology Bulletin*, 13, 95–102.

Morris, D., Collett, P., Marsh, P. and O'Shaughnessy, M. (1979) *Gestures: Their Origins and Distribution*. Stein and Day, New York.

Morrison, P., Burnard, P. and Hackett, P. (1991) A smallest space analysis of nurses' perceptions of their interpersonal skills. *Counselling Psychology Quarterly*, 4, 119–125.

Morton, T.L. and Douglas, M. (1981) Growth of relationships. In S. W. Duck and R. Gilmour (eds) *Personal Relationships 2: Developing Personal Relationships*. Academic Press, London.

Mosatche, H.S. and Bragonier, P. (1981) An observational study of social comparison in preschoolers. *Child Development*, 52, 314–322.

Mowrer, R. and Klein, S. (1989) A contract between traditional and contemporary learning theory. In S. Klein and R. Mowrer (eds) *Contemporary Learning Theory: Instrumental Conditioning Theory and the Impact of Biological Constraints on Learning*, Lawrence Erlbaum Assocs, Hillsdale, N.J.

Mulford, H.A. and Miller, D.E. (1964) Public acceptance of the alcoholic as sick. *Quarterly Journal of Alcohol Studies*, 25, 314–324.

Murray, E. (1956) The content analyses method of studying psychotherapy. *Psychological Monographs*, 70, No. 13 (Whole No. 420).

Murray, H.A. (1938) *Explorations in Personality: A Clinical and Experimental study of Fifty Men of College Age*. Oxford University Press, New York.

Murstein, B.I. (1972) Physical attractiveness and marital choice. *Journal of Personality and Social Psychology*, 22, 8–12.

Murstein, B.I. (1977) The stimulus value role (SVR) theory of dyadic relationships. In S. W. Duck (ed.) *Theory and Practice in Interpersonal Attraction*. Academic Press, London.

Murstein, B.I., MacDonald, M.G. and Cerreto, M. (1977) A theory and investigation of the effects of exchange-orientation on marriage and friendship. *Journal of Marriage and the Family*, 39, 543–548.

Nagata, D.K., Nay, W.R. and Seidman, E. (1983) Nonverbal and verbal content behaviors in the prediction of interviewer effectiveness. *Journal of Counseling Psychology*, 30, 85–86.

Nahemow, L. and Lawton, M.P. (1975) Similarity and propinquity in friendship formation. *Journal of Personality and Social Psychology*, 32, 205–213.

Nelson-Gray, R., Haas, J., Romano, B., Herbert, J. and Herbert, D. (1989) Effects of open-ended versus close-ended questions on interviewers' problem related statements. *Perceptual and Motor Skills*, 69, 903–911.

Nelson-Jones, R. (1983) *Practical Counselling Skills*. Holt, Reinhart and Winston, London.

Nicholls, J. (1978) The development of concepts of effort and ability, perception of own attainment, and the understanding that difficult tasks demand more ability. *Child Development*, 49, 800–814.

Nordhaug, O. (1989) Reward functions of personnel training. *Human Relations*, 42, 373–388.

Nosanchuk, T.A. and Erickson, B.H. (1985) How high is up? Calibrating social comparison in the real world. *Journal of Personality and Social Psychology*, 48, 624–634.

O'Brien, J. and Holborn, S. (1979) Verbal and nonverbal expressions as reinforcers in verbal conditioning of adult conversation. *Journal of Behaviour Psychiatry*, 10, 267–269.

O'Donnell, P., Kennedy, V. and McGill, P. (1983) Verbal operant conditioning, extinction trials and types of awareness statement. *Psychological Reports*, 53, 991–997.

O'Grady, K.E. (1989) Physical attractiveness, need for approval, social self-esteem, and maladjustment. *Journal of Social and Clinical Psychology*, 8, 62–69.

O'Leary, K. and O'Leary, S. (eds) (1977) *Classroom Management: The Successful Use of Behaviour Modification*. Pergamon, New York.

O'Leary, K., Poulos, R. and Devine, V. (1972) Tangible reinforcers: Bonuses or bribes? *Journal of Consulting and Clinical Psychology*, 38, 1–8.

Oliver, L. (1974) The effects of verbal reinforcement on career choice realism. *Journal of Vocational Behaviour*, 5, 275–284.

O'Reilly, C. and Puffer, S. (1989) The impact of rewards and punishments in a social context: A laboratory and field experiment. *Journal of Occupational Psychology*, 62, 41–53.

Overmeir, J.B. and Seligman, M.E.P. (1967) Effects of inescapable shock upon subsequent escape and avoidance learning. *Journal of Comparative and Physiological Psychology*, 63, 23–33.

Parker, S. and Kleiner, R.J. (1968) Reference group behaviour and mental disorder. In H.H. Hyman and E. Singer (eds) *Readings in Reference Group Theory and Research*. Free Press, New York.

Parsons, R. (1991) Empowerment – purpose and practice principle in social work. *Social Work with Groups*, 14, 7–23.

Parsons, J., Kaczala, C. and Meece, J. (1982) Socialization of achievement attitudes and beliefs. *Child Development*, 53, 322–339.

Patch, M.E. (1986) The role of source legitimacy in sequential request strategies of compliance. *Personality and Social Psychology Bulletin*, 12, 199–205.

Patterson, C.H. (1984) Reflections on client-centred therapy. Interviewed by Watkins, C. E. and Goodyear, R.K. *Counselor Education and Supervision*, 23, 178–186.

Patterson, M.L. (1976) An arousal model of interpersonal intimacy. *Psychological Review*, 83, 235–245.

Pattison, J.E. (1973) Effects of touch on self-exploration and the therapeutic relationship. *Journal of Consulting and Clinical Psychology*, 40, 170–175.

Pellegrini, R.J., Hicks, R.A., Meyers-Winton, S. and Antal, B.G. (1978) Physical attractiveness and self-disclosure in mixed sex dyads. *Psychological Record*, 28, 509–516.

Pendleton, M.G. and Batson, C.D. (1979) Self-presentation and the door-in-the-face technique for inducing compliance. *Personality and Social Psychology Bulletin*, 5, 77–81.

Perlman, D. (1986) Chance and coincidence in relationships. Paper presented at the International Conference on Personal Relationships, Tel Aviv, Israel.

Perlman, D. and Duck, S. W. (eds) (1987) *Intimate Relationships: Development, Dynamics and Deterioration*, Sage, Beverly Hills, Cal.

Perrott, E. (1982) *Effective Teaching*. Longman, London.

Perry, M. and Furukawa, M. (1986) Modelling methods. In F. Kanfer and A. Goldstein (eds) *Helping People Change*. Pergamon, New York.

Perry, R.P. and Penner, K.S. (1990) Enhancing academic achievement in college students through attributional retraining and instruction. *Journal of Educational Psychology*, 82, 262–271.

Pervin, L. (1989) *Goal Concepts in Personality and Social Psychology*. Lawrence Erlbaum, Hillsdale, N.J.

Peterson, C., Seligman, M.E.P. and Vaillant, G. (1988) Pessimistic explanatory style is a risk factor for physical illness: A thirty-five year longitudinal study. *Journal of Personality and Social Psychology*, 55, 23–27.

Phares, E. (1984) *Introduction to Personality*, C. Merrill, Columbus, Ohio.

Phillips, E. (1985) Social skills: History and prospect. In L. L'Abate and M. Milan (eds) *Handbook of Social Skills Training and Research*, Wiley, New York.

Pitman, E. (1984) *Transactional Analysis for Social Workers and Counsellors: An Introduction*. Routledge and Kegan Paul, London.

Podsakoff, P. (1982) Determinants of a supervisor's use of rewards and punishments: A literature review and suggestions for further research. *Organizational Behaviour and Human Performance*, 29, 58–83.

Poole, A., Sanson-Fisher, R. and Thompson, V. (1981) Observations on the behaviour of patients in a state mental hospital and a general hospital psychiatric unit: A comparative study. *Behaviour Research and Therapy*, 19, 125–134.

Pope, B. (1979) *The Mental Health Interview: Research and Application*. Pergamon, New York.

Porteous, J.D. (1977) *Environment and Behaviour*. Addison-Wesley, Reading, Mass.

Positano, S., Sandford, D., Elzing, R. and James J. (1990) Virtue rewarded: Reinforcement and punishment in an acute psychiatric admission ward. *Journal of Behaviour Therapy and Experimental Psychiatry*, 21, 257–267.

Poulson, C. (1983) Differential reinforcement of other-than-vocalization as a control procedure in the conditioning of infant vocalization rate. *Journal of Experimental Child Psychology*, 36, 471–489.

Powell, W. (1968) Differential effectiveness of interviewer interventions in an experimental interview. *Journal of Consulting and Clinical Psychology*, 32, 210–215.

Powers, P.C. and Geen, R.G. (1972) Effects of the behavior and perceived arousal of a model on instrumental aggression. *Journal of Personality and Social Psychology*, 23, 175–184.

Poyatos, F. (1983) *New Perspectives in Nonverbal Communication*, Pergamon, Oxford.

Premack, D. (1965) Reinforcement theory. In D. Levine (ed.) *Nebraska Symposium on Motivation*, Vol. 13. University of Nebraska Press, Lincoln.

Prue, D. and Fairbank, J. (1981) Performance feedback in organizational behaviour management: A review. *Journal of Organizational Behaviour Management*, 3, 1–16.

Purtilo, R. and Cassel, C. (1981) *Ethical Dimensions in the Health Professions*. Saunders, Philadelphia.

Rachlin, H. (1976) *Behaviour and Learning*. Freeman, New York.

Rapp, S., Carstensen, L. and Prue, D. (1983) Organizational behaviour management 1978–82: An annotated bibliography. *Journal of Organizational Behaviour Management*, 5, 5–50.

Raven, B. (1965) Social influence and power. In I.D. Steiner and M. Fishbein (eds) *Current Studies in Social Psychology*. Holt, New York.

Raven, B. (1988) Social power and compliance in health care. In S. Maes, C. Spielberger, P. Defares and I. Sarason (eds). *Topics in Health Psychology*. Wlley, New York.

Raven, B., Centers, R. and Rodrigues, A. (1975) The bases of conjugal power. In R.E. Cromwell and D.H. Olsen (eds) *Power in Families*. Wiley, New York.

Raven, B. and Rubin, J. (1983) *Social Psychology*. Wiley, New York.

Reece, M. and Whitman, R. (1962) Expressive movements, warmth and verbal reinforcement. *Journal of Abnormal and Social Psychology*, 64, 2324–2336.

Reid, D. and Whitman, T. (1983) Behavioural staff management in institutions: A critical review of effectiveness and acceptability. *Analysis and Intervention in Developmental Disabilities*, 3, 131–149.

Reis, H.T., Nezlek, J. and Wheeler, L. (1980) Physical attractiveness and social interaction. *Journal of Personality and Social Psychology*, 38, 604–617.

Rich, J. (1975) Effects of children's physical attractiveness on teachers' evaluations. *Journal of Educational Psychology*, 67, 599–609.

Rickard, H., Dignam, P. and Horner, R. (1960) Verbal manipulations in a psychotherapeutic relationship. *Journal of Clinical Psychology*, 16, 264–267.

Ridgeway, C.L., Berger, J. and Smith, L. (1985) Nonverbal cues and status: An expectation states approach. *American Journal of Sociology*, 90, 955–979.

Rierdan, J. and Brooks, R. (1978) Verbal conditioning of male and female schizophrenics as a function of experimenter proximity. *Journal of Clinical Psychology*, 34, 33–36.

Riesman, D. (1950) *The Lonely Crowd*. Yale University Press, New Haven, Conn.

Riesman, D. (1952) *Faces in the Crowd*. Yale University Press, New Haven, Conn.

Riess, M. and Schlenker, B.R. (1977) Attitude change and responsibility avoidance as modes of dilemma resolution in forced compliance situations. *Journal of Personality and Social Psychology*, 35, 21–30.

Riggio, R. and Friedman, H. (1986) Impression formation: The role of expressive behaviour. *Journal of Personality and Social Psychology*, 50, 421–427.

Rittle, R.H. (1981) Changes in helping behavior: Self versus situation perception as mediators of the foot-in-the-door effect. *Personality and Social Psychology Bulletin*, 7, 431–437.

Rodin, J. and Langer, E.J. (1980) Aging labels: The decline of control and the fall of self-esteem. *Journal of Social Issues*, 36, 12–29.

Rodin, M. (1982) Non-engagement, failure to engage and disengagement. In S. W. Duck (ed.) *Personal Relationships 4: Dissolving Personal Relationships*. Academic Press, London.

Rogers, C. (1957) The necessary and sufficient conditions of therapeutic personality change. *Journal of Counseling Psychology*, 21, 95–103.

Rogers, C. (1959) A theory of therapy, personality and interpersonal relationships, as developed in the client-centred framework. In S. Koch (ed.) *Psychology: A Study of Science*, Vol. 3. McGraw-Hill, New York.

Rogers, C. (1961) *On Becoming a Person*. Houghton Mifflin, Boston.

Rogers, C. (1964) Toward a modern approach to values: The valuing process in the mature person. *Journal of Abnormal and Social Psychology*, 68, 160–167.

Rogers, J. (1960) Operant conditioning in a quasi-therapy setting. *Journal of Abnormal and Social Psychology*, 60, 247–252.

Rosenblatt, P.C. (1977) Needed research on commitment in marriage. In G. Levinger and H. L. Raush (eds) *Close Relationships: Perspectives on the Meaning of Intimacy*. University of Massachusetts Press, Amherst.

Rosenfeld, H. (1987) Conversational control functions of nonverbal behaviour. In A. Siegman and S. Feldstein (eds) *Nonverbal Behaviour and Communication*. Lawrence Erlbaum Assocs, Hillsdale, N.J.

Rosenfeld, H. and Hancks, M. (1980) The nonverbal context of verbal listener responses. In M. Kay (ed.) *The Relationship of Verbal and Nonverbal Communication*. Mouton, The Hague.

Rosenshine, B. (1971) *Teaching Behaviour and Student Achievement*. National Foundation for Education Research in England and Wales, Windsor, Berks.

Rosenthal, R. and Jacobson, L. (1968) *Pygmalion in the Classroom*. Holt, Rinehart and Winston, London.

Ross, L.D., Rodin, J. and Zimbardo, P.G. (1969) Toward an attribution therapy: The reduction of fear through induced cognitive-emotional misattribution. *Journal of Personality and Social Psychology*, 12, 279–288.

Rotter, J.B. (1964) *Clinical Psychology: Foundations of Modern Psychology Series*. Prentice-Hall, Englewood Cliffs, N.J.

Rotter, J.B. (1966) Generalised expectancies for internal versus external control of reinforcement. *Psychological Monographs*, 80 (Whole No. 609).

Rotter, J. (1982) *The Development and Applications of Social Learning Theory: Selected Papers*. Praeger, New York.

Royce, W.S. and Weiss, R.L. (1975) Behavioural cues in the judgement of martial satisfaction: A linear regression analysis. *Journal of Consulting and Clinical Psychology*, 43, 816–824.

Ruffner, M. and Burgoon, M. (1981) *Interpersonal Communication*. Holt, Rinehart and Winston, New York.

Rule, B.G., Bisanz, G.L. and Kohn, M. (1985) Anatomy of a persuasion schema: Targets, goals and strategies. *Journal of Personality and Social Psychology*, 48, 1127–1140.

Rusbult, C.E. (1980) Commitment and satisfaction in romantic associations: A test of the investment model. *Journal of Experimental Social Psychology*, 16, 172–186.

Rusbult, C.E., Johnston, D.J. and Morrow, G.D. (1986) Impact of couple patterns of problem solving on distress and non-distress in dating relationships. *Journal of Personality and Social Psychology*, 50, 744–753.

Rusbult, C.E., Morrow, G.D. and Johnston, D.J. (1990) Self-esteem and problem solving behaviour in close relationships. *British Journal of Social Psychology* (in press).

Rusbult, C.E. and Zembrodt, I.M. (1983) Responses to dissatisfaction in romantic involvements: A multidimensional scaling analysis. *Journal of Experimental Social Psychology*, 19, 274–293.

Rushall, B. (1983) Using applied behaviour analysis for altering motivation. In G. Martin and D. Hrycaiko (eds) *Behaviour Modification and Coaching: Principles, Procedures and Research*. C.C. Thomas, Springfield, Ill.

Rushall, B. and Smith K. (1979) The modification of the quality and quantity of behaviour categories in a swimming coach. *Journal of Sport Psychology*, 1, 138–150.

Russell, A. and Linn, L. (1977) Teacher attention and classroom behaviour. *The Exceptional Child*, 24, 148–155.

Russell, J. (1971) *Motivation*. W.C. Brown, Dubuque, Iowa.

Rutter, D., Stephenson, G., Ayline, K. and White, P. (1978) The timing of looks in dyadic conversation. *British Journal of Social and Clinical Psychology*, 16, 191–192.

Sachs, P.R. (1982) Avoidance of diagnostic information in self-evaluation of ability. *Personality and Social Psychology Bulletin*, 8, 242–246.

Saigh, P. (1981) Effects of nonverbal experimenter praise on selected WAIS subtest performance of Lebanese undergraduates. *Journal of Nonverbal Behaviour*, 6, 84–88.

Sajwaj, T. and Dillon, A. (1977) Complexities of an 'elementary' behaviour modification procedure: Differential adult attention used for children's behaviour disorders. In B. Etzel, J. Le Blanc and D. Baer (eds) *New Developments in Behavioural Research: Theory, Method and Application*. Lawrence Erlbaum Assocs, Hillsdale, N.J.

Sakurai, S. (1990) The effects of four kinds of extrinsic rewards on intrinsic motivation. *Psychologia*, 33, 220–229.

Salmoni, A., Schmidt, R. and Walter, C. (1984) Knowledge of results and motor learning: A review and critical reappraisal. *Psychological Bulletin*, 95, 355–386.

Salzinger, K. and Pisoni, S. (1960) Reinforcement of verbal affect responses of normal subjects during the interview. *Journal of Abnormal and Social Psychology*, 60, 127–130.

Samaan, M. (1971) The differential effects of reinforcement and advice-giving on information seeking behaviour in counselling. *Dissertation Abstracts International*, 32, 189A.

Sapolsky, A. (1960) Effect of interpersonal relationships upon verbal conditioning. *Journal of Abnormal and Social Psychology*, 60, 241–246.

Sargent, L.W. (1965) Communicator image and news reception. *Journalist Quarterly*, 42, 35–42.

Saunders, C. (1986) Opening and closing. In O. Hargie (ed.) *A Handbook of Communication Skills*. Croom Helm, London.

Saunders C. and Caves, R. (1986) An empirical approach to the identification of communication skills with reference to speech therapy. *Journal of Further and Higher Education*, 10, 29–44.

Schachter, S. (1959) *The Psychology of Affiliation*. Stanford University Press, Stanford, Calif.

Scheflen, A.E. (1964) The significance of posture in communication systems. *Psychiatry*, 27, 316–331.

Scherer, K. and Ekman, P. (eds) (1982) *Handbook of Methods in Nonverbal Behaviour Research*. Cambridge University Press, Cambridge.

Schlenker, B. and Weigold, M. (1989) Goals and the self-identification process: Constructing desired identities. In L. Pervin (ed.) *Goal Concepts in Personality and Social Psychology*. Lawrence Erlbaum, Hillsdale, N.J.

Schmidt, G. and Weiner, B. (1988) An attribution–affect–action theory of motivated behavior: Replications examining help-giving. *Personality and Social Psychology Bulletin*, 14, 610–621.

Schroeder, H. and Rakos, R. (1983) The identification and assessment of social skills. In R. Ellis and D. Whittington (eds) *New Directions in Social Skill Training*. Croom Helm, London.

Schulman, R.F., Shoemaker, D.J. and Moelis, I. (1962) Laboratory measurements of parental behaviour. *Journal of Counseling Psychology*, 26, 109–114.

Schultz, C. and Sherman, R. (1976) Social class, development and differences in reinforcer effectiveness. *Review of Educational Research*, 46, 25–59.

Schwartz, B. (1989) *Psychology of Learning and Behaviour*, Norton, New York.

Scofield, M.E. (1977) Verbal conditioning with a heterogeneous adolescent sample: The effects on two critical responses. *Psychology*, 14, 41–49.

Segal, M.W. (1974) Alphabet and attraction: An unobtrusive measure of the effect of propinquity in a field setting. *Journal of Personality and Social Psychology*, 30, 654–657.

Seligman, A. (1973) Effect of noncontingent interviewer 'mm-hmms' on interviewer productivity. *Proceedings of the 81st Annual Convention of the American Psychological Association*, 8, 559–560.

Seligman, C., Brickman, J. and Koulack, D. (1977) Rape and physical attractiveness: Assigning responsibility to victims. *Journal of Personality*, 45, 554–563.

Seligman, M. (1970) On the generality of the laws of learning. *Psychological Review*, 77, 406–418.

Seligman, M. (1975) *Helplessness*. W. H. Freeman, San Francisco.

Seligman, M. and Maier, S.F. (1967) Failure to escape traumatic shock. *Journal of Experimental Psychology*, 74, 1–9.

Seyfried, B.A. (1977) Complementarity in interpersonal attraction. In S. Duck (ed.) *Theory and Practice in Interpersonal Attraction*. Academic Press, London.

Shapiro, J.G. (1968) Responsivity to facial and linguistic cues. *Journal of Communication*, 28, 104–111.

Sherman, S.J. (1980) On the self-erasing nature of errors of prediction. *Journal of Personality and Social Psychology*, 39, 211–221.

Sherman, W. (1990) *Behaviour Modification*. Harper and Row, New York.

Siegal, J. (1980) Effects of objective evidence of expertness, nonverbal behaviour and subject sex on client-perceived expertness. *Journal of Counseling Psychology*, 27, 117–121.

Siegman, A. (1973) Effect of nonverbal interviewer mm-hmms on interviewee productivity. Proceedings, 81 Annual Convention, American Psychological Association, 8, 5559–5560.

Siegman, A. (1979) Cognition and hesitation in speech. In A. Siegman and S. Feldstein (eds) *Of Time and Speech: Temporal Speech Patterns in Interpersonal Contexts*. Lawrence Erlbaum, Hillsdale, N.J.

Siegman, A. (1985) Expressive correlates of affective states and traits. In A. Siegman and S. Feldstein (eds) *Multichannel Integrations of Nonverbal Behaviour*. Lawrence Erlbaum, Hillsdale, N.J.

Siegman, A. (1987) The tell-tale voice: nonverbal messages of nonverbal communication. In A. Siegman and S. Feldstein (eds) *Nonverbal Behaviour and Communication*. Lawrence Erlbaum, Hillsdale, N.J.

Siegman, A. and Crown, C. (1980) Interpersonal attraction and the temporal patterning of speech in the initial interview: Replication and clarification. In W. P. Robinson, H. Giles and P. M. Smith (eds) *Language: Social Psychological Perspectives*. Pergamon, London.

Siegman, A. and Feldstein, S. (eds) (1987) *Nonverbal Behaviour and Communication* (2nd edn). Lawrence Erlbaum Assocs, Hillsdale, N.J.

Silva, D., Duncan, P. and Doudna, D. (1982) The effects of attendance-contingent feedback and praise on attendance and work efficiency. *Journal of Organizational Behaviour Management*, 3, 59–69.

Simpson, J.A. (1987) The dissolution of romantic relationships: Factors involved in relationship stability and emotional stress. *Journal of Personality and Social Psychology*, 53, 683–692.

Sims, H. and Manz, C. (1981) Social learning theory: The role of modelling on the exercise of leadership. *Journal of Organizational Behaviour Management*, 3, 55–63.

Singerman, H., Borkovec, T. and Baron, R. (1976) Failure of a 'mis-attribution therapy' manipulation to reduce speech anxiety. *Behavior Therapy*, 7, 306–313.

Skinner, B.F. (1938) *The Behaviour of Organisms*. Appleton-Century-Crofts, New York.

Skinner, B.F. (1953) *Science and Human Behaviour*, Collier Macmillan, London.

Skinner, B.F. (1957) *Verbal Behavior*. Appleton-Century-Crofts, New York.

Skinner, B.F. (1974) *About Behaviorism*, Vintage Books, New York.

Skinner, B.F. (1977) The force of coincidence. In B. Etzel, J. Le Blanc and D. Baer (eds) *New Developments in Behavioral Research: Theory, Method and Application*. Lawrence Erlbaum Assocs, Hillsdale, N.J.

Smith, R. and Smoll, F. (1990) Self-esteem and children's reactions to youth sport coaching behaviours: A field study of self-enhancement processes. *Developmental Psychology*, 2, 987–993.

Smith, V. (1986) Listening. In O. Hargie (ed.) *A Handbook of Communication Skills*. Croom Helm, London.

Smith-Hanen, S.S. (1977) Effects of nonverbal behaviors on judged levels of counselor warmth and empathy. *Journal of Counseling Psychology*, 24, 87–91.

Snyder, M. (1987) *Public Appearances, Private Realities: The Psychology of Self-Monitoring*. Freeman, New York.

Snyder, M. and Smith, D. (1986) Personality and friendship: The friendship worlds of self monitors. In V.J. Derlega and B. A. Winstead (eds) *Friendship and Social Interaction*. Springer-Verlag, New York.

Snyder, M., Tanke, E.D. and Berscheid, E. (1977) Social perception and interpersonal behavior: On the self-fulfilling nature of social stereotypes. *Journal of Personality and Social Psychology*, 35, 656–666.

Soloman, M.R. and Schopler, J. (1978) The relationship of physical attractiveness and punitiveness: Is the linearity assumption out of line? *Personality and Social Psychology Bulletin*, 4, 483–486.

Sommer, R. (1969) *Personal Space*. Prentice-Hall, Englewood Cliffs, N.J.

Spence, S. (1982) Social skills training with young offenders. In M. Feldman (ed.) *Developments in the Study of Criminal Behaviour*, Vol. 1, *The Prevention and Control of Offending*. Wiley, Chichester.

Spiegal, P. and Machotka, P. (1974) *Messages of the Body*. Free Press, New York.

Spielberger, C., Levin, S. and Shepard, M. (1962) The effects of awareness and attitude toward the reinforcement on the operant conditioning of verbal behaviour. *Journal of Personality*, 30, 106–121.

Staats, A.W. (1968) Social behaviorism and human motivation: Principles of the attitude-reinforcer – discriminative system. In A. G. Greenwald, T.C. Brock and T.M. Ostrom (eds) *Psychological Foundations of Attitudes*. Academic Press, New York.

Start, K.B. (1968) Rater–ratee attitude and personality in the assessment of teacher ability. *British Journal of Educational Psychology*, 38, 16–20.

Steele, C. (1988) The psychology of self-affirmation: Sustaining the integrity of the self. In L. Berkowitz (ed.) *Advances in Experimental Social Psychology*, Vol. 21. Academic Press, New York.

Steigleder, M., Weiss, R., Balling, S., Wenninger, V. and Lombardo, J. (1980) Drive-like motivational properties of competitive behavior. *Journal of Personality and Social Psychology*, 38, 93–104.

Steiner, C. (1974) *Scripts People Live*. Grove, New York.

Stewart, D. and Patterson, M. (1973) Eliciting effects of verbal and nonverbal cues on projective test responses. *Journal of Consulting and Clinical Psychology*, 44, 74–77.

Stewart, I. (1989) *Transactional Analysis Counselling in Action*, Sage, London.

Stewart, R.A., Powell, G.E. and Chetwynd, S.J. (1979) *Person Perception and Stereotyping*. Saxon House, Hampshire.

Stock, C. (1978) Effects of praise and its source on performance. *Perceptual and Motor Skills*, 47, 43–46.

Stone, L.J., Murphy, L.B. and Smith, H.T. (1973) *Competent Infant: Research and Commentary*. Basic Books, New York.

Stotland, E. (1969) Exploratory investigations of empathy. In L. Berkowitz (ed.) *Advances in Experimental Social Psychology*, Vol. 4. Academic Press, New York.

Strong, S., Taylor, R., Bratton, J. and Loper, R. (1971) Nonverbal behavior and perceived counselor characteristics. *Journal of Counseling Psychology*, 18, 554–561.

Stroufe, R., Chaikin, A., Cook, R. and Freeman, V. (1977) The effects of physical attractiveness and honesty: A socially desirable response. *Personality and Social Psychology Bulletin*, 3, 59–62.

Strupp, H.H., Wallach, M.S. and Wogan, M. (1964) Psychotherapy experience in retrospect: Questionnaire survey of former patients and their therapists. *Psychology Monographs*, 78, No. 11 (Whole No. 588).

Sullivan, H. (1955) *The Interpersonal Theory of Psychiatry*, Tavistock, London.

Swann, W., Hixon, J., Stein-Seroussi, A. and Gilbert, D. (1990) The fleeting gleam of praise: Cognitive processes underlying behavioral reactions to self-relevant feedback. *Journal of Personality and Social Psychology*, 59, 17–26.

Swann, W.B. and Snyder, M. (1980) On translating beliefs into action: Theories of ability and their application in an instructional setting. *Journal of Personality and Social Psychology*, 38, 879–888.

Swap, W.C. (1977) Interpersonal attraction and repeated exposure to rewarders and punishers. *Personality and Social Psychology Bulletin*, 3, 248–251.

Swensen, C. (1973) *Introduction to Interpersonal Relations*. Scott Foresman, Glenview, Ill.

Taffel, C. (1955) Anxiety and the conditioning of verbal behaviour. *Journal of Abnormal and Social Psychology*, 51, 496–501.

Tamase, K. (1989) Introspective–developmental counselling. *Bulletin of Nora University of Education*, 38, 161–177.

Tankard, J.W., McCleneghan, J.S., Ganju, V., Lee, E.B., Olkes, C. and Du Bose, D. (1977) Nonverbal cues and television news. *Journal of Communication*, 27, 106–111.

Tedeschi, J.T. (ed.) (1972) *The social influence processes*. Aldine, Chicago.

Tedeschi, J.T., Smith, R.B. and Brown, R.C. (1974) A reinterpretation of research on aggression. *Psychological Bulletin*, 81, 540–562.

Tepper, D. and Haase, R. (1978) Verbal and nonverbal communication of facilitative conditions. *Journal of Counseling Psychology*, 25, 35–44.

Tesser, A. (1988) Toward a self-evaluation maintenance model of social behaviour. In L. Berkowitz (ed.) *Advances in Experimental Social Psychology*, Vol. 21. Academic Press, New York.

Thelen, H.A. (1967) *Classroom Grouping for Teachability*. Wiley, London.

Thibaut, J.W. and Kelley, H.H. (1959) *The Social Psychology of Groups*. Wiley, New York.

Thorndike, E. (1898) Animal intelligence: An experimental study of the associative process in animals. *Psychological Review Monograph Supplement*, 2, No. 8.

Thorndike, E. (1911) *Animal Intelligence*. Macmillan, New York.

Thorne, A. (1987) The press of personality: A study of conversations between introverts and extroverts. *Journal of Personality and Social Psychology*, 53, 718–726.

Thorne, B. (1984) Person-centred therapy. In W. Dryden (ed.) *Individual Therapy in Britain*. Harper Row, London.

Thorne, B. (1990) Person-centred therapy. In W. Dryden (ed.) *Individual Therapy: A Handbook*. Open University Press, Milton Keynes.

Tolhuizen, J.H. (1989) Communication strategies for intensifying dating relationships: Identification, use and structure. *Journal of Social and Personal Relationships*, 6, 413–434.

Toukmanian, S.G. and Rennie, D.L. (1975) Microcounseling versus human relations training. *Journal of Counseling Psychology*, 22, 345–352.

Trout, D.L. and Rosenfeld, H.M. (1980) The effect of postural lean and body congruence on the judgement of psychotherapeutic rapport. *Journal of Nonverbal Behaviour*, 4, 176–190.

Trower, P. and Dryden, W. (1981) Psychotherapy. In M. Argyle (ed.) *Social Skills and Health*. Methuen, London.

Trower, P., Bryant, B. and Argyle, M. (1978) *Social Skills and Mental Health*. Methuen, London.

Truax, C.B. (1963) Effective ingredients in psychotherapy: An approach to involving the patient–therapist interaction. *Journal of Counseling Psychology*, 10, 256–263.

Truax, C.B. (1966) Therapist reinforcement of patient self-exploration and therapeutic outcome. *Journal of Abnormal Social Psychology*, 71, 1–9.

Truax, C.B. and Carkhuff, R.R. (1967) *Towards Effective Counselling and Psychotherapy*. Aldine Publishing Company, Chicago.

Truax, C.B. and Tatum, C.R. (1966) An extension from the effective psychotherapeutic model to constructive personality change in pre-school children. *Childhood Education*, 42, 456–462.

Tubbs, S. and Baird, J. (1976) *The Open Person... Self Disclosure and Personal Growth*. Merrill, Columbus, Ohio.

Turner, R. (1968) The self-conception in social interaction. In C. Gordon and K. Gergen (eds) *The Self in Social Interaction*. Wiley, New York.

Turney, C., Eltis, K., Hatton, N., Owens, L., Towler, J. and Wright, R. (1983) *Sydney Micro Skills Redeveloped: Series 1 Handbook*. Sydney University Press, Sydney.

Turney, C., Owens, L., Hatton, N., Williams, G. and Cairns, L. (1976) *Sydney Micro Skills: Series 2 Handbook*. Sydney University Press, Sydney.

Uhlemann, M.R., Lea, G.W. and Stone, G.L. (1976) Effect of instructions and modeling on trainees low in interpersonal communication skills. *Journal of Counseling Psychology*, 23, 509–513.

Upton, W. (1973) Altruism, attribution and intrinsic motivation in the recruitment of blood donors. *Dissertation Abstracts International*, 34, 6260B.

Van Lear, A. and Trujillo, N. (1986) On becoming acquainted: A longitudinal study of social judgement processes. *Journal of Social and Personal Relationships*, 3, 375–392.

Vargas, A.M. and Borkowski, J.G. (1982) Physical attractiveness and counseling skills. *Journal of Counseling Psychology*, 29, 246–255.

Veitch, R. and Griffith, W. (1976) Good news, bad news, affective and interpersonal effects. *Journal of Applied Social Psychology*, 6, 69–75.

Von Cranach, M., Kalbermatten, V., Indermuhle, K. and Gugler, B. (1982) Goal-directed action. *European Monographs in Social Psychology*, 30. Academic Press, London.

Vondracek, F. (1969) The study of self-disclosure in experimental interviews. *Journal of Psychology*, 72, 55–59.

Vroom, V. (1964) *Work and Motivation*. Wiley, New York.

Wachtel, P. (1973) Psychodynamics, behaviour therapy, and the implacable experimenter: An inquiry into the consistency of personality. *Journal of Abnormal Psychology*, 82, 324–334.

Wack, J. and Rodin, J. (1978) Nursing homes for the aged: The human consequences of legislation-shaped environments. *Journal of Social Issues*, 34, 6–21.

Waldron, J. (1975) Judgement of like–dislike from facial expression and body posture. *Perceptual and Motor Skills*, 41, 799–804.

Wallin, J. and Johnson, R. (1976) A positive reinforcement approach to controlling employee absenteeism. *Personnel Journal*, 55, 390–392.

Walster, E., Walster, G.W. and Berscheid, E. (1978) *Equity: Theory and Research*. Allyn and Bacon, Boston.

Washburn, P. and Hakel, M. (1973) Visual cues and verbal content as influences on impressions formed after simulated employment interviews. *Journal of Applied Psychology*, 58, 137–141.

Watzlawick, P. (1978) *The Language of Change*. Basic Books, New York.

Watzlawick, P., Beavin, J. and Jackson, D. (1967) *Pragmatics of Human Communication*. W.W. Norton, New York.

Wearden, J. (1988) Some neglected problems in the analysis of human operant behavior. In G. Davey and C. Cullen (eds) *Human Operant Conditioning and Behavior Modification*. Wiley, New York.

Weary, G.B. (1978) Self serving biases in the attribution process: A re-examination of the fact or fiction issue. *Journal of Personality and Social Psychology*, 36, 56–71.

Weight, D. (1974) Interviewers: locus of control and conditioning of interviewees' self-reference statements. *Psychological Reports*, 35, 1307–1316.

Weinberg, R. (1984) The relationship between extrinsic rewards and intrinsic motivation in sport. In J. Silva and R. Weinberg (eds) *Psychological Foundations of Sport*. Human Kinetics Pubs, Champaign, Ill.

Weiner, B. (1985) An attributional theory of achievement motivation and emotion. *Psychological Review*, 92, 548–573.

Weiner, B. (1986) *An Attributional Theory of Motivation and Emotion*. Springer, New York.

Weiner, B., Graham, S., Stern, P. and Lawson, M. (1982) Using affective cues to infer causal thoughts. *Developmental Psychology*, 18, 278–286.

Weiner, B. and Kukla, A. (1970) An attributional analysis of achievement motivation. *Journal of Personality and Social Psychology*, 15, 1–20.

Weiss, R.S. (1974) The provisions of social relationships. In Z. Rubin (ed.) *Doing unto Others*. Prentice-Hall, Englewood Cliffs, N.J.

Weiss, R., Krasner, L. and Ullmann, L.P. (1960) Responsivity to verbal conditioning as a function of emotional atmosphere and patterning of reinforcement. *Psychology Report*, 6, 415–426.

Weiss, R., Lombardo, J., Warren, D. and Kelley, K. (1971) Reinforcing effects of speaking in reply. *Journal of Personality and Social Psychology*, 20, 186–199.

Wheldall, K., Bevan, K. and Shortall, A. (1986) A touch of reinforcement: The effects of contingent teacher touch on the classroom behaviour of young children. *Educational Review*, 38, 207–216.

Wheldall, K. and Glynn, T. (1989) *Effective Classroom Learning: A Behavioural Interactionist Approach to Teaching*. Basil Blackwell, Oxford.

Wheldall, K. and Lam, J. (1987) Rows versus tables 11: the effects of two classroom seating arrangements on classroom disruption rate, on-task behaviour and teacher behaviour in three special school classes. *Educational Psychology*, 8, 303–312.

Wheldall, K., Wenban-Smith, J., Morgan, A. and Quance, B. (1988) *Reading: How do Teachers Typically Tutor?* Centre for Child Study, University of Birmingham.

White, R. (1948) *The Abnormal Personality*. Ronald Press, New York.

White, R. (1959) Motivation reconsidered: the concept of competence. *Psychological Review*, 66, 297–333.

White, B. and Sanders, S. (1986) The influence on patients' pain intensity ratings of antecedent reinforcement of pain talk or well talk. *Journal of Behaviour Therapy and Experimental Psychiatry*, 17, 155–159.

Whitehorn, J.E. (1964) Human factors in psychiatry. *Bulletin of New York Academy of Medicine*, 40, 451–466.

Whitehorn, J.E. and Betz, B.J. (1954) A study of psychotherapeutic relationships between physicians and schizophrenic patients. *American Journal of Psychiatry*, 3, 321–331.

Wiemann, J. and Giles, H. (1988) Interpersonal communication. In M. Hewstone, W. Stroebe, J.P. Codol and G. Stephenson (eds) *Introduction to Social Psychology*. Basil Blackwell, Oxford.

Wiener, M., Devoe, S., Rubinow, S. and Geller, J. (1972) Nonverbal behavior and nonverbal communication. *Psychological Review*, 79, 185–214.

Wikoff, M., Anderson, D. and Crowell, C. (1982) Behaviour management in a factory setting: Increasing work efficiency. *Journal of Organizational Behaviour Management*, 4, 97–127.

Wilensky, R. (1983) *Planning and Understanding: A Computational Approach to Human Reasoning*. Addison-Wesley, Reading, Mass.

Wilson, D.W. (1978) Helping behavior and physical attractiveness. *Journal of Social Psychology*, 104, 313–314.

Wilson, P.R. (1968) The perceptual distortion of height as a function of ascribed academic status. *Journal of Social Psychology*, 74, 97–102.

Wilson, S.R. and Benner, L.A. (1971) The effects of self-esteem and situation upon comparison choices during ability evaluation. *Sociometry*, 34, 381–397.

Winch, F.R. (1967) Another look at the theory of complementary needs in mate selection. *Journal of Marriage and the Family*, 29, 756–762.

Winthrop, H. (1958) Relation between appeal value and highbrow status on some radio and television programs. *Psychology Reports*, 4, 53–54.

Woll, S.B. and Cozby, P.C. (1987) Videodating and other alternatives to traditional methods of relationship initiation. In W. H. Jones and D. Perlman (eds) *Advances in Personal Relationships*, Vol. 1. JAI Press, Greenwich, Conn.

Woodside, A.G. and Davenport, J.W. Jnr (1974) The effect of salesman similarity and expertise on consumer purchasing. *Journal of Marketing Research*, 11, 198–202.

Woodward, W. (1982) The discovery of social behaviorism and social learning theory, 1870–1980. *American Psychologist*, 37, 396–410.

Wright, P.H. (1984) Self-referent motivation and the intrinsic quality of friendship. *Journal of Social and Personal Relationships*, 1, 115–130.

Zajonc, R. (1980) Feeling and thinking. *American Psychologist*, 35, 151–175.

Zimbardo, P.G. (1960) Involvement and communication discrepancy as determinants of opinion conformity. *Journal of Abnormal Social Psychology*, 60, 86–94.

Zimmer, J. and Anderson, S. (1968) Dimensions of positive regard and empathy. *Journal of Counseling Psychology*, 19, 161–166.

Zimmer, J. and Park, P. (1967) Factor analysis of counselor communications. *Journal of Counseling Psychology*, 14, 198–203.

Zimmerman, D.H. and West, C. (1975) Sex roles, interruptions and silences in conversations. In B. Thorne and N. Henley (eds) *Language and Sex*. Newbury House, Rowley.

Zoeller, C., Mahoney, G. and Weiner, B. (1983) Effects of attribution training on the assembly task performance of mentally retarded adults. *American Journal of Mental Deficiency*, 88, 109–112.

Name index

Abel, D. 72
Abramson, L.Y. 130
Acker, M. 64, 181
Adams, G.R. 114, 125
Adinolf, A.A. 117
Aho, L. 84
Albee, G. 138
Alicke, M.D. 116
Allen, K. 26
Allison, J. 30
Allison, M. 74
Alper, T. 82
Altmann, H. 97, 106
Anderson, C. 72, 74, 141
Anderson, D. 72
Anderson, S. 96
Antal, B.G. 90, 114
Arenson, S. 68
Argyle, M. 3, 7, 11, 12, 14, 58, 79, 87, 89, 160, 161
Aronfreed, J. 105
Aronson, E. 8, 125, 168, 181
Asch, S.E. 149
Ashby, K.L. 168
Aspy, D. 105, 107
At Emery Air Freight 72
Atkinson, J. 15
Authier, J. 5, 60, 96, 97, 98, 99, 104, 107, 109, 174
Ayline, K. 89
Ayllon, T. 28, 74
Azrin, N. 28

Baccus, G.K. 108
Bachmann, M. 133
Backman, C. 53, 54, 55
Baird, J. 77
Baldock, J. 4

Baldwin, J. 27
Balling, S. 37
Bandura, A. 14, 21, 28, 29, 36, 38, 41, 42, 43, 44, 45, 46, 76, 176, 177
Banspach, S.W. 97
Barker, G. 133, 136
Barnabei, F. 108
Barnard, D. 184
Barnes, D. 89
Barnett, F. 74
Barnlund, D. 14
Baron, A. 41
Baron, R. 46, 66, 139, 155
Barrios, B. 84
Barta, S. 10
Bartell, P. 26
Batson, C.D. 154
Baumeister, R. 66, 74, 183
Baxter, J. 83
Baxter, J.C. 100
Baxter, L.A. 167, 169
Bayes, M. 97
Beattie, G. 9
Beauchamp, T. 184
Beavin, J. 10, 11
Becker, H.S. 167
Becker, J. 100
Begley, P.J. 124
Beharry, E.A. 77, 108
Bell, R.Q. 156
Bellet, W. 89
Bem, D. 54
Bennett, M. 60, 183
Benson, P.L. 114
Bentley, B.J. 126
Berenson, B. 102
Berg, J.H. 62, 78, 164
Berger, C. 9, 151

Sergio, J. 72
Seyfried, B.A. 120
Shapiro, J.G. 80, 94
Shaver, P. 163
Sheinman, L. 140
Shell, R. 154
Shepard, M. 68
Sherman, S.J. 153, 154
Sherman, W. 27
Shoemaker, D.J. 100
Shortall, A. 81
Shukla, A. 67, 181
Siegal, J. 85
Siegman, A. 62, 79, 80, 102, 103, 104, 183
Silva, D. 72
Silver, M. 77
Simon, A. 5
Simpson, J.A. 170
Sims, H. 155
Singer, A. 27
Singerman, H. 139
Sirotnik, K. 184
Skinner, B.F. 19, 24, 28, 29, 31, 36
Smith, C. 85
Smith, D. 117
Smith, H.T. 156
Smith, J.R. 87
Smith, K. 75
Smith, L. 151
Smith, R. 6, 55, 74, 182
Smith, R.B. 146
Smith, R.H. 116
Smith, V. 109
Smith-Hanen, S.S. 85, 97, 102, 109
Smoll, F. 6, 55, 74, 182
Snyder, M. 21, 54, 67, 114, 117, 140, 181
Soder, R. 184
Solomon, M.R. 126
Sommer, R. 93
Spence, S. 25
Spiegal, P. 103
Spielberger, C. 35, 68
Spiller, H. 133
Staats, A.W. 118
Start, K.B. 119
Steele, C. 55
Steigleder, M. 37
Stein-Seroussi, A. 55, 62, 182
Steiner, C. 48, 49
Stephany, A. 109
Stephenson, G. 89
Stern, P. 135

Sternberg, W. 77
Stewart, D. 69
Stewart, I. 48, 57
Stewart, R.A. 116
Stich, M. 26, 37
Stock, C. 67, 180
Stokes, T. 26
Stone, G.L. 97, 109
Stone, L.J. 156
Stotland, E. 105
Strejc, H. 161
Strong, S. 102, 110
Stroufe, R. 90
Strupp, H.H. 99
Stuart, J.L. 115
Sugai, D. 3
Sullivan, H. 53
Swann, W. 55, 62, 140, 182
Swap, W.C. 162
Swensen, C. 53

Taffel, C. 68
Taguiri, R. 20
Tamase, K. 97
Tankard, J.W. 88
Tanke, E.D. 114
Tatum, C.R. 107
Taylor, R. 102, 110
Teasdale, J.D. 130
Tedeschi, J.T. 145, 146
Tepper, D. 91, 97, 109
Terry, D. 100
Tesser, A. 55, 161, 182
Thelen, H.A. 115
Thibaut, J.W. 160
Thompson, V. 69
Thorndike, E. 23
Thorne, A. 150, 163
Thorne, B. 51, 97
Timmons, E. 107
Tolhuizen, J.H. 165
Topping, J. 84
Toukmanian, S.G. 109
Towler, J. 5, 44, 64, 174
Traupmann, J. 160, 168
Trout, D.L. 86
Trower, P. 7, 14, 16, 60, 96, 185
Truax, C.B. 99, 102, 105, 106, 107
True, J.H. 89, 102, 109
Trujillo, N. 121, 166
Tryon, W. 60
Tubbs, S. 77

Subject index

acknowledgement 59–63
activity reinforcers 71; *see also*
    reinforcement
affiliation 11, 159, 162
altercasting 54
attending 62, 70, 73
attitudes 68, 74, 112, 118, 147, 177
attraction 112–14
attractiveness 54, 74, 83–4, 89–90, 112,
    159, 162, 182
attribution 20, 66–7, 128–30, 133, 175,
    180; and models of helping 137–9, 142
automatic effect of reinforcement 35; and
    awareness 35; and response/reinforcer
    relationship 35–6

bank tellers 72
behaviourist tradition of learning 24–5
body shape 115, 116

careers officer 62, 86
coach, 6, 55, 74, 174
coaching 73–6; recommended reinforcers
    75
cognitive dissonance 147–8
compliance 6
consummatory communication 9
counselling 124–5, 155, 174
counsellor 4, 51, 60, 82, 84, 85, 89, 90,
    95–6, 97, 101, 102–3, 106–7, 108–10,
    125, 127, 170, 173

dentist 82, 88
doctor 2, 4, 34, 49, 82, 88, 146, 152, 153,
    173
dress 116, 117, 118, 123, 125, 152, 155

empathy: components of 107–10; concept

of 98–9, 104–5; rewarding effects of
    105–7, 176
environment 92–4, 136–7, 142, 162
Expectancy-value theory 129

face 115, 116
facial expressions 87–8, 110
feedback 18–20, 59, 72, 132–3, 134–5,
    149–50, 164, 175, 176, 183; *see also*
    skill model components

gaze 88–9, 109, 110, 151
'generalised other' 53
gestures 86–7, 102, 110, 122, 175
goals 10, 14–17, 59, 71, 174; *see also* skill
    model components

health professional 4, 6, 61, 69–70, 83, 84,
    93, 137–9
height 117, 153

incentives 38
informational nature of rewards 38–40
ingratiation 41, 55, 119, 155, 183
interpersonal attraction 8, 104
interpersonal communication 2; a skill
    model 12–21; and skill 9–12
interpersonal professions 4–5
interviewer 61, 63, 76–7, 83, 85–6, 87,
    88–9, 108–9, 174; research 70; survey
    70
interviewing 5, 7, 67–70, 155, 174
intrinsic motivation 15, 40, 74

judge 114
jury 125, 126, 127

law of effect 22–4